# International Environmental Law

# International Environmental Law

**Third Edition**

**Mohammad Naseem**
**Saman Naseem**

This book was originally published as a monograph in the International Encyclopaedia of Laws/Environmental Law.

Founding Editor: Roger Blanpain
General Editor: Frank Hendrickx
Volume Editor: Kurt Deketelaere

Wolters Kluwer

*Published by:*
Kluwer Law International B.V.
PO Box 316
2400 AH Alphen aan den Rijn
The Netherlands
E-mail: lrs-sales@wolterskluwer.com
Website: www.wolterskluwer.com/en/solutions/kluwerlawinternational

*Sold and distributed by:*
Wolters Kluwer Legal & Regulatory U.S.
920 Links Avenue
Landisville, PA 17538
United States of America
E-mail: customer.service@wolterskluwer.com



ISBN 978-94-035-3308-7

e-Book: ISBN 978-94-035-3318-6
web-PDF: ISBN 978-94-035-3328-5

This title is available on www.kluwerlawonline.com

# The Author

Mohammad Naseem born and brought up in Sardarnagar, Pilibhit district, India, is a science graduate and Master of Laws with a specialization in Commercial Law from Aligarh Muslim University, India. He is an Environmental Law Expert and ex-Deputy General Manager (Legal) of ONGC Limited. He was also Vice President—Legal in ONGC-Videsh Limited (overseas arm of ONGC) for seven years. At present, he is the Chairman and Managing Partner of Global Law and Liaison Services, New Delhi. In his professional career spanning over more than three decades, he has dealt with a large number of high-value commercial matters, domestic and international arbitration, and litigation. He has been part of a large number of negotiation teams, having successfully negotiated various types of contracts worth billions of dollars, including acquisitions of petroleum properties in a number of countries. He is the author of monograph/book on *Energy Law of India*, *Energy Law-International*, *Environmental Law*, *Environmental Law-International*, *Sports Law, Religion Law*, *Medical Law of India*, *Medical Law-International* and *Islamic Law of Contracts* for Wolters Kluwer International, the Netherlands and has had to his credit a number of papers published in reputed national and international journals. He is the co-author of *Fuel and Energy* II (*Petroleum and Natural Gas*) of Halsbury's Laws of India Series (volume 21) published by LexisNexis Butterworths India Limited. Edward Elgar Publishing Limited has published "World Petroleum Regimes" a paper authored by him in the *Hand Book on International Energy Law* and another article on "Natural Gas Provisions in Host Government Contracts—Regulatory and Contractual Aspects in India" published by Oil, Gas and Energy Law Intelligence (OGEL), United Kingdom. He is the visiting faculty and guest expert speaker of the Indian Academy of International Law and Diplomacy, University of Petroleum and Energy Studies, Dehradun and Indian School of Petroleum, New Delhi. He has traveled extensively throughout the world in relation to negotiation and conducting training programs. He has been a speaker in Seminars organized by IBC Asia Limited at Singapore, Oil and Gas IQPC at Bangkok, Thailand, Kuala Lumpur, Malaysia, and Tehran, and in a seminar conducted by Oil Industry Pension Fund (OIPF), Iran. For conducting negotiations, he has visited Myanmar, Singapore, Vietnam, Japan, South Korea, Hong Kong, Thailand, Iran, U.A.E., Iraq, Jordan, Syria, Turkey, Egypt, Libya, Sudan, South Sudan, Italy, Russia, Kazakhstan, Denmark, Netherlands, Switzerland, France, U.K.,

U.S., Canada, Ecuador, Venezuela, and Uzbekistan. He is a life member of very prestigious bodies like Indian Society of International Law and a permanent member of India International Law Foundation. With more than thirty-five years of varied practical and on-the-job legal experience in negotiation, drafting, interpretation and vetting of legal documents and dealing with arbitration and litigation on the one hand and acting as a trainer, speaker and author on the other, Mr. M. Naseem has been part of an exclusive team of trainers, negotiators, advisors and strategists and is a legal luminary of international repute in his own right.

**Co-Author**

Saman Naseem holds her post-graduation in Commercial Law from Aligarh Muslim University with her graduation from the Symbiosis International University, India and is a Founder Partner of Global Law and Liaison Services, a firm providing professional advice in the field of law in general and environmental law in particular. She is an active participant in seminars and conferences and has presented research papers on various topics. She is the co-author of the monograph/books on *Energy Law India*, *Energy Law-International*, *Environmental Law*, *Environmental Law-International*, *Medical Law*, *Medical Law-International*, *Islamic Law of Contracts* and *Religion Law of India* for Wolters Kluwer International, the Netherlands. Edward Elgar Publishing Limited has published an article co-authored by her by the title "World Petroleum Regimes" and another article on "Natural Gas Provisions in Host Government Contracts—Regulatory and Contractual Aspects in India" published by OGEL, United Kingdom. She is a promising environmental law expert and has been a practicing advocate. She has been connected with Nongovernmental Organizations (NGOs), namely the Madad Foundation Trust which supports various social causes.

# Table of Contents

# List of Abbreviations

| | |
|---|---|
| ADP | Ad Hoc Working Group on the Durban Platform for Enhanced Action |
| AI | Artificial Intelligence |
| ARIES | Artificial Intelligence for Environment and Sustainability |
| ASEAN | Association of Southeast Asian Nations |
| ATCM | Antarctic Treaty Consultative Meeting |
| BAT | Best Available Technique |
| BC3 | Basque Centre for Climate Change |
| BEA | Bilateral Environmental Agreement |
| BIT | Bilateral Investment Treaty |
| BOEM | Bureau of Ocean Environment Management |
| BOEMRE | Bureau of Ocean Energy Management, Regulation and Enforcement |
| BSEE | Bureau of Safety and Environmental Enforcement |
| CBD | Convention on Biological Diversity |
| CCPCJ | Commission on Crime Prevention and Criminal Justice |
| CDM | Clean Development Mechanism |
| CEC | Commission for Environmental Cooperation |
| CFCs | Chlorofluorocarbons |
| $CH_4$ | Methane |
| CHM | Common Heritage of Mankind |
| CIL | Customary International Law |
| CITES | Convention on International Trade in Endangered Species of Wild Fauna and Flora |
| CLC | Civil Liability Convention |
| CLCS | Commission on the Limits of the Continental Shelf |
| $CO_2$ | Carbon Dioxide |
| COLREG | Convention on the International Regulations for Preventing Collisions at Sea, 1972 |
| COMNAP | Council of Managers of National Antarctic Programs |

## List of Abbreviations

| | |
|---|---|
| COP | Conference of the Parties |
| CSD | Commission on Sustainable Development |
| CTBT | Comprehensive Nuclear-Test-Ban Treaty |
| CTBTO | Comprehensive Nuclear-Test-Ban Treaty Organization |
| CWA | Clean Water Act |
| DC | Developing Countries |
| DDE | Dichlorodiphenyldichloroethylene |
| DDT | DichloroDiphenyl Trichloroethane |
| DECC | Department of Energy and Climate Change |
| DU | Depleted Uranium |
| EA | Environmental Assessment |
| EC | European Community |
| ECHA | European Chemicals Agency |
| ECHR | European Court of Human Rights |
| ECJ | European Court of Justice |
| ECOSOC | Economic and Social Council |
| EEZ | Exclusive Economic Zone |
| EIA | Environmental Impact Assessment |
| ENMOD | Convention on the Prohibition of Military or any Other Hostile Use of Environmental Modification Techniques |
| EPA | Environmental Protection Agency |
| EU | European Union |
| FAO | Food and Agriculture Organization |
| FFS | Fossil Fuel Subsidy |
| FMCT | Fissile Material Cut-Off Treaty |
| FTA | Free Trade Agreement |
| FUND | International Convention on the Establishment of an International Fund for Oil Pollution Damage |
| GATT | General Agreement on Tariffs and Trade |
| GCF | Green Climate Fund |
| GDP | Gross Domestic Product |
| GEF | Global Environmental Facility |
| GHGs | Greenhouse Gases |
| GMO | Genetically Modified Organism |
| HAL | Halliburton |
| HELCOM | The Baltic Marine Environment Protection Commission |
| HFCs | Hydrofluorocarbons |
| IA | Investment Agreement |
| IAEA | International Atomic Energy Agency |

| | |
|---|---|
| ICJ | International Court of Justice |
| IEA | International Environmental Agreement |
| IEC | International Electrotechnical Commission |
| IFC | International Finance Corporation |
| IFNEC | International Framework for Nuclear Energy Cooperation |
| ILC | International Law Commission |
| ILO | International Labour Organization |
| IMF | International Monetary Fund |
| IMO | International Maritime Organization |
| INES | International Nuclear Event Scale |
| INTERPOL | International Criminal Police Organization |
| ISA | International Seabed Authority |
| ISM | International Safety Management |
| ISPS | International Ship Port Facility Security |
| ITLOS | International Tribunal for the Law of the Sea |
| ITTA | International Tropical Timber Agreement |
| ITTC | International Tropical Timber Council |
| ITTO | International Tropical Timber Organization |
| IUCN | International Union for the Conservation of Nature |
| LDN | Land Degradation Neutrality |
| LRTAP | Convention on Long-Range Transboundary Air Pollution |
| LULUCF | Land-Use, Land-Use Change and Forestry |
| MARPOL | International Convention for the Prevention of Pollution from Ships |
| MDL | Multidistrict Litigation |
| MEA | Multilateral Environmental Agreement |
| mg/l | Milligrams/Liter |
| MMS | Mineral Management Services |
| $N_2O$ | Nitrous Oxide |
| NAAEC | North American Agreement on Environmental Cooperation |
| NACEC | The North American Commission on Environmental Cooperation |
| NAFTA | North American Free Trade Agreement |
| NDC | Nationally Determined Contribution |
| NEPA | National Environmental Policy Act |
| NGO | Nongovernmental Organizations |
| $NO_2$ | Nitrogen Dioxide |
| NOx | Oxides of Nitrogen |
| NPT | Nuclear Non-Proliferation Treaty |
| NSG | Nuclear Suppliers Group |

**List of Abbreviations**

| | |
|---|---|
| NWFZ | Nuclear Weapon-Free Zone |
| NWS | Nuclear Weapon States |
| $O_3$ | Tropospheric Ozone |
| ODS | Ozone-Depleting Substances |
| OECD | Organisation for Economic Co-operation and Development |
| OEIGWG | Open-Ended Intergovernmental Working Group |
| OGEL | Oil, Gas and Energy Law |
| OGUK | Oil & Gas UK |
| OPA | Oil Pollution Act |
| OPEP | Oil Pollution Emergency Plans |
| OPRC | International Convention on Oil Pollution Preparedness, Response and Co-operation |
| OSLTF | Oil Spill Liability Trust Fund |
| OSPAR | The Convention for the Protection of the Marine Environment of the North-East Atlantic |
| PERAC | Protection of Environment in Relation to Armed Conflicts |
| PC | Preparatory Committee |
| PCA | Permanent Court of Arbitration |
| PCB | Polychlorinated Biphenyl |
| PCIJ | Permanent Court of International Justice |
| PM | Particulate Matter |
| POP | Persistent Organic Pollutant |
| PPMs | Process and Production Methods |
| PPP | Polluter Pays Principle |
| PSA | Petroleum Safety Authority |
| PSC | Production Sharing Contracts |
| Pu | Plutonium |
| PV | Photovoltaic |
| SDGs | Sustainable Development Goals |
| SDR | Special Drawing Rights |
| SEEA | System of Environmental-Economic Accounting |
| SFM | Sustainable Forest Management |
| SLCFs | Short-Lived Climate Forcers |
| SNT | Sensitive Nuclear Technologies |
| $SO_2$ | Sulfur Dioxide |
| SOLAS | Safety of Life at Sea |
| SORT | Strategic Offensive Reductions Treaty |
| STCW | International Convention on Standards of Training Certification and Watch Keeping for Seafarers |
| TBT | Technical Barriers to Trade |

| | |
|---|---|
| TNC | Transnational Corporation |
| UKCS | UK Continental Shelf |
| U.N. | United Nations |
| UNCCD | United Nations Convention to Combat Desertification |
| UNCED | United Nations Conference on Environment and Development |
| UNCLOS | United Nations Convention on the Law of the Sea |
| UNDP | United Nations Development Programme |
| UNEA | United Nations Environment Assembly |
| UNECE | United Nations Economic Commission for Europe |
| UNEP | United Nations Environment Programme |
| UNESCO | United Nations Educational, Scientific and Cultural Organization |
| UNFCCC | United Nations Framework Convention on Climate Change |
| UNFF | United Nations Forum on Forests |
| UNFI | United Nations Forest Instrument |
| UNGA | United Nations General Assembly |
| UNODC | United Nations Office on Drugs and Crime |
| UNSPF | United Nations Strategic Plan for Forests |
| UNU 2011 | United Nations University 2011 |
| U.S.-EPA | United States Environmental Protection Agency |
| UV-B | Ultraviolet-B |
| WCR | Well Control Rule |
| WHC | World Heritage Convention |
| WHO | World Health Organization |
| WMO | World Meteorological Organization |
| WSSD | World Summit on Sustainable Development |
| WTO | World Trade Organization |
| WWF | World Wide Fund for Nature |

## List of Abbreviations

# Acknowledgments

We would like to thank and express our sincere gratitude to Mrs. Rana Naseem and Mr. Faraz Naseem who have not only spared us to take time out of their share but also helped in the collection of valuable material on *Environmental Law-International*, typographic help and in all other respect so that this task could be completed successfully.

*Mohammad Naseem*
*Saman Naseem*
*New Delhi 2024*

## Acknowledgments

# General Introduction

*1.* International environmental law[1] is a field of international law dealing with and within limitations of international law as practiced by the sovereigns, regulating the behavior of states and international organizations with respect to the environment.[2] The core domains for international environmental regulation include management and prevention of pollution on land, water, oceans management, and protection of the world's fauna, flora, and the regulation of carbon and other particulate emissions into the atmosphere. It also covers topics such as population, biodiversity, climate change, ozone depletion, toxic and hazardous substances, air, land, sea, and trans-boundary water pollution, conservation of marine resources, desertification, waste disposal, and nuclear damage. The International Environmental law is concerned with the attempt to control pollution and the depletion of natural resources within a framework of sustainable development. It is a branch of public international law created by states for states to govern problems that arise between and among them.

*2.* In the face of devastating nature of environmental degradation in some parts of the world, the international community has continuously evolved and developed national and international laws to protect, manage, and conserve environment, natural resources, and living species for current and future generations. In this respect, environmental laws provide the platform on which institutions, policies, and compliance are judged and enforcement regimes at different levels are built in order to regulate and bring in harmony in the process of interactions with the environment. Environmental law is an evolving and constantly changing legal field. The understanding of natural resources and biodiversity and their impact is improving day by day, so there is a need that the legal framework that governs planning, use, and management of the environment must also adapt accordingly. The domestic environmental law has evolved through enactment of various legislations by the states mainly after the Industrial Revolution when environmental problems posed a potential threat to the survival of human beings. The early examples of enactments designed to preserve the environment, for its own sake or human enjoyment, are found throughout history. Around AD 80, the Senate of Rome passed legislation to protect the city's supply of clean water for drinking and bathing. In the fourteenth century, England prohibited both the burning of coal in London and the disposal of

---

1. Also termed as international ecological law.
2. *See* Phillipe Sands, *Principles of International Environmental Law* (2nd ed., Cambridge 2003).

waste into waterways. In 1681, the Quaker leader of the English colony of Pennsylvania, William Penn, ordered that one acre of forest be preserved for every five acres cleared for settlement, and in the following century, Benjamin Franklin led various campaigns to curtail the dumping of waste. In the nineteenth century, in the midst of the Industrial Revolution, the British government passed regulations to reduce the deleterious effects of coal burning and chemical manufacturing on public health and the environment.

Under common law, the primary protection was provided in the law of nuisance, but this only allowed for private actions for damages or injunctions if there was harm to the land. Private enforcement, however, was limited and totally inadequate with respect to major environmental threats to common resources, and examples are smells emanating from pigsties,[3] strict liability against dumping rubbish,[4] or damage from exploding dams.[5] During the "Great Stink" of 1858, because of the dumping of sewerage into the River Thames, it began to smell so ghastly in the summer heat that Parliament had to be evacuated. Ironically, the Metropolitan Commission of Sewers Act, 1848 had allowed the Metropolitan Commission for Sewers to close cesspits around the city in an attempt to "clean up," but this simply led people to pollute the river. In nineteen days, Parliament passed a further act to build the London sewerage system. London also suffered from terrible air pollution, and this culminated in the "Great Smog" of 1952, which in turn triggered the legislative response that resulted in the enactment of the Clean Air Act 1956. The basic regulatory structure was to set a limit on emissions for households and businesses particularly on burning coal.

## §1. Concept of Environmental Law

*3.* The concept of "environmental law" as a separate and distinct body of law is a twentieth-century development.[6] It was only in the 1960s that the fragile nature of environment was recognized, and the need was felt for legal protection. Subsequently, this recognition was translated into basic legal norms which developed into a body of "environmental law" and influenced its evolution relating to natural resource laws. At the same time other influences like a growing awareness of the unity and fragility of the biosphere, increasing concern over the impact of industrial activity on natural resources and human health, and the increasing strength of the regulatory state, etc. resulted in the development of a new body of environmental law. By the end of the twentieth century, environmental law was established as a component of the legal body in developed as well as in many developing nations of the world.

3. *Aldred*'s Case (1610) 9 Co Rep 57b; (1610) 77 ER 816.
4. *R v. Stephens* (1866) LR 1 QB 702.
5. *Rylands v. Fletcher* (1868) UKHL 1.
6. *See* generally R. Lazarus, *The Making of Environmental Law* (Cambridge Press 2004); P. Gates, *History of Public Land Law Development* (Zenger Pub 1968).

§2. Growth of International Environmental law

*4.* Environmental law cut across other areas of international law, such as commercial law, trade and human rights. International cooperation in the form of treaties, agreements, and resolutions created by intergovernmental organizations as well as national laws and regulations are used to protect the environment. The documents from the major organizations concerned with protection of the environment such as the United Nations Environment Programme (UNEP), the European Union (EU), the Organisation for Economic Co-operation and Development (OECD), and the Council of Europe are helpful in understanding the development of environmental law. Since ultimate responsibility for the protection of the environment remains with governments and its other bodies, at the national and local level, municipal laws and regulations related to the environment are also very important to understand and appreciate the growth of international environmental law.

*5.* Environmental law, principles, policies, directives, and regulations enacted and enforced by local, national, or international entities aim to regulate human treatment of the nonhuman world. During the late twentieth century, environmental law developed from a modest adjunct of the law of public health regulations into an almost universally recognized independent field protecting both human health and nonhuman nature. Prior to the twentieth century, there were few International Environmental Agreements (IEAs). The accords that were reached focused primarily on boundary waters, navigation, and fishing rights along shared waterways, and no importance was given to pollution and other ecological issues. In the early twentieth century, conventions to protect commercially valuable species were reached, including the Convention for the Protection of Birds Useful to Agriculture (1902), signed by twelve European governments; the Convention for the Preservation and Protection of Fur Seals (1911), concluded by the United States (U.S.), Japan, Russia, and the United Kingdom (U.K.); and the Convention for the Protection of Migratory Birds (1916), adopted by the U.S. and the U.K. (on behalf of Canada) and later extended to Mexico in 1936. In the 1930s, Belgium, Egypt, Italy, Portugal, South Africa, Sudan, and the U.K. adopted the Convention Relative to the Preservation of Fauna and Flora in their Natural State, which committed those countries to preserve natural fauna and flora in Africa by means of national parks and reserves. Spain and France signed the Convention but never ratified it, and Tanzania formally adopted it in 1962. India, which acceded to the agreement in 1939, was subject to the sections of the document prohibiting "trophies" made from any animal mentioned in the annexure.

Beginning in the 1960s, environmentalism became an important political and intellectual movement in the West. In the U.S., the publication of biologist Rachel Carson's Silent Spring (1962), a passionate and persuasive examination of chlorinated hydrocarbon pesticides and the environmental damage caused by their use, led to a reconsideration of a much broader range of actual and potential environmental hazards. In subsequent decades, the U.S. government passed an extraordinary number of environmental laws—including enactments addressing solid-waste disposal, air and water pollution, and the protection of endangered species—and created an Environmental Protection Agency (EPA) to monitor compliance. These new laws dramatically increased the national government's role in the area of environment previously left primarily to state and local regulation. Thirty-four countries in 1971 adopted the Convention on Wetlands of International Importance Especially as Waterfowl Habitat, generally known as the Ramsar Convention as it was signed in the Ramsar city of Iran. It required all countries to designate at least one protected wetland area, and it recognized the important role of wetlands in maintaining the ecological equilibrium. Following the U.N. Conference on the Human Environment, held in Stockholm in 1972, the U.N. established the UNEP as the world's principal international environmental organization. Although UNEP oversees many modern-day agreements, it has little power to impose or enforce sanctions on non-complying parties. Nevertheless, a series of important conventions arose directly from the conference, including the Convention on the Prevention of Marine Pollution by Dumping of Wastes or Other Matter (1972) and the Convention on International Trade in Endangered Species of Wild Fauna and Flora (CITES) (1973).

*6.* Until the Stockholm conference, the countries generally had been slow to enact legal standards for environmental protection—although there had been some exceptions, such as the passage of the conservationist Countryside Act in the U.K. in 1968. In October 1972, the leaders of the European Community (EC) declared that the goal of economic expansion had to be balanced with the need to protect the environment. In the following year, the European Commission, the EC's executive branch, produced its first Environmental Action Programme, and since then European countries have been at the forefront of environmental policymaking. In Germany, for example, public attitude toward environmental protection changed in the early 1980s, when it became known that many German forests were being destroyed by acid rain. During the 1980s, the "trans-boundary effects" of environmental pollution in individual countries spurred negotiations on several international environmental conventions. The effects of the 1986 accident at the nuclear power plant at Chernobyl in Ukraine (then part of the Soviet Union) were especially significant. European countries in the pollution's downwind path were forced to adopt measures to restrict their populations' consumption of water, milk, meat, and vegetables. In Austria, traces of radiation were found in cow's milk as well as in human breast milk. As a direct result of the Chernobyl disaster, two international agreements—the Convention on Early Notification of a Nuclear Accident and the Convention on Assistance in the Case of Nuclear Accident or Radiological Emergency, both adopted in 1986—were drafted to ensure notification and assistance in the event of a nuclear accident. In the following decade, a Convention on Nuclear Safety (1994) established incentives for countries to adopt basic standards for the safe operation of land-based nuclear power plants.

*7.* There are often conflicting data about the environmental impact of human activities and scientific uncertainty which complicate the drafting and implementation of environmental laws and regulations, particularly for international conferences attempting to develop universal standards. Consequently, such laws and regulations are designed to be flexible so as to accommodate changes in scientific understanding and technological capacity. The Vienna Convention for the Protection of the Ozone Layer (1985), for example, neither did specify the measures that signatory states were required to adopt to protect human health and the environment from the effects of ozone depletion nor did it mention any of the substances that were thought to damage the ozone layer. Similarly, the United Nations Framework Convention on Climate Change (UNFCCC), or Global Warming Convention, adopted by 178 countries at the 1992 United Nations Conference on Environment and Development (UNCED) held in Rio de Janeiro (popularly known as the "Earth Summit"), did not set binding targets for reducing the emission of the "greenhouse" gases which was thought to cause global warming.

*8.* In 1995, the Intergovernmental Panel on Climate Change, which was established by the World Meteorological Organization (WMO) and UNEP to study changes in the Earth's temperature concluded that, "the balance of evidence suggests a discernible human influence on global climate." Although cited by environmentalists as final proof of the reality of global warming, the report was faulted by some critics for relying on insufficient data, for overstating the environmental impact of global warming, and for using unrealistic models of climate change. Two years later in Kyoto, Japan, a conference of signatories to the Framework Convention on Climate Change adopted the report.

*9.* Its market mechanisms included the sale of "emission reduction units," which are earned when a developed country reduces its emissions below its commitment level, to developed countries that have failed to achieve their emission targets. Developed countries could earn additional emission reduction units by financing energy-efficient projects (e.g., clean development mechanisms (CDMs)) in developing countries (DC). Since its adoption, the protocol has encountered stiff opposition from some countries, particularly the U.S., which has not ratified it.

*10.* The first session of the UN Environment Assembly (UNEA)—the highest-level U.N. body ever convened on the environment—was held on June 23, 2014, at the UNEP headquarters in Nairobi. The UNEA feeds directly into the General Assembly and has universal membership of all 193 U.N. Member States as well as other stakeholder groups. With this wide reach into the legislative, financial, and development arenas, the new body presents a groundbreaking platform for leadership on global environmental policy.

## §3. Challenges to Environment

*11.* The current issues and challenges faced by international environmental law include ozone layer depletion, global warming, desertification, destruction of tropical rain forests, marine plastics pollution from ships, international trade in endangered species, shipment of hazardous wastes to Third World countries, dumping of waste, deforestation, protection of wetlands, oil spills, trans-boundary nuclear radiation, groundwater depletion, international trade in pesticides, acid rain etc.

*12.* Some of the key challenges that exist at present and can be envisaged for the progressive development of environmental law are:

(a) time lags between scientific understanding of environmental issues and corresponding development of appropriate laws at the national, international, and regional levels;
(b) outdated or inadequate national legislation or international agreements cannot effectively address certain environmental issues;
(c) lack of environmental laws to adequately preserve and protect natural resources and ecosystems, especially in DC; and
(d) insufficient capacity to implement environmental laws, especially in DC.

*13.* The global environmental situation has deteriorated post-Stockholm conference (1972) that created the UNEP. Keeping in view the current developments, any solutions must cope with threats from cyber wars, nuclear war, genetic mutations, and artificial intelligence (AI). There is also a tendency to minimize economic impact at the expense of environmental protection which requires harmonization. State sovereignty is another hurdle in implementing effective environmental conservation and sustainable development. International law makes states responsible for adapting regulations and securing compliance which is not uniform and varies from country to country. With respect to the direct and indirect impacts of armed conflicts on the natural environment, states can integrate legal protections for the environment into their armed forces' doctrines. The human rights groups may commit resources and expertise to help to deal with the environmental consequences of conflict. Since the 1960s, the United Nations General Assembly (UNGA) has been the main body for the protection of the global environment, and it is the time that the United Nations (U.N.) takes this problem with needed urgencies. The U.N. Trusteeship Council which is dormant may be revived with a mandate for the environment and the global commons. The UNEP may be developed into a specialized agency to elevate its status with the necessary competence and financial stability.

## §4. Artificial Intelligence and Pollution

*14.* AI is being applied in many areas dealing with environmental protection, including natural resource conservation, wildlife protection, energy management, water management, carbon footprint management, clean energy, waste management, pollution control, agriculture and weather forecast. AI is considered the biggest development in the global economy. It is estimated that by 2030, AI will contribute up to 15.7 trillion of the global economy. AI is steadily becoming a part of our daily lives, and its impact can be seen through the advancements made in the field of environmental sciences and environmental management. AI is very beneficial for environmental analysis, as it enables to process a huge amount of data quickly so as to draw conclusions that may not have been possible by human mind alone. For instance, in China, IBM's Green Horizon project uses AI technology to forecast air pollution, track pollution sources and provide potential solutions to deal with it. World Health Organization (WHO) estimates that exposure to air pollution causes around 4.2 million mortalities across the globe each year. As per its further estimation, around 91% of the global population lives in places where the air pollution is much more than the guidelines of WHO which is a concern for the communities around the globe. Several companies offer AI solutions for environmental protection and for controlling global warming. The key players in AI in environmental protection market adopt various strategies for retaining their position in the market. These strategies include geographical expansion, collaborations and partnerships, new product or service launches, and mergers and acquisitions. For instance, in November 2018, AI company One Concern launched an AI-powered platform that allows companies to forecast levels of potential flooding up to five days in advance.

### I. Energy Efficiency

*15.* The use of AI has led to improvement in energy efficiency as organizations like Microsoft, Google and Tesla have made considerable efforts in developing "Earth Friendly" AI systems. For example, Google's DeepMind AI has helped to reduce the data center energy usage by 40% making them more energy efficient and reducing overall greenhouse gas (GHG) emissions. As data centers alone consume 3% of global energy each year, development of such AI's not only improves the energy efficiency but also assists in providing energy access to remote communities, setting up micro-grids and integrating renewable energy resources. Installation of smart grids can utilize AI techniques to regulate and control parts of neighborhood power grid to deliver exactly the amount of electricity needed or requested from consumers. AI-driven autonomous vehicles with techniques like route optimization, eco-driving and ride-sharing may help in reducing the carbon footprint. The smart buildings and the smart cities with the use of AI can have built-in sensors to ensure the efficient use of energy. The building material has been developed from natural resources, such as cement that captures carbon dioxide ($CO_2$) and cooling systems that use wind and sun.

### II. Waste Management

*16.* Controlling industrial emissions and waste management is another challenge that can be dealt with the advanced learning machines and smart networks that could detect leaks, potential hazards and diversions from industrial standards and governmental regulations.

### III. Climate Change

*17.* In 2017, Microsoft announced a scheme that is Microsoft's AI for Earth, which will use AI to find solutions to various challenges related to climatic changes, agriculture, water and biodiversity. Other similar AI-infused Earth applications are iNaturalist and eBirds that collect data from experts on the species encountered, helping to keep track of their population, favorable ecosystems and migration patterns.

## IV. Agriculture

*18.* The application of AI is increasing in agriculture for automated data collection, detection of crop diseases and optimizing agricultural inputs and returns based on demand and supply. A Berlin-based agricultural tech startup (Progressive Environmental & Agricultural Technologies) PEAT has developed a deep learning application called Plantix that identifies potential defects and nutrient deficiencies in soil. Analysis is conducted by software algorithms which correlate particular foliage patterns with certain soil defects, plant pests and diseases. AWhere and FarmShots, both U.S.-based companies, use machine learning algorithms in connection with satellites to predict weather, analyze crop sustainability and evaluate farms for the presence of diseases and pests.

## V. Protecting Oceans

*19.* The application of AI in environment protection includes machine learning for protecting the oceans, monitoring shipping, ocean mining, fishing, coral bleaching or the outbreak of marine disease. For instance, the Nature Conservancy is collaborating with Microsoft on using AI for carbon storage, seafood harvesting, and conservation of marine life.

## VI. System of Environmental-Economic Accounting Ecosystem Accounting

*20.* On April 29, 2021, an innovative AI tool was launched by the U.N. and the Basque Centre for Climate Change (BC3). Developed by the Statistics Division of the United Nations Department of Economic and Social Affairs (UN DESA), the UNEP, and BC3, this tool can accelerate implementation of the new standard for valuing the contributions of nature that was adopted by the U.N. Statistical Commission. The tool makes use of Artificial Intelligence for Environment and Sustainability (ARIES) platform to support countries as they apply the new international standard for natural capital accounting, the System of Environmental-Economic Accounting (SEEA) Ecosystem Accounting.

### *A. ARIES for SEEA*

*21.* The new open-source and user-friendly digital tool, called the ARIES for SEEA Explorer, enables rapid and standardized yet customizable ecosystem accounting. The ecosystem accounts produced by countries will track the extent, condition and services provided by nature's ecosystems—such as forests and wetlands—in the form of physical and monetary accounts and indicators. The adoption of the SEEA Ecosystem Accounting is viewed as a historic step for the Sustainable Development Goals (SDGs). Building economic systems that value nature as a central source of human well-being, environmental health and economic prosperity is essential. The ARIES for SEEA Explorer is available on the U.N. Global Platform: a cloud-service environment supporting international collaboration among all countries in the world by sharing scientific knowledge, data, methods and technology. Some countries have started using the ARIES for SEEA Explorer.

## §5. COVID-19 AND ENVIRONMENT

### I. Effect on Normal Human Life

*22.* The COVID-19 Pandemic started in December 2019 has resulted in lockdowns in the whole world. As the disease spread to most of the countries making it the largest pandemic in the world. Coronavirus, a zoonotic virus has caused infection and death in hundreds and thousands. The virus is thought to have originated from bats, and the first was reported in December 2019, in Wuhan, Hubei province, China, and initial cases were related to source infection from a seafood wholesale market (Huang et al., 2020). Lockdown imposed has resulted in cessation of activities and closure of industries throughout the world. The COVID-19 pandemic has also brought drastic changes in everyday lives as well as on economy which may have immediate and long-term impacts on environmental law. There have been long-lasting impact on behaviors, values, demographics, and available resources. Normative and political values have also shifted, especially surrounding COVID-19-related risks such as human-wildlife interactions and single-use plastics. Increased time spent indoors and closures of national and state parks lead to reevaluation of the importance of nature. The behavioral changes forced by the pandemic brought optimism about the capacity for mass behavioral shifts leading to climate change mitigation.

*23.* COVID-19 has also brought into focus a number of socioeconomic problems that affect vulnerable sections of society. If COVID-19 leaves populations weaker and more susceptible to disease than they were prior to the pandemic, previously "tolerable" levels of air pollution under existing environmental regulations may lead to disproportionate harm. This pandemic is a call to infuse a sense of morality and solidarity into global manner of thinking. The crippling effects should be recognized that can result in a disregard for animal welfare. The global community has to put the health of the planet and all of its inhabitants before the objective of profit margins.

### II. Improvement in Environment

*24.* The lockdown and other actions taken by the countries to stop the spread of COVID-19 have led to improvement in the quality of environment. Some changes, such as decreased travel, closure of industries, have led to environmental benefits like cleaner air and reduced GHG emissions. There was encouragement to employees to work from home. According to WHO, lockdown and consequent cessation of a large number of daily activities had a good influence on the environment. Change in air pollution levels was first observed over Wuhan, China, the city which first reported incidents of coronavirus leading to COVID-19 disease. During the lockdown, there was an improvement in the quality of environment facilitating the implementation of legal obligations on various environmental indicators. Due to a pause in industrial effluent discharge into the canals of the city of Venice, Italy, its water was found to glitter. The effect of lockdown on air quality in Milan was assessed and studied through the trends of nine pollutants. Lockdown resulted in a significant reduction of PM10, PM2.5, BC, benzene, CO and oxides of nitrogen (NOx). Part of the ozone increase was probably due to the lower NO measured during lockdown.

# Part I. International Environmental Law: Evolution and Sources

*25.* In the present-day world, environmental laws set the parameters and form the standards that governments follow to manage natural resources and environmental quality in the country and also take measures so that there is no spread of trans-boundary pollution. The broad categories of "natural resources" and "environmental quality" include air and water pollution, forests and wildlife, hazardous waste, agricultural practices, wetlands, and land use planning. The body of environmental law includes not only the text of these laws but also the regulations that implement and the judicial decisions that interpret existing legislation and treaties. In general, the standards set forth in environmental laws can be applied either to private parties or to the government. The Clean Air and Clean Water Acts, in the U.S., for example, are frequently used to regulate the polluting activities of private enterprises. These laws mandate certain pollution-reducing technology or limit the levels of pollution for power plants and factories. The National Environmental Policy Act (NEPA) applies only to the actions of the U.S. government. NEPA requires that the federal government undertake a comprehensive Environmental Impact Assessment (EIA) before it proceeds with projects that are likely to harm the environment.

*26.* By the end of the twentieth century, international environmental law had been established as a component of the legal landscape in all developed nations of the world and many developing ones. Global and regional environmental issues became the subject of international law. Debates over environmental concerns implicate core principles of international law and have been the subject of numerous international agreements and declarations. The Stockholm and Rio texts have provided a foundation for the development of national and international environmental law and policy. The Johannesburg World Summit on Sustainable Development (WSSD) produced a political declaration known as the Johannesburg Declaration on Sustainable Development, a Plan of Implementation of the WSSD, and "Type II" non-negotiated, partnership commitments by governments and other stakeholders, including business and nongovernmental organizations (NGOs).

*27.* In the 1960s, the concern with respect to environmental protection gained importance in international community when it became the focus of law and policy in many states. Public opinion, increasingly aware of environmental harm due to major oil spills and other sources of pollution, played a major role in this development. In this background, the government of Sweden, in 1968, proposed that the U.N. convene an international conference on the human environment. The aim was to focus attention on the importance of environmental problems, so as these problems could be comprehensively considered by the U.N. The UNGA endorsed the proposal and convened an international conference[7] which was held in Stockholm from June 5–16, 1972.

## §1. Stockholm Conference

*28.* The Stockholm Conference came out with[8] a declaration of principles, a resolution on institutional and financial measures, and contained an action plan with recommendations. Out of the five texts that emerged from the UNCED, three were nonbinding instruments: the Rio Declaration on Environment and Development, Agenda 21, and the non-legally binding authoritative statement of principles for a global consensus on the management, conservation, and sustainable development of all types of forests ("Forest Principles"; Forests, International Protection). In addition, two treaties, the Convention on Biological Diversity (CBD) and the Framework Convention on Climate Change, were opened for signature at the UNCED.

### I. Declaration on Environment

*29.* In September 1968, an Intergovernmental Conference of Experts on the Scientific Basis for Rational Use and Conservation of the Resources of the Biosphere, sponsored by the United Nations Educational, Scientific and Cultural Organization (UNESCO), first suggested the idea of a declaration on the environment. Resolution 1448 of August 6, 1969 of the UN Economic and Social Council (ECOSOC) and UNGA Resolution 2581 (XXIV) of December 15, 1969, convening the Stockholm meeting, supported the objective of adopting basic premises to guide the future actions on the environment. The resolutions also established a special committee consisting of twenty-seven states, advising the U.N. Secretary-General to undertake preparations for the Stockholm Conference. The Preparatory Committee (PC) was able to resolve most issues facing the conference, leaving few matters to be debated at the Stockholm Conference itself.

7. UNGA Res 2398 (XXIII) of Dec. 3, 1968.
8. Around 114 States participated in Stockholm Conference.

## II. Preparatory Committee

*30.* The PC initially had before it a background paper prepared by the U.N. Secretary-General recommending that the PC drafts a declaration on the "rights and obligations of citizens and Governments with regard to the preservation and improvement of the human environment." After consulting the Member States, PC agreed on the objectives of a declaration: to have a document of basic principles, calling attention to environmental problems and to the rights and obligations of all parts of society in relation thereto; to stimulate public opinion and community participation for the protection and improvement of the environment in the interest of present and future generations; to provide guiding principles for governments to formulate policy; and to set objectives for future international cooperation. Throughout its text, the declaration was to take due account of the environmental stresses caused by differences in social and economic development.[9] On this basis and with suggestions from the Secretary-General as to the content, the PC established an intergovernmental working group to prepare a draft.

## III. Intergovernmental Working Group

*31.* The working group and the committee debated during the drafting process whether the declaration should primarily seek to outline broad goals and objectives, or whether it should embody legal principles elaborating the rights and duties of states with respect to the environment. In the end, the drafters merged the two approaches and opted to include specific guidelines for future action as well as statements primarily aimed at stimulating public and governmental awareness of environmental issues. The PC and the Declaration of the U.N. Conference on the Human Environment ("Stockholm Declaration") thus expressed their aim as providing "a common outlook and common principles to guide the world in the preservation and enhancement of the human environment."[10]

*32.* After the working group presented the first draft of seventeen principles, many of which were contested, the PC instructed it to develop further the text based on well-established principles of international law. The working group returned with a new preamble and twenty-three principles, a text which the chairman said recognized the right of individuals to an adequate environment, state responsibility for extraterritorial damage to the environment, and the particular interests of DC.[11] The committee forwarded the draft without change or comment to the conference.

9. UN Doc A/CONF.48/PC/6 paras 27–38.
10. Preamble of Stockholm Declaration.
11. UNGA Preparatory Committee for the United Nations Conference on the Human Environment: Report of the Preparatory Committee on its Fourth Session.

*33.* Several states at the Stockholm Conference sought to amend the draft and, at the request of China, the conference established a working group on the declaration. Negotiations in the working group continued until the last day of the conference and the final text that emerged retained twenty-one of the committee's principles and added four new ones. One principle, on the duty of states to inform others of activities within their territories that might have an adverse extraterritorial effect, was removed and referred to the UNGA. The principle referring to nuclear weapons was referred to the plenary session for final decision and was ultimately retained as Principle 26, the concluding provision. The plenary session adopted the declaration and submitted it, along with other final texts, to the UNGA.

## §2. Stockholm Declaration

*34.* This declaration comprehensively deals with the environmental problem faced by the international community and has the following main features.

### I. Preamble and Principles

*35.* The preamble to the Stockholm Declaration begins with the statement that man is the creature who moulds his environment and that the natural element and the manmade are essential to human well-being and the full enjoyment of basic human rights, including the right to life. Protecting the human environment is a major issue for economic development. The preamble recognizes that the natural growth of the world population continuously poses problems for preserving the environment but expresses faith that scientific and social progress in improving the environment strengthens each day.

*36.* The preamble reflects the divergent views of the participants at Stockholm on whether the Stockholm Declaration should be primarily inspirational or whether it should provide specific guidelines for action. It also reflected disagreement over whether the Stockholm Declaration should be addressed to governments, to individuals, or to all sections of society. The introductory phrases of the preamble recall the beginning of the U.N. Charter in referring to the peoples of the world, although most principles address governmental action.

### II. Principles

*37.* The second part of the Stockholm Declaration contains twenty-six principles approved by the conference to inspire and guide future action. During the drafting, more than half a dozen delegations at the conference thought that the Stockholm Declaration should begin with a general affirmation of every human being's right to a safe or wholesome environment, arguing that it was implicit in the right to an adequate standard of living recognized in Article 25(1) of Universal Declaration of Human Rights (1948). Man has the fundamental right to freedom, equality, and adequate conditions of life in an environment of a quality that permits a life of dignity and well-being, and he bears a solemn responsibility to protect and improve the environment for present and future generations. In this respect, policies promoting or perpetuating apartheid, racial segregation, discrimination, colonial and other forms of oppression, and foreign domination stand condemned and must be eliminated as per Principle 1 of the Stockholm Declaration. This principle links human rights and environmental protection and refers to the most prominent international human rights problems while condemning apartheid, colonialism, and racial discrimination.

*38.* Principles 2–7 of the Stockholm Declaration set forth the rationale for environmental protection and specific threats to the environment. These principles embody that the natural resources of the globe are not only oil and minerals but also air, water, earth, plants and animals as well as representative samples of natural ecosystems. These should be preserved in the interest of present and future generations. Renewable resources must maintain their ability to replenish themselves, and non-renewable resources should not be wasted.[12] The Stockholm Declaration emphasizes the necessity of adequate resource management and the responsibility of mankind to protect wildlife and habitats.[13] This section calls for a halt to the production of toxic wastes or other matters that cannot be absorbed by the environment and/or a prevention of marine pollution.[14] Principle 7 of the Stockholm Declaration is the only principle in this group that includes language of obligation, providing that states shall take steps to prevent marine pollution and may reflect the negotiations then concluding to adopt the Convention on the Prevention of Marine Pollution by Dumping of Wastes and Other Matters.

*39.* Principles 8–20 of the Stockholm Declaration identify means of environmental protection and their relationship to economic and social development. Four provisions concern the particular situation of DC. After stating that economic and social development is indispensable to an environment favorable to the existence and work of man (Principle 8 of the Stockholm Declaration), Principle 9 affirms that the best means to remedy underdevelopment is to enhance financial assistance and technical assistance. National environmental policies should assist the potential progress of poorer countries, and they should be accorded supplementary international assistance.

*40.* Principles 10–12 of the Stockholm Declaration relate to international trade and economic consequences of environmental protection, particularly for DC. Principle 10 of the Stockholm Declaration provides that the stability of prices and an

12. Principles 3–5 of the Stockholm Declaration.
13. Principle 4 of the Stockholm Declaration.
14. Principle 6 of the Stockholm Declaration.

adequate remuneration for primary products and goods are essential for the management of the environment. Principles 13–15 of the Stockholm Declaration underline the necessity of integrated, coordinated, and rational development planning. Demographic issues produced a recommendation in Principle 16 of the Stockholm Declaration in favor of policies which respect fundamental human rights and are judged adequate by the concerned governments. Principles 18–20 of the Stockholm Declaration mention other instruments of environmental policy: recourse to science and technology, exchange of information, and finally, teaching and information about environmental matters.

*41.* The last group of principles, Principles 21–26 of the Stockholm Declaration, is of particular interest for the development of international law. Principle 21 expresses a basic norm of customary international environmental law. The states have, in accordance with the U.N. Charter and the principles of international law, the sovereign right to exploit their own resources pursuant to their own environmental policies, and the responsibility to ensure that the activities within their national jurisdiction or control do not cause damage to the environment of other states or of areas beyond the limits of national jurisdiction.

*42.* The Stockholm Declaration also affirms that states should cooperate to develop international law regarding liability and compensation for victims of pollution and other environmental damage produced outside their boundaries.[15] They should define criteria and norms in environmental matters, taking into consideration the system of values prevailing in each country, in particular, in DC.[16] States should cooperate to protect and improve the environment and ensure that international organizations play a coordinated, effective, and dynamic role in this field.[17] The final principle condemns nuclear weapons and all other means of mass destruction.

## III. Legal Status

*43.* The Stockholm Declaration was not adopted as a treaty hence not legally binding as such. Moreover, few of the principles in the Stockholm Declaration purport to be normative. Instead, most of them represent an agreed statement of the environmental problems identified during the Stockholm Conference, the then-current understanding of the causes of these problems, and a set of relevant economic and political considerations to be taken into account in resolving the problems.

15. Principle 22 of the Stockholm Declaration.
16. Principle 23 of the Stockholm Declaration.
17. Principles 24–25 of the Stockholm Declaration.

## IV. Legal Value and Practical Significance

*44.* Despite its formally nonbinding character, the Stockholm Declaration is legally significant. The articulation of global values and policies it represents was a prerequisite to establishing international legal norms. Principles 2–4 of the Stockholm Declaration, for example, represented new values in affirming the importance of all components of the biosphere and the responsibility to safeguard them. This idea of conservation became the foundation of national and international measures over the succeeding decades. Further, the Stockholm Declaration stimulated joint action globally and regionally, as it stressed planning and cooperation, taking into account the needs of DC and future generations.

## V. International Court of Justice

*45.* Several Stockholm principles of normative content have emerged as legal norms. A majority opinion of the International Court of Justice (ICJ) declared in 1996 that the obligation of states to ensure that activities within their jurisdiction and control respect the environment of other states, a reformulation of Principle 21 of the Stockholm Declaration, "is now part of the corpus of international law relating to the environment."[18] The duty to cooperate, contained in Principle 24 of the Stockholm Declaration, was called a "fundamental principle" of international law by the International Tribunal for the Law of the Sea (ITLOS).[19] Principle 22 of the Stockholm Declaration has led to the adoption of a growing number of treaties on responsibility and liability for extraterritorial environmental harm.

## VI. Duty to Consult and Duty to Inform

*46.* The developments and debate at Stockholm itself had an impact on the subsequent development of the environmental law. The working group's original Principle 20, on the duty to inform, generated two UNGA resolutions on the duty to consult and to inform states about activities that might cause significant transboundary environmental harm. Brazil presented a resolution, co-sponsored by other developing states, on the duty to cooperate in the field of the environment, including by the provision of information about activities, while strongly reaffirming state sovereignty over natural resources. Other states countered with a resolution affirming that no UNGA resolution could affect Principles 21 and 22 of the Stockholm Declaration. Both resolutions were adopted without a dissenting vote.[20]

18. Legality of the Threat of Use or Use of Nuclear Weapons (Nuclear Weapons Advisory Opinions) 241–42; *Gabcíkovo-Nagymaros* Case 41.
19. *See also* MOX Plant Arbitration and Cases (*UK v. Ireland*) (Provisional measures) Order of Dec. 3, 2001 (*see also* Interim (Provisional) Measures of Protection)).
20. (UNGA Res 2995 (XXVII) of Dec. 15, 1972 and UNGA Res 2996 (XXVII) of Dec. 15, 1972).

## VII. Declaration as Prime Mover

*47.* The Stockholm Conference stimulated numerous international activities to protect the environment. Governments in different countries took action to counter marine oil pollution through preventive and remedial measures and concluded new instruments to conserve wild animals like the 1972 London Convention for the Conservation of Antarctic Seals. The Stockholm Declaration provided a rationale for legal and political action to address the identified problems. Institutions created after Stockholm, in particular, the UNEP, relied on the Declaration and Action Plan in developing their agendas. Stockholm also stimulated institutions concerned with other fields of international law to consider environmental issues. The International Maritime Organization (IMO), the Food and Agriculture Organization (FAO) of the U.N., and regional bodies such as the United Nations Economic Commission for Europe (UNECE) and the Association of Southeast Asian Nations (ASEAN) acted in response to the principles set forth in the Stockholm Declaration.

*48.* The U.N. reaffirmed and developed the general principles of the Stockholm Declaration in 1982 by UNGA adopting the World Charter for Nature.[21] The Stockholm Conference had an impact on legal developments in other fields of international law as well. Examples include the negotiations which began in 1972 at the U.N. Conference on the Law of the Sea. The resulting United Nations Convention on the Law of the Sea (UNCLOS) reaffirmed and detailed global and regional regulations to combat marine environmental injury and affirmed the principle that states have a general obligation to protect and preserve the marine environment. Similarly, Article 30 of Charter of Economic Rights and Duties of States (1974), adopted by the UNGA in 1974, proclaims that the protection, preservation, and management of the environment for present and future generations are the responsibilities of all states.

## §3. Rio Conference

*49.* In 1983, the UNGA voted to create the World Commission on Environment and Development, an independent body linked to but outside the U.N. system. Commonly known as the Brundtland Commission, it was to examine critical environment and development issues and to formulate realistic proposals for dealing with them; to propose new forms of international cooperation on these issues to influence policies in the direction of needed changes; and to raise the levels of understanding and commitment to action of individuals, organizations, businesses, and governments. The conclusions of the Brundtland Report stressed the need for an integrated approach to development policies and projects which, if environmentally sound, should lead to sustainable economic development in both developed countries and DC.

21. UNGA Res. 37/7 of Oct. 28, 1982.

*50.* The Brundtland Report led the U.N. to organize a second global conference on the environment in 1992 in Rio de Janeiro, the UNCED, twenty years after the Stockholm Conference, to assess events during the intervening years and to focus on the relationship between environmental protection and economic development.[22] The UNCED was originally designed as the successor to the Stockholm Conference, but legal and political developments as identified in the Brundtland Report shifted the focus of the conference. UNCED took place in Rio de Janeiro, Brazil in June 1992, with representatives from 178 countries. The convening resolution identified nine issues of major concern: (1) protection of the atmosphere; (2) protection of freshwater resources; (3) protection of the marine environment; (4) protection of land resources; (5) conservation of biological diversity; (6) environmentally sound management of biotechnology; (7) environmentally sound management of wastes; (8) improvement of living and working environments; and (9) protection of human health and improvement of the quality of life. The UNGA created a PC open to all U.N. Member States, members of specialized agencies, and accredited observers. UNCED represented one of the largest conferences ever held, with 172 states participating and some 116 heads of state or government attending.

## I. Origin, Purpose, and Meaning

*51.* The three sessions of the PC negotiated legal, institutional, and financial questions. One initial goal was to proclaim an Earth Charter, built on the foundation of the Stockholm Declaration, going beyond codification of existing norms to establish standards based on the best practices then emerging in environmental law and policy. After negotiations, the idea of an Earth Charter was abandoned in favor of adopting a declaration of principles, a compromise between the DC seeking only political commitments and industrialized countries, mainly Member States of the OECD, which insisted on legal norms. There were competing views on the contents of a declaration. The industrialized countries considered it essential to include principles on public information and participation, and the polluter pays principle (PPP), while DC demanded inclusion of the rights to development, poverty alleviation, and recognition of common but differentiated responsibilities.

## II. Rio Principles

*52.* The Rio Declaration on Environment and Development ("Rio Declaration"), a short statement of twenty-seven principles, has a composite and compromise character due to the competing aims and priorities of the participating states. The result represents a carefully negotiated balance between the priorities and interests of the developed and developing states. Given the number of participating states, it also represents the consensus of the time on the issue of integrating environment and development. The result is a document of mixed content, with several principles reflecting a restatement of existing rules on trans-boundary environmental matters,

22. UNGA Res. 44/228 of Dec. 22, 1989.

other principles setting forth new or developing principles of law concerned with environmental and development, and yet a third set of principles proclaiming policy goals and ideals.

### *A. Sustainable Development*

*53.* The central concept of the Rio Declaration is sustainable development, as defined by the Brundtland Report, which integrates development and environmental protection. This new focus is illustrated in Principle 2 of the Rio Declaration, which repeats the formulation of Principle 21 of the Stockholm Declaration that balances sovereignty with the duty to prevent trans-boundary environmental harm, but adds the word "developmental" in providing that states have the right to exploit their resources in accordance with their own environmental and developmental policies. Principle 3 of the Rio Declaration proclaims a right to development, while Principle 4 of the Rio Declaration affirms that environmental protection shall constitute an integral part of the development process and cannot be considered in isolation, in order to achieve sustainable development.

### *B. Environment Protection with Economic Development*

*54.* The linking of environment and development is also seen in Principle 7 of the Rio Declaration which addresses common but differentiated responsibilities. The principle bases the differentiated responsibility on two elements namely responsibility for creating environmental problems and capacities of states to address or remedy the problems. Principle 8 of the Rio Declaration adds that states should reduce and eliminate unsustainable patterns of production and consumption and promote demographic policies. Although it is not made explicit, the first part of this principle mainly concerns industrialized states, while the second part is aimed at DC.

The Rio Declaration also shifts away from the rights-based approach of the comparable opening provision in the Stockholm Declaration. It states: "Human beings are at the center of concerns for sustainable development. They are entitled to a healthy and productive life in harmony with nature" (Principle 1 of the Rio Declaration). This principle serves to refocus action away from environmental protection alone to environmental protection in the context of economic development, an approach reflected also in provisions concerned with the equitable demands of present and future generations (Principles 3, 5, 7, 11 of the Rio Declaration). The Rio Declaration reiterates some existing legal norms and has added several new ones as well. Statements of obligation given in Principle 10 of the Rio Declaration affirm that states shall provide rights of public information, participation, and access to justice. Principle 13 of the Rio Declaration calls for the development of liability rules. Principles 18 and 19 of the Rio Declaration require notifying other states about emergencies and projects that may affect their environment.

*C. Development of Principles of Environmental Law*

*55.* The formulation of emerging principles of environmental law includes the precautionary principle,[23] the "polluter pays" principle that requires internalization of environmental costs[24] and the general requirement for an EIA.[25] Principle 11 of the Rio Declaration stresses the importance of enacting effective environmental legislation, noting that standards applied by some countries may not be appropriate to others because of the economic and social costs involved. These principles were not widely known or practiced at the time of the Stockholm Conference but became common in the intervening years and were thus included in the Rio Declaration. Some of the principles, especially Principle 17 of the Rio Declaration on EIA, have been widely accepted since UNCED, while the normative status of the precautionary principle remains highly debated.

*56.* Other Declarations are more in the nature of policy guidelines. Principle 3 of the Rio Declaration aims at the eradication of poverty, Principle 6 of the Rio Declaration claims special priority for the needs of DC, and Principle 9 of the Rio Declaration relates to the strengthening of endogenous capacity building for sustainable development by improving scientific understanding. Principle 12 of the Rio Declaration advocates a "supportive and open economic system" and international consensus and condemns discriminatory trade measures or disguised restrictions on international trade, as well as unilateral actions. Finally, Principle 14 of the Rio Declaration aims to discourage or prevent the relocation and transfer to other states of activities and substances that cause severe environmental degradation or are harmful to human health. Principles 20–22 of the Rio Declaration stresses the importance of the participation of women, youth, and indigenous peoples.

## III. Legal Status

*57.* Like the Stockholm Declaration, the Rio Declaration was not adopted as a legally binding instrument. Its preamble provides that the participating states reaffirm the Stockholm Declaration and aim to do two things: (1) establish new and equitable partnerships and new levels of cooperation among states, key sectors of societies and peoples and (2) work toward international agreements to protect the integrity of the global environmental and developmental system. Several principles repeat and confirm international legal rules widely contained in treaties and national law and, in some instances, recognized as Customary International Law (CIL). Principle 2 of the Rio Declaration and its predecessor Principle 21 of the Stockholm Declaration, in particular, are accepted statements of CIL. Article 3 of CBD, the preamble of the Framework Convention on Climate Change, and Article 1(a) Statement of Forest Principles proclaim the same rule. The duty to cooperate, specified

23. Principle 15 of the Rio Declaration.
24. Principle 16 of the Rio Declaration.
25. Principle 17 of the Rio Declaration.

in Principle 24 of the Stockholm Declaration and Principle 7 of the Rio Declaration, derives from general international law and the U.N. Charter. Principle 24 of the Rio Declaration adds that cooperation shall be conducted in good faith and that it shall also include further development of international law in the field of sustainable development.

The precautionary principle is the most debated of the Rio Principles, to the point that some states refer to it as an "approach" and deny that it is a legal principle. Its invocation has been particularly contentious in matters of international trade, where states cite precaution as a justification for trade restrictions. It has also been invoked to suspend the performance of treaty obligations or to demand that states demonstrate the lawfulness of certain activities.[26]

## IV. Legal and Practical Significance

*58.* The Rio Declaration reiterated the key legal principles of the Stockholm Declaration and incorporated other legal principles which emerged in the intervening years as well as elaborated new principles. After Rio, virtually every major international convention concerning multilateral cooperation included environmental protection as one of the goals of the states parties. An increase in the number of treaties adopted after the Rio Conference shows the impact of the meeting and its concluding texts. The legal work of the UNEP, first set forth in 1981 in the Montevideo Programme for the Development and Periodic Review of the Environmental Law, was revised in September 1992 on the basis of the UNCED outcomes. The significance of the Rio Declaration also lies in the contents of the declaration. Sustainable development became the main concept with environmental protection seen as one of its pillars. Like the Stockholm Declaration, the Rio Declaration has also helped in evolution and shaping of international environmental law.

## §4. The Emergence of Concept of Sustainable Development

*59.* A decade after the Rio Conference, the WSSD was held in Johannesburg, South Africa from August 26 to September 4, 2002, in order to "reinvigorate the global commitment to sustainable development."[27] The meeting sought to assess progress in the implementation of the outcome of the UNCED and to identify areas where further efforts are needed to implement Agenda 21. It also sought to address new challenges and opportunities and was intended to result in renewed political commitment and support for sustainable development consistent with the principle of common but differentiated responsibilities. The Stockholm and Rio Conferences created a global awareness and consensus on basic principles of international environmental law and led to the conclusion of numerous global and regional environmental agreements. The Rio Declaration contains "fundamental principles for the

---

26. *Gabcíkovo-Nagymaros* Case; *Southern Bluefin Tuna* Cases; *Mox Plant Arbitration* and Cases.
27. UNGA Res. 55/199 (2000) of Feb. 2, 2001.

achievement of sustainable development, based on a new and equitable global partnership," as the UNGA stated when it endorsed the Rio Declaration.[28] As such, it has contributed to the codification and progressive development of international law relating to the environment. In the decades after the Stockholm and Rio Conferences, environmental concerns encountered increasing competition on the international agenda from economic globalization, an emphasis on free trade, and the development crises of poor countries. Motivated by the developments, the U.N. convened a conference to mark the tenth anniversary of the Rio meeting as the WSSD.

### I. Development Agenda

*60.* Between August 26, 2002 and September 4, 2002, the representatives of more than 190 countries met in Johannesburg, South Africa, in order to reaffirm their "commitment to the Rio Principles, the full implementation of Agenda 21 and the Programme for the Further Implementation of Agenda 21."[29] At the end of the conference, a Declaration on Sustainable Development was adopted which affirmed the will of the participating states to "assume a collective responsibility to advance and strengthen the sustainable development—economic development, social development and environmental protection—at local, national, regional and global levels."[30] The text recognized that the global environment continues to suffer, and realization is there for the loss of biodiversity, the depletion of fish stocks, the progress of desertification, the evident adverse effects of climate change as well as the pollution of the air, water, and sea. However, the declaration mainly focused on development and poverty eradication, especially in the poorest countries. A plan of implementation declares that "poverty eradication, changing unsustainable patterns of production and consumption, and protecting and managing the natural resource base of economic and social development are overarching objectives of and essential requirements for sustainable development."[31] Further, it proposes to ensure access, at the national level, to environmental information and judicial and administrative proceedings in environmental matters, as well as public participation in decision-making.

*61.* The instruments adopted at the World Summit did not affect the validity of Agenda 21 which remains the key governing text for the environmental program of international institutions and a general guideline for governments, regional and local authorities as well as for non-state actors. Indeed, the WSSD reaffirms the texts adopted at Rio and calls for priority attention to two matters: the implementation of and compliance with IEAs by contracting states, and the coordination among the

28. UNGA Res. 48/190 of Dec. 21, 1993.
29. Draft Plan of Implementation of the World Summit on Sustainable Development, para. 1.
30. Johannesburg Declaration on Sustainable Development, para. 5.
31. Draft Plan of Implementation of the World Summit on Sustainable Development, para. 2.

secretariats of Multilateral Environmental Agreements (MEAs). This recommendation in itself is an affirmation of the growth and development of international environmental law, in which the Stockholm and Rio Declarations have been fundamental guiding documents.

§5. The Kyoto Protocol

## I. Introduction

*62.* The Kyoto Protocol extended the 1992 UNFCCC that commits state parties to reduce GHG emissions, based on the scientific consensus that (a) global warming is occurring and (b) likely $CO_2$ emissions predominantly caused it. The Kyoto Protocol adopted in Kyoto, Japan, on December 11, 1997, entered into force on February 16, 2005. There are currently 192 parties (Canada withdrew effective December 2012) to the Protocol. The Kyoto Protocol implemented the objective of the UNFCCC to fight global warming by reducing GHG concentrations in the atmosphere to "a level that would prevent dangerous anthropogenic interference with the climate system" (Article 2). The Protocol is based on the principle of common but differentiated responsibilities. It puts the obligation to reduce current emissions on developed countries being historically responsible for the current levels of GHGs in the atmosphere. The Protocol's first commitment period started in 2008 and ended in 2012. A second commitment period was agreed on in 2012, known as the Doha Amendment to the protocol, in which thirty-seven countries had fixed binding targets. Australia, the EU (and its twenty-eight Member States), Belarus, Iceland, Kazakhstan, Liechtenstein, Norway, Switzerland, and Ukraine. Belarus, Kazakhstan, and Ukraine have stated that they may withdraw from the Protocol or not put into legal force the Amendment with second-round targets. Japan, New Zealand, and Russia have participated in Kyoto's first round but have not taken on new targets in the second commitment period. Other developed countries without second-round targets are Canada (which withdrew from the Kyoto Protocol in 2012) and the U.S. (which has not ratified the Protocol). As of October 2020, 147 states had accepted the Doha Amendment. It entered into force on December 31, 2020.

## II. Carbon Credits

*63.* $CO_2$, the GHG produced by combustion of fuels, has become a cause of panic as its concentration in the Earth's atmosphere has been rising alarmingly. This has been turned into an incentive namely carbon credits which helps people, countries, consultants, traders, corporations, and even farmers earn billions of rupees through carbon credits. As nations have progressed, there has been emission of more and more carbon and other gases resulting in global warming. Therefore, countries came together and Kyoto Protocol was signed. The Kyoto Protocol created a mechanism under which countries emitting more carbon and other gases (GHG include ozone, $CO_2$, methane, nitrous oxide ($N_2O$) and even water vapor) have voluntarily decided that they will bring down the level of carbon to the levels of early 1990s.

In 2008, developed countries decided on different norms to bring down the level of emission fixed for the companies and factories. A company has two ways to reduce emissions. One, it can reduce GHG by adopting new technology or improving upon the existing technology to attain the new norms for emission of gases. Or it can tie up with developing nations and help them set up new technology that is eco-friendly, thereby helping a developing country or its companies "earn" credits. Any company, factories or farm owner in a developing country can get linked to UNFCCC and know the "standard" level of carbon emission allowed for its outfit or activity. The extent to which one is emitting less carbon (as per standard fixed by UNFCCC) one gets carbon *credits in a developing country*. These credits are bought over by the companies of developed countries which are mostly Europeans as the U.S. has not signed the Kyoto Protocol.

*64.* Carbon credits are a part of international emission trading norms. They incentivize companies or countries that emit less carbon. The total annual emissions are capped, and the market allocates a monetary value to any shortfall through trading. Businesses can exchange, buy, or sell carbon credits in international markets at the prevailing market price. The total value of global carbon markets grew nearly 20% in 2020, reaching EUR 229 billion. This marks the fourth consecutive year of record growth and more than five times the value in 2017. India is one of the countries that have "credits" for emitting less carbon. India and China have surplus credit to offer to countries that have a deficit. By December 2019, Indian companies had registered 1,669 projects under CDM and earned 246.6 million credits; another 526 projects were registered under the "voluntary" market and these have earned 89 million credits. Thus, in all, Indian companies have roughly got 350 million credits which they can sell and make money. Assume that British Petroleum is running a plant in the U.K., and it is emitting more gases than the accepted norms of the UNFCCC, it can tie up with its own subsidiary in, say, India or China under the CDM. It can buy the "carbon credit" by making Indian or Chinese plant more eco-savvy with the help of technology transfer. It can also tie up with any other company or anybody else in the open market.

*65.* Under the CDM, a deal can be made for carbon credit. Only a portion of the total earnings of carbon credits of the company can be transferred to the company of the developed countries under CDM. There is a fixed quota on buying of credit by companies in Europe.

## §6. Paris Agreement

*66.* The Paris conference was the twenty-first session of the Conference of the Parties (COP) to the UNFCCC, known as COP21. The conference concluded a round of negotiations launched in Durban, South Africa, in 2011 with the aim of producing a new legal agreement among national governments to strengthen the global response to climate change. The Paris Agreement formally entered into force on November 4, 2016. As of January 2021, 190 parties have ratified this agreement. The Paris Agreement builds upon the Convention and brought all nations into a common cause to undertake ambitious efforts to combat climate change and adapt to its effects, with enhanced support to assist DC to do so. The Paris Agreement's central aim is to strengthen the global response to the threat of climate change by keeping a global temperature rise in this century well below 2°C above preindustrial levels and pursuing efforts to limit the temperature increase even further to 1.5°C. To reach these ambitious goals, appropriate financial flows, a new technology framework, and an enhanced capacity-building framework will be put in place, thus supporting action by DC and the most vulnerable countries, in line with their own national objectives. The agreement also provides for enhanced transparency of action and support through a better transparency framework. The Paris agreement set out principles but did not contain the details. On December 15, 2018, delegates to COP24, hosted in Katowice, Poland, adopted most of a comprehensive "rulebook" containing the operational details of the Paris Agreement.

### I. Nationally Determined Contribution

*67.* The Paris Agreement requires all parties to put forward their best efforts through "nationally determined contributions" (NDCs) and to strengthen these efforts in the years ahead. This includes requirements that all parties report regularly on their emissions and implementation efforts. The countries which attended United Nations Climate Change Conference (COP21) made emission-cutting pledges. The achievement by a party of its NDCs is not a legally binding obligation. The Paris Agreement encourages parties to formulate and communicate "long-term low greenhouse gas emissions development strategies" and invited parties to communicate those strategies to the UNFCCC.

### II. Talanoa Dialogue

*68.* The 2018 facilitative dialog, renamed the "Talanoa Dialogue," concluded a year-long assessment of progress toward the Paris Agreement's long-term goals and was meant to inform parties as they prepare for a new round of NDCs. The Paris Agreement was to apply post-2020. But under a decision accompanying the agreement, parties chose to jumpstart the five-year cycle with a "facilitative dialogue" on collective progress in 2018, and the submission by 2020 of NDCs running through 2030. The Talanoa Dialogue sent clear signals to the entire world and aimed to be inclusive due to the consensus-building nature of the debate. The outcome of this dialogue was initiation of the political momentum, and it helped concerned parties to prepare for NDC, beneficial for a better future for everyone.

### III. Transparency System

*69.* The transparency system under the UNFCCC sets different requirements for developed countries and DC, but the new transparency framework will apply to all countries but provide "built-in flexibility" to accommodate varying national capacities. The aim is for all parties to work toward the same standards of accountability as their capacities strengthen over time. In addition, the agreement establishes a new mechanism to "facilitate implementation and promote compliance." This "non-adversarial" committee of experts will seek to help countries falling behind on their commitments get back on track. There are no penalties for noncompliance.

## IV. U.S. Stand on Paris Agreement

*70.* In December 2015, under the leadership of Barack Obama, U.S. had committed to the Paris Climate Agreement, but in November 2020, the then-President, Donald Trump withdrew U.S. from the agreement taking the position that it would begin negotiations to reenter either the Paris accord or an entirely new transaction on terms that are fair to the U.S. The move dealt a significant blow to efforts to slow the rise of global temperatures and reduce $CO_2$ emissions. This decision of U.S. was motivated by economics, saying the Paris agreement harms U.S. businesses and workers to the exclusive benefit of other countries. U.S. wanted to renegotiate the Paris climate accord. The deal required countries to set their own targets for reducing emissions by 2020. The Obama administration had committed the U.S. to reduce carbon emissions by 26%–28% by 2025. The agreement also established a USD 100 billion fund to help vulnerable countries deal with the effects of climate change.

*71.* The U.S. took the lead in negotiating the deal, signed the agreement in April 2016, along with China, the EU, and 171 other nations. China and the U.S. account for nearly 40% of global carbon emissions. The agreement took effect in November 2016 after nations accounting for 55% of global emissions ratified the treaty. The U.S took steps to roll back Mr. Obama's climate change agenda. In March 2017, President Trump signed an executive order scrapping the Obama administration's "Clean Power Plan," which mandated steep reductions in GHG emissions by power plants. As the world's second-biggest polluter and richest nation, the U.S. is very important in the fight against climate change. But the withdrawal of U.S. under the Donald Trump regime put that in jeopardy. However, in November 2020, after the election of Joe Biden as President and Kamala Harris as Vice President, U.S. officially rejoined the Paris Agreement on February 19, 2021, positioning the country to once again be a part of the global climate solution.

*72.* At present, China accounts for 26% of the world's $CO_2$ emissions, followed by the U.S., India, Russia and Indonesia. Combined these five nations account for half of the world's annual emissions. China remains the world's biggest annual emitter despite a surge in renewable energy development, as it remains heavily reliant on coal for power. It has set a goal for $CO_2$ emissions to "peak before 2030 and achieve carbon neutrality before 2060". China also pledged to track and detect leaks in methane, which holds more warmth than carbon dioxide but is shorter lived and regarded as the quickest way to limit global warming in the near-term.

*73.* The U.S., the second-biggest emitter on an annual basis but the biggest historically, has failed to improve its target in the past year, after the Biden administration in 2021 set an economy-wide target of cutting net emissions by 50%–52% below 2005 levels by 2030.

Some progress has also been made in Indonesia, where emissions declined by 23% over the past year as renewable energy accounted for a greater proportion of its total electricity production. The third biggest annual emitter, India, is trying to make headway, after setting a goal in 2022 to reduce its emissions intensity by 45% by 2030 compared with 2005 levels.

## §7. COP28

*74.* The United Nations Climate Change Conference (COP28) ended on December 13, 2023. It laid the ground for a just and equitable transition. Nearly 200 parties came together in Dubai with a decision on first "global stocktake" to ratchet up climate action before the end of the decade with the aim to keep the global temperature limit of 1.5°C within reach. World leaders at COP28 were joined by civil society, business, Indigenous Peoples, youth, philanthropy, and international organizations in a spirit of shared determination to close the gaps to 2030. The Global Climate Action space at COP28 provided a platform for governments, businesses and civil society to collaborate and showcase their real-world climate solutions.

### I. Global Stocktake

*75.* The global stocktake is the main outcome of COP28 – as it contains elements that were under negotiation and can now be used by countries to develop better climate action plans due by 2025. The stocktake recognizes the science that indicates global GHG emissions need to be cut 43% by 2030, compared to 2019 levels, so as to limit global warming to 1.5°C. The fact remains that parties are off track when it comes to meeting their Paris Agreement goals. The stocktake calls on parties to take actions toward a tripling of renewable energy capacity and doubling energy efficiency improvements by 2030. The list also includes accelerating efforts toward the phase-down of unabated coal power, phasing out inefficient fossil fuel subsidies, and other measures that drive the transition away from fossil fuels in energy systems, in a just, orderly and equitable manner.

### II. Different Funds

*76.* Parties reached to agreement on the operationalization of the loss and damage fund and funding arrangements. Commitments to the fund started coming and, totaled more than USD 700 million to date. There was also progress on the loss and damage agenda with an agreement that the UN Office for Disaster Risk Reduction and the UN Office for Project Services will host the secretariat of the Santiago Network for Loss and Damage. This platform will catalyze technical assistance to developing countries that are particularly vulnerable to the adverse effects of climate change. The Green Climate Fund (GCF) received a boost with six countries pledging new funding at COP28 with total pledges standing at a record USD 12.8 billion from thirty-one countries, with expectation of further contributions. Eight donor governments announced new commitments to the Least Developed Countries Fund and Special Climate Change Fund totaling more than USD 174 million to date, while new pledges, totaling nearly USD 188 million were made to the Adaptation Fund.

*77.* At COP28, discussions continued on setting a "new collective quantified goal on climate finance" in 2024, taking into account the needs and priorities of developing countries. The new goal, which will start from a baseline of USD 100 billion per year, will be a building block for the design and subsequent implementation of national climate plans that need to be delivered by 2025. The negotiations on the "enhanced transparency framework" at COP28 laid the ground for a new era of implementing the Paris Agreement. UN Climate Change is developing the transparency reporting and review tools for use by parties, which were showcased and tested at COP28. The final versions of the reporting tools should be made available to parties by June 2024.

## III. COP29

*78.* COP28 also saw parties agree to Azerbaijan as host of COP29 from 11 to 22 November 2024, and Brazil as COP30 host from 10 to 21 November 2025. At COP29, governments must establish a new climate finance goal, reflecting the scale and urgency of the climate challenge. And at COP30, they must come prepared with new NDCs that are economy-wide, cover all GHGs, and are fully aligned with the 1.5°C temperature limit.

# Chapter 2. Sources of International Environmental Law

*79.* International environmental law has developed as a critical part of the international legal system. As such it has evolved in a body of legal rules and procedures, and this body constitutes international law. A fundamental question that underpins law generally is what its sources are. A fundamental source of English and American law is the Magna Carta. In legal systems based on the common law, law comprises decisions made by courts, legislation, and constitutional documents. The other principal legal system in the world is civil law. In civil law system, the authority of the law is based on legislation and codes of law. In distinction to international law, these national or domestic systems of law are termed municipal laws. The sources of international environmental law comprise of rules developed through practice of signing of treaties and entering into conventions, decisions of international forums, and practice of states regarding regulation of relation with other states pertaining to environment.

## §1. International and Domestic Law Interaction

*80.* To understand the nature and sources of international environmental law, one must first understand the difference between national and international law. National law is law that is adopted by the government of an individual country. In the U.S., the most common examples of national law are federal and state legislation and judicial decisions. Delegated legislation like regulations and executive orders would fall within this category. Although these national laws are adopted by an individual country, some of them can have international impacts as well. A foreign manufacturer whose defective product injures a person living in the U.S. may be held liable for resulting damages under U.S. law. The U.S. Corrupt Practices Act prevents a U.S. corporate executive from bribing a foreign government official. While these laws affect international activities and nonnational parties, they are generally not considered international law. Rather, they are considered extraterritorial applications of national law. International law, on the other hand, concerns agreements among different nations, or between citizens or corporations of different nations. Agreements or treaties among different nations are generally referred to as public international law. Contracts between private parties whether corporations or citizens residing in different countries fall under private international law. Because the field of international environmental law focuses on the relations and agreements among nations, it is part of public international law as well. So environmental law exists at many levels and is only partly constituted by international declarations, conventions, and treaties.

*81.* The bulk of environmental law is statutory—i.e., encompassed in the enactments of legislative bodies—and regulatory—i.e., generated by agencies charged by governments with protection of the environment. In addition, many countries have included some right to environmental quality in their national constitutions. Since 1994, for example, environmental protection has been enshrined in the German Grundgesetz ("Basic Law"), which states that the government must protect for "future generations the natural foundations of life." Similarly, the Chinese constitution declares that the state "ensures the rational use of natural resources and protects rare animals and plants"; the South African constitution recognizes a right to "an environment that is not harmful to health or well-being; and to have the environment protected, for the benefit of present and future generations"; the Bulgarian constitution provides for a "right to a healthy and favourable environment, consistent with stipulated standards and regulations;" and the Chilean constitution contains a "right to live in an environment free from contamination." As originally enforced, there was no explicit provision dealing with environmental protection in the Constitution of India. In 1976, the Constitution (forty-second Amendment) Act was passed which, *inter alia*, inserted Part IV A in the Constitution wherein Article 48 A provided that, "The State shall endeavor to protect and improve the environment and to safeguard the forests and wildlife of the country." In addition, Article 51A(g) of the Constitution imposes a constitutional obligation and makes it a fundamental duty of every citizen of India "to protect and improve the natural environment including forests, lakes and wildlife, and to have compassion for living creatures."

*82.* A large body of environmental law is embodied in the decisions of international, national, and local courts. Some of it is manifested in arbitrated decisions, such as the Trail Smelter arbitration (1941), which enjoined the operation of a smelter located in British Columbia, Canada, near the international border with the U.S. state of Washington and held that "no State has the right to use or permit the use of its territory in such a manner as to cause injury by fumes in or to the territory of another or the properties or persons therein." Some environmental law also appears in the decisions of national courts. For example, in *Scenic Hudson Preservation Conference v. Federal Power Commission* (1965), a U.S. federal appeals court voided a license granted by the Federal Power Commission for the construction of an environmentally damaging pumped-storage hydroelectric plant (i.e., a plant that would pump water from a lower to an upper reservoir) in an area of stunning natural beauty, demonstrating that the decisions of federal agencies could be successfully challenged in the courts. Significant local decisions included *National Audubon Society v. Superior Court (1976)*, in which the California Supreme Court dramatically limited the ability of Los Angeles to divert water that might otherwise fill Mono Lake in California's eastern desert.

## I. Characteristics of International Law

*83.* Compared with national law, or municipal law, international law lacks two basic legal characteristics namely an overall legislative body with powers of enforcement and a centralized judicial system with empowerment enforcement authority. The absence of these two poses the question whether international law is law in the true sense or even it exists? But the fact remains that regardless of the theoretical discussions and disagreements, international law works in actual practice. Prior to the twentieth century, international law functioned even without any formal overall stated basis for its rules. International trade, communications, and travel all operated with reasonable safety except in the state of war. Until the early twentieth century, peaceful settlement of disputes was conventionally sought through some temporary body set up by agreement of the parties in dispute such as a Claims Commission or an Arbitration tribunal. A permanent organization for this purpose is the Permanent Court of Arbitration (PCA) which was established under the Hague Convention for the Pacific Settlement of International Disputes. Its title is a misnomer in that it is not a court but simply an organization to facilitate arbitration and other forms of dispute resolution. As such, the PCA cannot develop jurisprudence. It was to provide for jurisprudence that the idea of a Permanent Court of International Justice (PCIJ) was nurtured and established through the Council of the League of Nations in the early 1920s. This was the precursor to the ICJ established after World War II. Under Article 92 of the Charter of the U.N., the Court of Justice is the principal judicial organ of the U.N.

## §2. Hard and Soft Law

*84.* On the basis of enforcement capability of a law, it is considered as hard or soft law. A law which parties consider themselves bound to observe will fall in the domain of hard law whereas a law which parties are not so convinced of its applicability will fall in the category of soft law. This type of situation exists when a law is being applied between or among sovereigns.

### I. Soft Law

*85.* The international soft law refers to those norms which are not binding per se, but which play an important interpretive role in the construction and interpretation of principles and rules of formal international environmental law. A universally respected academic lawyer, Sir Robert Jennings[32] claimed that he would not recognize a norm even if he should meet one in the street. The concept of soft law, as a legal rule may not be binding but has some legal significance as a country may follow it voluntarily. Thus, even though guidelines, codes of conduct, and declarations are not binding but, nevertheless, may gain some effect and over time may develop into hard law. Examples of the principles of international environmental soft law are the principle of sustainable development, the precautionary principle, and the PPP. The hard law and soft law in international environmental law create a disparate system of global environmental protection. In response to the challenges posed by environmental degradation, a body of nonbinding agreements, statements, declarations, resolutions, and recommendations has emerged in international environmental law. These declarations, recommendations, resolutions, or guidance documents that are not legally binding and are discretionary, are referred to as soft laws. The most important example is the Agenda 21 plan of action adopted at the 1992 UNCED (Rio Earth Summit) which comprises a series of nonbinding chapters

32. President of the International Court of Justice.

on institutional and substantive topics such as trans-boundary air pollution, biodiversity, access to environmental information, biotechnology, and chemicals. As evidenced by the impact of Agenda, "soft" does not mean irrelevant. Since the founding of the U.N., international soft-law regimes governing everything from human rights to outer space have proliferated in quantity, in scope, and in the influence of public and private-sector behavior and have been followed by the countries voluntarily.

*86.* Soft law has influenced domestic regulatory developments and served as guidance to domestic decision-makers like legislators, regulators, or judges who are faced with new or emerging environmental challenges at the domestic level. This is particularly the case with respect to nonbinding decisions by conferences of the parties to global treaties serving as highly instructive interpretive guidance to flesh out the details of these broad framework agreements. The main examples of nonbinding fora that generate influential nonbinding soft law are UNEP Governing Council decisions, which frequently evolve into negotiated treaties (The Governing Council was replaced in 2013 with a successor body namely U.N. Environment Assembly). UNEP's approach to mercury provides a good example. UNEP's attention to the issue of mercury pollution began with a Governing Council decision in 2001 calling for, *inter alia*, comprehensive studies of the anthropogenic sources of mercury, existing toxicity studies, and prevention and control technologies. Subsequent decisions built on those studies led to legally binding instrument on mercury called the Minamata Convention on Mercury.

## II. Hard Law

*87.* The hard law contains norms which could be enforced or capable of being enforced after certain procedural requirements are met. The law applied by ICJ is a good example of hard law. The PCIJ was the first international body with responsibility for general jurisdiction. Its statute contained sixty-eight articles including Article 38 which authoritatively stated the legal sources the court would use and apply. Article 38 was carried forward into the Charter of the successor, the ICJ as follows:

(1) The Court, whose function is to decide in accordance with international law such disputes as are submitted to it, shall apply:
  (a) international conventions, whether general or particular, establishing rules expressly recognized by the contesting states;
  (b) international custom, as evidence of a general practice accepted as law;
  (c) the general principles of law recognized by civilized nations;
  (d) subject to the provisions of Article 59, judicial decisions and the teachings of the most highly qualified publicists of the various nations, as subsidiary means for the determination of rules of law.

(2) This provision shall not prejudice the power of the Court to decide a case *ex aequo et bono*, if the parties agree thereto.

This wording is identical with the earlier Article 38 except it adds the clause: "whose function is to decide in accordance with international law such disputes as are submitted to it." This emphasizes that the court will apply international law in its proceedings. However, paragraph 2 was also an addition to the earlier article. The Latin phrase *ex aequo et bono* means in equity and good conscience. In other words, the court has the reserved authority to decide a case in accordance with equity and fairness rather than according to the strict letter of the law. In its broadest sense, equity is fairness. As a legal system, equity can be considered a body of law addressing the concerns that fall outside the jurisdiction of common law. The duality of legal judgment based on equity or on common law has a long history. For example, equity and the common law were once opposing values in the English legal system. The common law was created by a judiciary independent from the Crown and was based on the strict interpretation of statutes and precedents. Equity was determined by the king's chancellor and thus was considered arbitrary and a royal encroachment on the power of an independent judiciary. Despite this criticism, equity assumed a permanent place in the English legal system, as the powers of the Chancery became more defined, and judgments became consistent enough to be compiled and used as precedent. Despite the apparent lack of clarity and consistency, other legal systems have also recognized the advantages of allowing judges to determine remedies in cases not covered by well-established common law or statutes.

The above-mentioned four categories of sources of law are not set up as a hierarchy. Nor are they entirely exclusive. The formal sources of law for ICJ referred to above are also known as "hard law" and establish legally binding obligations on states.

### A. *Distinction Between Hard and Soft International Law*

*88.* The distinction between hard and soft international law is that hard international law refers to agreements or principles that are directly enforceable by a national or international body. Soft international law refers to agreements or principles that are meant to influence individual nations to respect certain norms or incorporate them into national law. Soft international law by itself is not enforceable and serves to articulate standards widely shared, or aspired to, by nations. Similar parallels can be found at the national level. Sometimes official, a legislative body, or an agency will announce a new public policy or priority. In this announcement, or proclamation, there are commitments to incorporate this new policy or priority into specific legal provisions. While the announcement itself is not enforceable in court, it can have a powerful influence on the development and implementation of specific legal provisions. In some jurisdictions like India, these are included in the Constitution with the title "Directive Principles of State Policy."

*89.* Private international law concerns business transactions, regulations of relations, etc. between citizens or corporations of different countries. Because most of the rules governing these private transactions are enforceable in the courts of the concerned countries, these rules are considered as hard international law. However, international environmental law concerns general principles agreed upon among nations. Although these principles sometimes oblige countries to adopt implementing legislation, they are not usually enforceable on their own in court unless specific legislation is made or agreement containing these principles is ratified. The soft status of international environmental law, and most international law, is a result of concerns over sovereignty because of which nations are reluctant to surrender their sovereign authority and control over their territory, peoples, and affairs to external international authorities. Even when nations have joined in international agreements, many of them add reservations or exceptions to preserve their right to decline to be bound by certain parts of the agreement and take exceptions or apply principles of reciprocity to them. The exercise of this power weakens the total effectiveness of many international agreements.

### §3. Customary International Law

*90.* CIL is also an important source of international environmental law. These are the norms and rules that countries follow as a matter of custom, and they are so prevalent that they bind all states in the world. Examples of CIL relevant to the environment include the duty to warn other states promptly about icons of an environmental nature and environmental damages to which another state or states may be exposed, and Principle 21 of the Stockholm Declaration relating to good neighborliness.

### §4. International Treaties and Agreements

*91.* A number of legally binding international agreements and treaties encompass a wide variety of issues like terrestrial, marine, and atmospheric pollution, wildlife, and biodiversity. IEAs may be bilateral or multilateral treaties or even protocols. Protocols are subsidiary agreements arising from a primary treaty. They exist in many areas of international law but are especially useful in the environmental field, where they may be used to regularly incorporate recent scientific knowledge. They also permit countries to reach an agreement on a framework that would be contentious if every detail were to be agreed upon in advance. The most widely known protocol in international environmental law is the Kyoto Protocol, which followed from the UNFCCC.

## I. International Conferences

*92.* The significant international conferences like the 1972 U.N. Conference on the Human Environment, the 1983 World Commission on Environment and Development, the 1992 UNCED, and the 2002 WSSD have contributed to the development of international environmental law. MEAs sometimes have created international organization or institutions responsible for implementing the agreement. Major examples are the CITES and the International Union for Conservation of Nature (IUCN). The deliberations in these bodies or institutions also help in development of international environmental law.

## II. Bilateral Treaties

*93.* Bilateral agreements/treaties are frequently concluded between states in relation to either a shared natural resource (e.g., a shared watershed) or a transboundary pollution source. These agreements impose binding obligations on the parties, who in turn may impose obligations on private individuals within their jurisdiction through domestic laws. Notable examples include the U.S.–Canada Air Quality Agreement of 1991, which focused on measures to reduce acid rain and the Boundary Waters Treaty of 1909, which established the International Joint Commission (IJC) to look into water resource issues involving the U.S. and Canada.

Relevant obligations may also be found in bilateral treaties that are not, strictly speaking, environmental agreements. The bilateral U.S. trade promotion agreements include provisions that impose environment-related obligations. These include obligations to effectively enforce domestic environmental laws and regulations and obligations to take measures to implement certain MEAs. Both, mature, long-standing treaties relating to "Friendship, Commerce, and Navigation" and newer bilateral investment agreements (IAs), may implicate environmental issues.

## III. Regional Agreements

*94.* The environmental obligations are also created through regional treaties or agreements. These regional agreements take a variety of forms. In some cases, regional agreements may be independent regimes designed to unique environmental circumstances of a given region. This is the case, for example, with the regional seas agreements adopted under UNEP, such as the Convention for the Protection and Development of the Marine Environment of the Wider Caribbean Region and its protocols.[33] These regional agreements fit comfortably within the institutional architecture of ocean environmental management established under the better-known UNCLOS, but their obligations are distinct from or in addition to obligations set out in the Convention itself.

*95.* In some cases, regional environmental agreements cover the same substantive area as global environmental agreements, but additional obligations apply only to the parties to the regional agreement. For example, the Bamako Convention,[34] adopted in 1991 under the auspices of the Organization of African Unity, amplifies

33. Convention for the Protection and Development of the Marine Environment of the Wider Caribbean Region, Mar. 24, 1983, 1984 U.S.T. LEXIS 254.
34. Bamako Convention on the Ban of the Import into Africa and the Control of Trans-boundary Movement and Management of Hazardous Wastes Within Africa, adopted in 1991 under the auspices of the Organization of African Unity.

and extends obligations set out in its global predecessor, the Basel Convention.[35] In still other cases, regional environmental agreements may overlap with but impose slightly different obligations than those set out in comparable international agreements. This arises where the regional agreement may have preceded and served as a model for the subsequent global agreement. This is the case, for example, with the Protocol on Persistent Organic Pollutants (POPs) to the Convention on Long-Range Trans-boundary Air Pollution (LRTAP Protocol), which predates a global agreement that was adopted on the same topic: the Stockholm Convention on POPs (Stockholm Convention). Although their basic structure and function are very similar, there are some distinctions among the obligations in each agreement as well as in the lists of chemicals that they cover.

## IV. Global Multilateral Environmental Treaties/Agreements

*96.* Global MEAs are an important source and help in the development of international environmental law. Indeed, for many people, "international environmental law" begins and ends with the MEAs. And although their impact and influence may be overrated, the MEAs do matter in international environmental law. A key-defining feature of the MEAs is that they are purpose-built agreements aimed at particular topics with limited mandates and scopes. A large number of MEAs have been negotiated including chemicals/waste (e.g., Stockholm Convention; Basel Convention); biodiversity (e.g., Convention on International Trade of Endangered Species of Wild Fauna and Flora (CITES), CBD, Cartagena Protocol); atmosphere and climate (e.g., UNFCCC), and oceans (UNCLOS).

### *A. Conferences of the Parties*

*97.* The international environmental sphere does not have a common global institutional framework that can serve as a platform for all related activities. Instead, each negotiated agreement brought into force establishes its own institutional governance structure and quasi-regulatory processes. The plenary body for most MEAs is known as the COP. The COP comprises representatives from each party, who meet periodically. The MEA designates the COP as the main decision-making authority for the treaty. The COP is given the power to review compliance with and implementation of the treaty and also the authority to create subsidiary bodies, etc. In addition, the MEAs designate a secretariat comprising a permanent administrative staff to facilitate and record the meetings of the COP and its subsidiary bodies.

35. Basel Convention on the Control of Trans-boundary Movements of Hazardous Wastes and Their Disposal, Mar. 22, 1989, 1989 U.S.T. LEXIS 240.

*B. Framework Agreements and Protocols*

*98.* Some of the MEAs are expressly designated or otherwise function as "framework" agreements which serve as platforms for more focused negotiations. They include most notably (a) the Vienna Convention on the Protection of the Ozone Layer, which spawned the much better-known Montreal Protocol; (b) the UNFCCC, which created the Kyoto Protocol; and (c) the CBD, which has given rise to a series of targeted protocols including the Cartagena Protocol on trade in transgenic organisms and Nagoya Protocol on Access and Benefit Sharing (ABS). While such protocols typically share the institutional framework (i.e., shared secretariats and, often, shared meeting events) with their progenitors, the protocols are themselves unique MEAs with a separate legal standing.

*C. COP Technical Work, Amendments, and Decisions*

*99.* The technical processes and activities COP sets in motion can indirectly influence national regulatory developments. The COP decision-making can lead to new legal obligations through amendments and the adoption of new protocols. Pursuant to amendments that may be adopted according to detailed procedures set out in the treaties, MEAs are frequently designed to evolve over time. The procedures vary by agreement but typically provide that amendments are adopted by majority decision within the COP. The amendments do not enter into force until ratified by a minimum threshold number of parties. The recent MEAs have embraced a practical approach to address the problem of delay at the national ratification level by providing that amendments shall enter into force automatically after one year for all parties except those that have affirmatively provided notice of their rejection of the amendment. Certain COP "decisions" can have impacts that, for the practitioner, are equal to or even more important than formal amendments. For example, COP decisions can take the form of guidance to the parties and the private sector about the meaning of ambiguous treaty terms.

*100.* Some MEAs expressly provide for the adoption of decisions having legally binding effect. These decisions allow for rapid evolution of legal obligations without triggering the more burdensome process for treaty amendments or national ratification decisions. This is the case with respect to decisions to list or delist species by the COP for CITES, which triggers obligations on parties to impose trade restrictions on those species, and decisions to "adjust" the phase-out schedule for ozone-depleting substances (ODS) under the Montreal Protocol. In many cases, the agreements provide detailed procedures to be followed before an issue is considered ripe for adoption by the COP, either as a nonbinding decision, a binding decision, or as an amendment.

§5. JUDICIAL DECISIONS AS A SOURCE

*101.* Although the Statute of the ICJ refers to judicial decisions as a subsidiary source for determining rules of law, however, the judgments and advisory opinions of the World Court and arbitral or other international tribunals are quite important and considered as the affirmation or the revelation of CIL. So international environmental law includes the opinions of international courts and tribunals as a source. The decisions carry much weight with legal commentators and are quite influential on the development of international environmental law. One of the biggest challenges in international decisions relating to environment is to determine an adequate compensation for environmental damages.[36] The courts include the ICJ; the ITLOS; the European Court of Justice (ECJ); the European Court of Human Rights (ECHR);[37] and other regional treaty tribunals.

## I. *Trail Smelter* and Other Cases

*102.* The arbitral judgment of March 11, 1941, in the *Trail Smelter* case is considered to have laid the foundations of international environmental law regarding interstate pollution which has emerged as a big issue and a leading case in the area of state liability for trans-boundary pollution. It resulted from injuries caused in the American state of Washington from sulfur dioxide ($SO_2$) released by a smelter plant in British Columbia, Canada. After protests by the U.S., the two countries agreed to submit the case to arbitration. In the arbitration decision, the tribunal proclaimed a general principle of international law that would be very helpful for establishing the liability of the U.S. for GHG emissions. It is stated that "[a] State owes at all times a duty to protect other States against injurious acts by individuals within its jurisdiction," and went on saying that: No state has the right to use or permit the use of its territory in such a manner as to cause injury by fumes in or to the territory of another or the properties or persons therein, when the case is of serious consequences and the injury is established by clear and convincing evidence.

*103.* Subsequently, it was confirmed by a more general principle prohibiting causing harm to another state, enunciated in the *Corfu Channel* case,[38] and referred to in the 1956 Lake Lanoux Arbitration[39] in the context of transfrontier water pollution, the announced rule undoubtedly forms part of positive international law. Thus, the case law relating to environmental issues may emerge out of decisions of the ICJ, the ECJ, the European and Inter-American Courts of Human Rights, decisions of the General Agreement on Tariffs and Trade (GATT) Dispute Settlement Panels, awards of international arbitral tribunals, and decisions of the International Tribunal on the Law of the Sea.

36. T. Hardman Reis. *Compensation for Environmental Damages under International Law* (Kluwer Law International, The Hague 2011, ISBN 978-90-411-3437-0).
37. "ECtHR case-law factsheet on environment" (PDF). Retrieved Nov. 8, 2012.
38. *U.K. v. Albania*, 1949 I.C.J. 4.
39. *Spain v. France*, 12 U.N.R.I.A. 281 (1957).

## II. Responses of Judges

*104.* Judicial decisions have a central role in developing and enforcing effective laws for the protection of the environment and ensuring access to justice. The response of judges in different parts of the world to the problems created by the Industrial Revolution in the nineteenth century, using the tools of the domestic law, has been mirrored in the responses of judges around the world to the environmental challenges of their own countries, using a range of legal mechanisms, derived from their respective constitutions. In developing and enforcing local laws, judges have sometimes been criticized for not respecting the proper limits of the judicial role, when dealing with issues of political controversy or allocation of economic resources. With the support of UNEP, judges have been at the forefront in programs for improving judicial capacity in the field of environmental law, and for sharing skills and experiences. Although the legal frameworks may differ, many of the problems and their solutions are of universal application. The emerging principles can be seen as the foundation of a system of "common laws of the environment" suitable for environmental challenges of the present-day world.

## III. The *Birmingham Corporation* Case

*105.* The great *Birmingham Corporation* case of 1858 is a landmark case which asserted the rights of the individual to defend his environment against nuisance, regardless of any countervailing public interest. The action was brought by Charles Adderley who was the owner of a large estate through which ran the River Tame. Raw effluent was being discharged into the River Tame from the sewers of the Birmingham Corporation, which was finding it very difficult to cope with the needs of its growing population. The court appeared to show remarkably little concern about those problems. In the words of Page Wood V-C "it was a matter of almost absolute indifference whether the decision will affect a population of [(250,000]) … I am not sitting here as a committee for public safety, armed with arbitrary power to prevent what it is said will be a great injury to Birmingham only, but to the whole of England; that is not my function."[40]

*106.* Although Charles Adderley was nominally suing as a landowner in his own right, he also took on the role of representative of some 27,000 tenants within his ancestral estate and more generally as an MP for the area, his efforts were motivated by personal conviction in relation to the environment. These came to the fore some years later, by his contribution to the development of environmental law as chairman of the Royal Sanitary Commission. Its report to Parliament became the basis for the first comprehensive legislation in this field, namely Public Health Act 1875. This Act was precursor of many legislations that followed and is still the foundation of much of modern environmental law. In explaining the Bill to Parliament, Adderley described it as recognizing Parliament's general duty to protect "the right

40. *Attorney General v. Birmingham Corporation* (1858) 4 K&J 539.

of the public as a whole to clear water, air and land."[41] The Vice-Chancellor's judgment in 1858 was an affirmation of the principle that private interests are not to be overridden by public interest considerations, unless that interference is sanctioned by the Parliament. The injunction required the defendant to take such steps as may be necessary and proper, "due time being allowed," to prevent the continuation of the nuisance. In the meantime, the injunction was in effect suspended. So, life in Birmingham did not grind to a halt overnight. Sewage did not cease to pour into the River Tame.[42]

*107.* The judgment marked the beginning of a long period of post-action negotiations during which the corporation struggled to find adequate and longer-term technical solutions to their problems. In fact, as Pontin records, it was not until the 1870s, after Adderley had returned to the Chancery Division to enforce the original injunction, that the council devoted serious time and money to sewage treatment. The corporation's consultant failed in 1874 to persuade the court that the discharge from its sewage works was "inodorous, colorless, and clearer than the water of the river Tame." Eventually, as Pontin explains, "after a series of eclectic but unconvincing experiments, the council stumbled upon what was now being recognized as one of Britain's first systems of tertiary treatment."[43] It was not until 1895, thirty-seven years after the original decision, that the treatment was deemed adequate to enable the injunction to be discharged.[44]

## IV. *Oposa* Case in Philippines

*108.* The Philippines Supreme Court in the famous *Oposa* case[45] upheld a challenge to the state's policies for granting consent to fell trees in the countries' virgin forests, brought by some forty-three children from all over the Philippines, on behalf of themselves and "generations yet unborn." In December 2008, a Philippine's court upheld an action by a group of citizens for an order requiring the government to clean up Manila Bay. The court ordered the government to prepare a plan of action to remedy the pollution in the bay and restore the productive state of its marine resources. The government was required to submit to the Supreme Court written reports every ninety days on its progress. In 2011 after three years, the Chief Justice and other justices took a tour of the bay to inspect progress for themselves.[46] In the Philippines, the legitimacy of the court's intervention in such matters is founded on broadly expressed constitutional provisions. The Constitution of

41. HC Debates Jul. 25, 1871 col 238.
42. Ben Pontin, *The Secret Achievements of Nineteenth Century Nuisance Law*, 19 ELM 271 (2007). *See also* Ben Pontin, *Nuisance Law and Environmental Protection: A Study of Nuisance Injunctions in Practice* (Lawtext Publishing Ltd 2013) Ch. 2. Vide Carlwath CVO Lord, *Judges and the Common Laws of the Environment –At Home and Abroad*, 26(2) J. Envtl. L. 177–187 (2014).
43. *Ibid.*, 48–49.
44. *Ibid.*, 50.
45. *Oposa v. Factoran* GR No. 101083 (SC Jul. 30, 1993) (Phil).
46. *Metropolitan Manila Development Authority v. Concerned Citizens of Manila Bay* GR 171947-48 (SC Dec. 18, 2008) (Phil).

Philippines (1987 Constitution) embodies a "right of the people to a balanced and healthful ecology in accord with the rhythm and harmony of nature."[47] Similar provisions are found in many modern constitutions.[48]

## V. Protecting Mother Earth

*109.* The thinking that people have a right to a balanced environment was taken to a further stage in Bolivia's Mother Earth law ("Ley de derechos de la Madre Tierra").[49] Mother Earth is defined as: "She is sacred, fertile and the source of life that feeds and cares for all living beings in her womb. She is in permanent balance, harmony and communication with the cosmos. She is comprised of all ecosystems and living beings, and their self-organisation."

On the occasion of the United Nations Conference (June 2012) on Sustainable Development, commonly referred as Rio+20, the outcome document paragraph 39 states:

> "We recognize that planet Earth and its ecosystems are our home and that 'Mother Earth' is a common expression in a number of countries and regions, and we note that some countries recognize the rights of nature in the context of the promotion of sustainable development."[50]

For the purpose of protecting and enforcing her rights, Mother Earth is given "the character of a collective subject of public interest, "[51] so enabling actions to be taken on her behalf.

*110.* In the U.K., there are no express constitutional provisions of this kind. But the common law may sometimes fill the gap. In the Supreme Court, Lord Hope highlighted the need for the law to protect nature for its own sake, apart from direct property or financial interests of particular litigants. He gave as an example the plight of an osprey, whose routes to a favorite fishing loch might be threatened by wind-farm development affecting its routes to a favorite fishing loch:

> Lord Hope highlighted the need for the law to protect nature for its own sake. The fact that a proposal cannot reasonably be said to affect any individual's property rights or interests should not mean that it is not open to any individual to challenge the proposal. It would otherwise "seem to be contrary to

47. *Ibid.*
48. Article 42 of the Constitution of Kenya states, "Every person has the right to a clean and healthy environment, which includes the right—(a) to have the environment protected for the benefit of present and future generations through legislative and other measures."
49. The law defines seven specific rights: to Life itself; to the Diversity of Life; to water; to clean air; to equilibrium; to restoration of life systems affected by direct or indirect human activities'); and to live free from contamination. *See* Begonia Filgueira, *And About Time for Rights to Nature? The Bolivian Mother Earth Rights Law*, 23 ELM 144 (2011).
50. http://www.harmonywithnatureun.org/environmentalProvisions/.
51. *Supra* 49.

the purpose of environmental law, which proceeds on the basis that the quality of the natural environment is of legitimate concern to everyone", so someone has to be allowed to speak up on its behalf.[52]

*111.* The judgment of Chief Justice Preston in the 2006 *Telstra* case can be taken up as an example.[53] The issue was the familiar one of a proposed mobile telecommunications antenna in the genteel Sydney suburb of Cheltenham, and the fears of the local community of harm from radiation caused by electromagnetic energy. Before allowing the proposal to proceed, the judge not only conducted a detailed examination of the technical evidence but also took the opportunity for a discussion of the principles of what he called "the basic concept of ecologically sustainable development," as embodied in the relevant statute.[54] He outlined six basic principles: in summary, (a) sustainable use, (b) integration (c) the precautionary principle; (d) the principle of equity, including intergenerational equity; (e) the conservation of biological diversity; and (f) the internalization of environmental costs—the need for full account to be taken of the short-term and long-term costs of any major project.[55] These principles are derived from the interpretation of local legislation but are of much wider application.

*112.* In the case of *Massachusetts v. EPA*,[56] the claim was brought by twelve states against the EPA to regulate emissions of GHG. On one view, the case turned on relatively narrow issues about the construction of the word "pollutant." But on another it went wider, the judgments giving judicial recognition at the highest level to scientific theories linking the rise in global temperatures with man-made emissions of GHG, and the need to take action. The majority of the judges affirmed the standing of the states to bring these proceedings, citing Justice Holmes' reference in a case 100 years before to the state's role as "quasi-sovereign" with an interest "independent of and behind the titles of its citizens, in all the earth and air within its domain, with the last words as to whether its mountains shall be stripped of forests and its inhabitants shall breathe pure air."[57] The case had the effect of leading the EPA to revise its view, to identify six GHGs which were a danger to public health, and to resist a challenge in the U.S. Court of Appeals by a body named the Coalition for Responsible Regulation, with the support of another group of states.[58]

*113.* These examples dating from the nineteenth century to the present show that national judges have big influence in moulding and shaping the law of the environment and the public's response to it. Judge Weeramantry has said in his introduction to the UNEP Judicial Handbook on Environmental Law published in 2004:

52. *Walton v. Scottish Ministers* (2012) UKSC 44 (152).
53. *Telstra Corporation v. Hornsby Shire Council* (2006) 146 LGERA 10.
54. *Ibid.*, 35.
55. *Ibid.*, 35–37.
56. 549 US 497 (2007).
57. *Ibid.*, 518–519 citing *Georgia v. Tennessee Copper Co* 206 US 230, 237 (1907).
58. *Coalition for Responsible Regulation v. EPA* 684 F 3d 102 (DC Cir 2012).

> The judiciary is ... one of the most valued and respected institutions in all societies. The tone it sets through the tenor of its decisions influences societal attitudes and reactions towards the matter in question. This is all the more so in a new and rapidly developing area. Judicial decisions and attitudes can also play a great part in influencing society's perception of the environmental danger and of the resources available to society with which to contain it.[59]

## VI. Environmental Justice

*114.* Judge Weeramantry, the Sri Lankan judge of the ICJ in a remarkable judgment in the *Hungarian Dams* case[60] reaffirmed that the environment "is not an abstraction but represents the living space, the quality of life and the very existence of human beings, including generations yet unborn"; and that the "general obligation to ensure that activities within their jurisdiction and control, respect the environment of other states or areas beyond national control is now part of the corpus of the international law of the environment." The judgments affirmed the role of the judiciary in the development and enforcement of environmental law but pointed out a deficiency in the knowledge, relevant skills, and information which is to be addressed by international action. These principles for development of national legislation on access to information have since been incorporated in guidelines endorsed by UNEP's governing Council.[61] The congress was followed in November 2012 by the establishment by UNEP of International Advisory Council on Environmental Justice, which in turn provided input in February 2013 to the meeting of UNEP's Governing Council.

*115.* In the *Oposa* case, the Supreme Court made clear that the rights of the unborn to protection of their future environment were not dependent on any particular constitutional structure or legal system. Such rights, the court asserted, concern:

> nothing less than the right to self-preservation and self-perpetuation ... the advancement of which may even be said to predate all government and constitutions ... these basic rights need not even be written in the Constitution for they are assumed to exist from the inception of humankind.[62]

---

59. Dinah Shelton & Alexandre Kiss, *Judicial Handbook on Environmental Law* (UNEP 2004) https://elaw.org/system/files/UNEP.judicial.handbook.enviro.law.pdf.
60. Case concerning the *Gabcíkovo-Nagymaros* project (Hungary/Slovakia) (1997) ICJ Rep 7.
61. UNEP, Guidelines for the Development of National Legislation on Access to Information, Public Participation and Access to Justice in Environmental Matters, adopted by the Governing Council of the United Nations Environment Programme in decision SS.XI/5, pt A of Feb. 26, 2010; https://www.unep.org/resources/publication/guidelines-development-national-legislation-access-information-public.
62. *Oposa v. Factoran* GR No. 101083 (SC Jul. 30 1993) (Phil).

§6. Scholarly Writing

*116.* The writings of eminent jurists also provided a material source for identifying environmental law and helped in its evolution. International bodies like the International Law Commission (ILC) of the U.N. as well as national institutes and professional organizations may study and publish authoritative restatements or commentaries on different aspects of the law. Individual writer's author treatises and articles examining particular issues in depth that may be of use to judges as input for decision-making.

*117.* The international law of environment has developed from many sources like CIL, treaties and agreements bilateral as well as multilateral, judicial decisions, international conferences, writings of the scholars, and these also form the main sources of international environmental law.

# Chapter 3. Role of State and Non-state Actors in Development of International Environmental Law

*118.* The present international environmental law encompasses a complex array of state actors and non-state actors like international institutions, private individuals, NGOs, scientists, business concerns, and technical experts. NGOs can be international or domestic, large membership organizations or small think tanks, advocacy or programmatic organizations. International institutions include traditional international organizations, as well as treaty bodies and regional integration organizations. The actors responsible for development of environmental laws can be viewed along several interrelated dimensions. First, the types and degree of influence they exercise at different junctures in the policy cycle can be studied. Further, their agenda setting, normative development, implementation, and enforcement can be considered.

## §1. States

*119.* States are dominant players in both the development and implementation of international environmental law. Most of the substantive content of international environmental law is in the form of treaties and some softer instruments such as codes of conduct or guidelines. These have developed through a process of interstate negotiation. The implementation of norms depends primarily on national action: enactment of international standards into domestic law, establishment of domestic permitting procedures, monitoring and reporting on regulated activities, punishment of violations, and judicial application.

As a matter of fact, states remain central, but the nature of the state system itself is changing. The state is becoming more porous not only economically but also environmentally. As a result, it is increasingly difficult to draw a clear separation between international and domestic environmental policy. A problem such as climate change is not just a foreign relations problem instead has implications for every aspect of domestic policy, e.g., energy, transportation, construction, land use. As the *Trail Smelter* case illustrates, even more localized trans-boundary pollution problems implicate a variety of governmental, and nongovernmental, actors and will not necessarily be resolved through traditional interstate channels.

*120.* The development of international environmental law has to some extent eroded the principle of the sovereign equality of states by differentiating among states in terms of both their obligations and their rights. This development also acknowledges that states are heterogeneous rather than homogeneous which is reflected not only in the principle of common but also in differentiated responsibilities. As per the principle of differentiated responsibilities, differentiation is made among states according to their contributions to a given problem and their capacity for problem solving. This principle finds expression in the decision-making procedures of institutions such as the Global Environmental Facility (GEF), the Montreal Protocol and Kyoto Protocol compliance committees.

§2. PRIVATE INDIVIDUAL

*121.* The activity of humans as private individuals involves consumption of resources resulting in the generation of wastes which contributes to environmental problems. The challenge for international environmental law is to develop effective ways of regulating these private activities. In understanding the special characteristics of international environmental law, it is helpful to consider several features of environmental problems that serve to distinguish them from other international problems. International environmental problems are caused primarily by private conduct, whereas international law primarily addresses questions of governmental conduct so there is a paradox of how to deal with the individuals under international law. The areas covered by international law are claiming territory, using force against other states, protection of human rights, exercising jurisdiction, etc. Some environmental problems are also the products of governmental conduct—for example, the blowing up of Kuwaiti oil wells by Iraq during the first Gulf War and thereafter bombardment of Iraq by the U.S. However, most pollution and natural resource depletion result from private activities like climate change. Emissions of $CO_2$ and other "greenhouse gases" results from generating and consuming electricity, driving cars, manufacturing products, growing food, and cutting trees. The same is true of other international environmental problems as well. For example, threats to African elephants come from the consumers who wish to purchase ivory products and from the poachers who satisfy that demand by killing elephants. The oil pollution results from the combined activities of oil producers, shipbuilders, shippers, and, ultimately, individuals who consume oil for transportation and other purposes. Similarly, deforestation results from demand by local populations for fuel wood, timber and agricultural land.

*122.* Most environmental problems are caused primarily by conduct that is mainly private rather than governmental, and the business community has an unusually high stake in international environmental regimes. The states are the direct addressees of international environmental obligations, whereas private actors are the ultimate regulatory targets. Some international environmental regimes actually define the applicable standards of private conduct directly. For example, the International Convention for the Prevention of Pollution from Ships (MARPOL Convention) establishes detailed construction and design standards for oil tankers, which shipbuilders and vessel operators, must follow. The states act as transmission belts, applying the MARPOL Convention's standards to their flag vessels. Other IEAs require states to adopt elaborate regulatory mechanism to control private conduct, including permitting schemes for waste disposal or for trade in endangered species, or prior informed consent requirements for transport of hazardous materials. Still other international environmental regimes, such as the Kyoto Protocol, simply require states to bring about a particular result but leave it up to states to decide how to influence private conduct in order to achieve this result.

## §3. Nongovernmental Organizations

*123.* The environmental NGOs play a significant role in virtually every aspect of the international environmental process. Depending on their membership, they may be regarded either as "giving the environment a voice" and thus acting in the common interest or as representing the particular interests of their members in preserving a specific natural environment. Although typically, NGOs wield influence by attempting to influence states, in some cases, NGOs play a more direct role in international environmental regimes. For example, under the Montreal Protocol, they may provide information on state compliance to the Secretariat, while under the CITES, NGOs have quasi-official roles in monitoring and reporting processes. NGOs may also act directly in the national or international marketplace by using or threatening consumer boycotts. Relevant examples are the campaigns against the consumption of ivory and seal fur. NGOs help define an issue, promote it on the policy agenda, exert pressure on national delegations during the negotiations, monitor state compliance, and, in some cases, even bring complaints regarding inadequate enforcement. International institutions such as UNEP traditionally have played a catalytic role in helping to set the environmental agenda, but, today, international institutions are increasingly a site of normative development.

The NGOs can be seen in terms of the basis on which they exercise influence or power. The basis of scientists' influence is, of course, expertise, and, for this reason, they tend to be less influential in the process of normative development, which involves questions of value, and more influential at stages in the policy process that involve issues with objective answers. Some NGOs also play an expert role, but others have a representative basis, deriving their influence from their membership.

*124.* The environmental actors can be analyzed by focusing on the different causal pathways through which they exercise influence. For example, many NGOs and businesses still operate primarily through states. They exercise influence by pushing their own state to support a policy internationally or to implement its international obligations. Increasingly, however, NGOs and the business sector participate more directly in international institutions. And, sometimes, NGOs also act directly in the national or international marketplace through the threat or use of consumer boycotts. The intervention of NGOs can have significant influence, as is evidenced by the famous Brent Spar case, where the intervention of Greenpeace prevented Shell from sinking an oil platform in the North Sea, by channeling public opinion against this form of decommissioning.

## §4. International Institutions

*125.* The development of international environmental law during the second half of the twentieth century and, in particular, after the Stockholm Conference in 1972 can be grasped taking into consideration the role of international institutions. These institutions are not a homogenous set of actors, and they perform a variety of functions in the development and implementation of international environmental law. Within the complex web of institutions, the U.N., through, in particular, the UNGA, the Economic and Social Commission, and the Commission on Sustainable Development (CSD), plays a coordinating role. The UNGA, for example, convened the three major environmental summits namely Stockholm, Rio, and Johannesburg and established UNEP. These summits have played an important role in generating political consensus on the issues to be addressed in international law and policy-evolving principles of international environmental law.

The major organizations involved in environmental matters include the WMO, the U.N. FAO and the IMO. The main function of these organizations is to coordinate the efforts of states in a specific area of regulation. Most MEAs create organs such as a COP and a secretariat. Examples of this include the COP and secretariats established by the Basel Convention, the UNFCCC, the CBD, the Convention on Desertification and the Stockholm Convention. These institutions facilitate the development of a specific regime by hosting regular negotiations sometimes resulting in more specific treaties or other legal instruments. The subsidiary bodies established by a principal organ of a treaty is a by-product of the previous types of organizations. For example, the U.N. General Assembly, one of the principal organs of the U.N., has established several subsidiary bodies, two of which are very important in environmental matters, namely the UNEP and the U.N. Convention of the WMO, which is a subsidiary body of the U.N. General Assembly. COPs are also empowered to create subsidiary bodies. Thus, the Conference of the Parties Serving as the Meeting of the Parties to the Kyoto Protocol (CMP) has set up bodies to manage the flexible mechanisms under Articles 6 and 12 of the Protocol. In some cases, subsidiary bodies may, in turn, be involved in the creation of a new organization. For example, in 1991, UNEP and United Nations Development Programme (UNDP), together with the World Bank, created the GEF which became an independent organization in 1994. This change took place, largely under pressure from DC, in order to limit the influence of the World Bank. The fourth type of organizations are known by their relative organizational informality as these are forums for discussion among states and, in some cases, also among some other entities.

*126.* International institutions, such as UNEP and various U.N. specialized agencies have a catalytic role in problem identification, and in the negotiation and further development of environmental regimes. They play a role in problem identification by providing forums for coordinating scientific research; they support the development and implementation of international environmental treaties by hosting the secretariats for negotiating conferences and for MEAs. MEAs, in turn, also have generated a large number of international institutions, including conferences of the parties, which are not international organizations, as traditionally understood, but have traits and perform roles that closely resemble those generally attributed to international organizations. International financial institutions, such as the World Bank and the GEF, coordinate the transfer of financial and technological resources. Monitoring and verification programs and compliance procedures are coordinated through, in particular, institutions associated with MEAs. In addition, a number of courts and tribunals, at least in principle, have jurisdiction to consider environmental disputes.

In the course of performing these functions, many international institutions both engage in normative development and administer international environmental law.

These activities have contributed to the emergence of a distinctive type of law, now often referred to as global administrative law. Institutions are sometimes said to be the means by which international regimes are implemented. It was the 1972 Stockholm Conference on the Human Environment which triggered international institutionalization, particularly the establishment of the UNEP, and the 1992 Rio Conference on Environment and Development (the Earth Summit). Since 1992, attention has been shifted from institution building to implementation and consolidation. The main functions of international environmental institutions may be summarized as facilitating international treaties and agreements; framing new principles, policies, and laws; acting as a forum for the negotiation of further measures and regulations; receiving reports on treaty implementation by states; coordinating environmental monitoring; facilitating independent monitoring and inspection; promoting scientific research; providing technical and financial support; and facilitating the participation of civil society in environmental activities. The coordination of the policies of the many international organizations with environmental mandates has generally fallen to the U.N., in particular, the General Assembly and the ECOSOC.

## §5. Scientific Developments

*127.* Scientific developments figure prominently in international environmental regimes as many environmental problems were noticed and came on the surface as scientific understanding increased. The role of scientists is perhaps greatest in the agenda-setting process, although technical experts can also play a significant role in the process of elaborating and implementing international environmental regimes. Many pressing environmental problems, such as climate change or ozone depletion, were not immediately felt; they were identified and recognized as problems only as a result of scientific development. For example, when chlorofluorocarbons (CFCs)[63] were first invented in the 1920s, they were considered completely benign—not flammable, explosive, or toxic. They became an international issue only much later, in the 1970s, as a result of the Nobel Prize winning work of two atmospheric chemists who realized that, over time, CFCs would migrate to the upper atmosphere and catalytically react with ozone, thereby destroying the stratospheric ozone layer.

The climate change became an important political issue due to both significant advances in basic science and the entrepreneurship of a small number of scientific knowledge brokers, who pushed the issue through a series of international meetings and hearings at the national level. Their efforts provided knowledge about the existence of the problem, raised public awareness and concern, influenced national policymakers, and helped begin an international dialogue, initially at the nongovernmental level but gained prominence among governments as well.

63. The principal ozone-depleting substance.

*128.* The private actors are the ultimate targets of most international environmental regulation, so they are particularly active in the international standard setting and implementation processes. Businesses typically influence policy and rulemaking in order to further their own business interests. For example, in the case of "green" business, the prime mover is gaining a competitive advantage through the adoption of more stringent environmental measures and in the case of "brown" business, by seeking to stall the adoption of more stringent measures in order to continue doing business as usual. Sometimes industries develop environmental standards on their own in order to enhance their image, forestall governmental regulation, or influence the development of internationally uniform standards in anticipation of governmental regulation. These private and quasi-private standard-setting efforts are an increasingly significant feature of international environmental law.

§6. Financial Institutions

*129.* The growing role and grassroots participation in environmental issues by financial institutions is an important aspect in the present-day world. Since the early 1990s, the financial institutions in developed countries have been trying to identify, quantify, and manage environmental risk resulting from new era industrial and other developments. So, nowadays, financial institutions, mainly investment banks and long-term credit institutions, apply modern techniques to handle environmental risk. For example, some banks in the U.S. have special structures at the highest level of the organization to deal with both environmental risk and environmental products.

## I. Surveys on Risk Perception

*130.* As a result of the changes in the surrounding circumstances, environmental risk is definitely an important issue for financial institutions worldwide. The international survey carried out by European Bank for Reconstruction and Development (EBRD) in 1993 provides evidence of the extent to which environmental risks have affected banking practices internationally. The survey incorporated the experiences of fifty-six lenders from seven countries and found out that over one-third of the banks stated that they had experienced significant losses resulting directly or indirectly from environmental risks. This included all the participating U.S. banks and a very high proportion of Banks in Germany and the U.K. The findings were that:

- The most common sources of loss were defaulted loans, written off in preference to exercising rights over collateral which could have exposed lenders to the costs of undertaking remedial works.
- Large numbers of financial institutions also reported losses arising from remedial works undertaken by the lender after foreclosure and from loans which defaulted as a result of environmental upgrading or costs for remedial works incurred by the borrower.

- Smaller but significant numbers of banks testified to reduced share values and dividend payments, resulting from environmental violations or costs incurred by customers, together with increased volatility of share prices as a result of increased environmental risk across their equity portfolios.

Another survey sponsored by UNEP, Global Survey on Environmental Policies and Practices of the Financial Services Industry,[64] identified similar trends with respect to the environmental credit risks and loss exposure of many financial institutions. Financial institutions in central and eastern European countries and former Soviet Union countries report two phenomena occurring when nations embark on governmental reform. They have experienced consequences of environmental risk in only a few cases.

## II. Banking Transactions

*131.* Almost all banking transactions involve risk, and the financial institution's ability in identifying and quantifying the different levels of risk is the key to separate good decisions from bad ones. Environmental risk is one of several kinds of risks that financial institutions must take into account when assessing new lending or investment opportunities. They have to and are increasingly focusing on environmental risk and implementing policies and procedures to mitigate it. The general aim is to focus upon environmental issues associated with lending investments and thus to increase the opportunities for environmentally acceptable or sustainable development and to minimize exposure to environmental or financial risks.

Virtually all forms of credit corporate transactions undertaken by financial institutions operate within the context of environmental concerns. Notwithstanding, financial institutions explicitly recognize that some forms of transaction are inherently more exposed to credit risk than others. Typical responses may include increasing the level of risk assessment procedures before lending or adjusting credit terms or security requirements. The main determinant of environmental risk is the nature of a borrower's business activity and previous activities carried out on the borrower's site or any sites offered as collateral. The environmental risks also vary according to different forms of transactions. For example, the associated environmental risk to a short-term credit for a retail company is considerably shorter than a long-term credit to support the construction of a big petrochemical plant.

## III. Financial Institutions and Banks: Environmental Risk

*132.* The financial institutions also deal with and provide for the economic risk associated with environmental issues. Some of them are described below.

64. Refer to Cambridge Centre for Sustainable Finance (2016), *Environmental Risk Analysis by Financial Institution*; A Review of Global Practice, Cambridge Institute for Sustainability Leadership, U.K.

*A. United Nations Environment Programme*

*133.* UNEP was established in 1972 as U.N. body for the environment. It promotes effective action and ensures that environmental interests are given importance in international policymaking. UNEP has also helped in some of the most important global treaties involving environmental issues. The UNEP provides the secretariats for the following agreements:

(1) Washington Convention on International Trade in Endangered Species (1973).
(2) Vienna Convention on the Protection of the Ozone Layer (1979) and its Montreal Protocol on Substances That Deplete the Ozone Layer (1985).
(3) Bonn Convention on Migratory Species (1979).
(4) Basel Convention on Trans-boundary Movements of Hazardous Wastes and Their Disposal (1989) and its Protocol on Liability and Compensation (1999).
(5) CBD (1992) and its Cartagena Protocol on Biosafety (2000).
(6) Rotterdam Convention on the Prior Informed Consent (PIC) Procedure for Certain Hazardous Chemicals and Pesticides in International Trade (1998) (joint secretariat with the U.N. FAO).
(7) Intergovernmental Negotiating Committee for a treaty on POPs.

UNEP brings together financial institutions around the world by promoting an annual roundtable meeting to discuss environmental issues that affect financial institutions, including commercial banks, investment banks, insurance companies, etc. These meetings take place in a specific country and are attended by financial institutions. The agenda includes strategic discussions about the challenges and opportunities for the financial market related to sustainable development of environment. It also works as a forum where financial institutions can share views about contentious issues and interchange experiences in order to improve the role of financial sector with respect to environment.

*B. World Bank*

*134.* World Bank is also engaged with environmental questions and deals this aspect through the International Finance Corporation (IFC). IFC is the World Bank's body to finance the private sector either directly or through another financial institution. IFC has strict rules to deal with environmental questions during the evaluation of credit applied for an investment project becoming a model for financial institutions around the world. For example, IFC requires environmental assessment (EA) of projects proposed for its financing to help ensure that they are environmentally sound and sustainable. EA evaluates a project's potential environmental risks and impacts in its area of influence. It examines project alternatives, identifies ways of improving project selection, planning, design, and implementation by preventing, mitigating, or compensating for adverse environmental impacts. EA also includes the process of mitigating and managing adverse environmental impacts throughout project implementation.

### §7. Financial Institution and Harmonization of Environmental Regulation

*135.* Attempts have been made for harmonizing environmental legislation with equivalent legislation in Western European countries. Progress toward harmonization of environmental legislation is most rapid in some countries of central Europe (Poland, Hungary, The Czech Republic and Slovakia), which have signed association agreements with the EU. This harmonization of environmental legislation has focused on contamination (environmental emissions and effluents standards). Both, direct and indirect environmental risks are in large part a result of environmental regulation. In the case of indirect risk, environmental regulations can determine levels of permitted emissions and effluents as well as the enforcement actions intended to discourage companies from exceeding these levels by imposing and recovering damages. In the case of goods received in guarantee, environmental regulation and enforcement play an important role in determining the value held in collateral. Direct liability risk is a product of regulatory intervention when regulations or directives or associated common law judgments explicitly state such risks and penalties.

# Chapter 4. Environmental Agreements

*136.* IEAs play an important role in the present-day globalized economy. These agreements are also important in the context of coalition formation theory and in many cases, they form the basis of development of environmental law. Given the incentives to free ride, associated with the environment as a public good and to the presence of spill overs, the profitability and the optimality of environmental agreements are separated from their stability (i.e., self-enforcement). The partial coalitions and multiple agreements prevail among subsets of players, and that agreements among all players are most unlikely to exist. The design of the agreements, moreover, can be crucial in determining the number of signatory countries.

## §1. Common Provisions and Characteristics

*137.* IEAs are legally binding intergovernmental outcomes directed at reducing impacts on the environment caused by human activity. Using a clear definition allowed creation of a comprehensive database listing over MEAs and bilateral environmental agreements (BEAs), which included treaties, protocols, and amendments. MEAs and BEAs address pollutants; preservation of species; and protection of habitats. Variation in the effects of these agreements on environmental behavior may depend as much on characteristics of member countries, the international context, and the underlying environmental problem as on the differences in agreement design.

## §2. Environmental Clauses in Trade Agreements

*138.* The trade agreements as a matter of fact did not contain provisions dealing with environmental concerns. However, largely as a result of the tuna/dolphin dispute ruling, which prompted environmentalists, environmental issues became part of the trade negotiations, and many trade agreements include important environmental provisions. Nonetheless, MEAs remain the primary way that international environmental issues are addressed, and some MEAs include trade provisions, generally referred to as Specific Trade Obligations or STOs.

Prior to the North American Free Trade Agreement (NAFTA) and the Uruguay Round GATT agreement, environmental issues were not factors in trade negotiations, although it had been discussed in the context of Technical Barriers to Trade (TBT) during the Tokyo Round (World Trade Organization (WTO) 2002). However, environmental provisions were included in both the NAFTA and Uruguay round agreements, have been factors in many subsequent negotiations, and are included in recent trade agreements.

The membership of the WTO encompasses a large number of nations of the world, while many MEAs have limited membership with some missing major players such as the U.S. Some free-trade supporters, however, demand inclusion of environmental issues in trade agreements.[65] This position is taken, in part, because its proponents believe that it may be easier to get agreement on trade barriers than for separate environmental agreements. Thus, including environmental issues in the trade agreement is a way to get broader acceptance and approval of the environmental provisions. Further, trade agreements also have enforcement mechanisms which generally are missing from the MEAs.

## I. The Tuna/Dolphin Ruling

*139.* The U.S., at the urging of environmentalists, had adopted the Marine Mammal Protection Act that prohibited the importation of tuna that had been caught in such a method that killed dolphins, which often accompany and feed on schools of the fish (National Oceanic and Atmospheric Administration (NOAA) 2002). Mexico brought this to the trade dispute process of the GATT, claiming it was an illegal trade constraint under GATT.[66] The GATT appeals process ruled in favor of Mexico which produced an immediate and very unfavorable reaction from environmentalists in the U.S. who felt the ruling unfairly removed an important protection for an endangered species. Among the procedures affected was the NAFTA, the Uruguay Round of GATT negotiations, and its final agreement; it was a factor in the organization of opposition to and scuttling of the WTO's Seattle meeting which was to launch the next round of trade liberalization talks.

*140.* While the tuna/dolphin ruling was unfavorable for trade restrictions based on environmental protection, a subsequent case—the shrimp/sea turtle dispute—reversed that ruling, at least to a limited extent.[67] This case was brought by a group of East Asian nations against the U.S. as a result of a ban on the imports of shrimp caught under techniques that result in harm to sea turtles. Although the dispute panel ruled in favor of the complainants, the appeals panel largely reversed the ruling while calling on the U.S. to enter good faith negotiations to resolve remaining issues. The U.S. was held to have applied the regulations in a discriminatory way, but the ruling seemed to allow the ban if applied equitably.[68] The U.S. claimed victory as a result of the appeal panel's ruling.[69]

---

65. Gray, Krissoff and Tsigas 1996.
66. *See* Dale Calyer, *Environmental Provisions in Trade Agreements*, paper presented at the short course *Trade and the Environment: Dealing with Pollution and Natural Resource Management in a Globalizing World*, at World Bank, Washington D.C., Dec. 8, 2004.
67. *Ibid.*
68. *Ibid.*
69. *Ibid.*

## II. GATT Group on Environmental Measures

*141.* The GATT Secretariat in 1971 prepared a study entitled "Industrial Pollution Control and International Trade." In November 1971, the GATT Council of Representatives agreed to set up the GATT Group on Environmental Measures and International Trade (EMIT) with participation open to all members. However, the group had never met until the European Free Trade Association requested a meeting to help prepare for the 1992 U.N. Conference on Environment and Development. According to the WTO, factors that led to this request included the TBT discussions during the Uruguay Round negotiations, developing country concerns about exports to them of chemicals whose use was prohibited in the exporting countries, and the U.S.-Mexican tuna/dolphin dispute and its consequences, as well as a rising international awareness of the importance of environmental problems and issues.

## III. NAFTA and the Environment

*142.* Negotiations for NAFTA included environmental issues in response to opposition by environmentalists who feared that it would aggravate environmental problems, especially in Mexico.[70] Consequently, it was decided to address the problems in both the negotiations and a parallel process, a decision that:

> suggested that the NAAEC be considered as a model trade and environmental institution.[71] Thus, NAFTA became the first trade liberalization agreement to explicitly include environmental issues, although it was implicit in previous GATT agreements. In NAFTA, environmental objectives were achieved primarily through the side agreement.[72] The preamble to the NAFTA agreement indicates that the provisions will be carried out in a manner consistent with environmental protection and in ways to promote sustainable growth.

*143.* The important factor in view of sovereignty is that each country enforces its own environmental laws. The Commission for Environmental Cooperation (CEC) has some enforcement powers through investigation of citizen's complaints that a country is not enforcing its environmental laws and regulations. The CEC functions include overseeing implementation of the side agreement, providing a forum for discussing issues, and cooperating in solving environmental problems. It incorporates cooperation through the exchange of information, technical assistance, consultation, and coordination of environmental laws. It also operates through contention or conflict resolution under provisions for observing/monitoring, receiving, and evaluating complaints, and enforcement if the complaints are judged valid.[73]

---

70. *Ibid.*
71. *See Is NACEC a Model Trade Environment Institution? Lessons from Mexican Industry*, Working Paper No. 01–08, Global Development and Environment Institute, Tufts University, Medford, M.A.
72. Hauer and Runge 1999; Hufbauer and Orejas 2001.
73. De Janvry, Sadoulet and Davis 1997, p. 13; Kotvis 1995.

## IV. The Environmental Issues and WTO

*144.* The WTO contributes to the protection and preservation of the environment through its objective of ensuring sustainable development and avoiding protectionism, through its rules and enforcement mechanism and its work in different WTO bodies. Sustainable development and protection and preservation of the environment are fundamental goals of the WTO enshrined in the Marrakesh Agreement, which established the WTO. It complements the WTO's objective to reduce trade barriers and eliminate discriminatory treatment in international trade relations. While there is no specific agreement dealing with the environment, under WTO rules members can adopt trade-related measures aimed at protecting the environment provided there is no misuse of such measures for protectionist purposes. WTO practices have resulted in environmental issues becoming an established part of the multilateral trading system. "At the end of the Uruguay Round, Trade Ministers adopted the Decision on Trade and the Environment which anchored environment and sustainable development in WTO work."[74] With the implementation of the WTO agreement, a Committee on Trade and Environment (CTE) was established in 1995 with a mandate to consider all aspects of the trade-environmental interface (Sampson, 2000); however, environmental issues also are considered by other parts of the WTO regime. The WTO Secretariat cooperates with implementing bodies for MEAs, following their work and providing information on WTO rules and mechanisms.

### A. *WTO Rules Setting Framework*

*145.* The WTO rules, with their fundamental principles of non-discrimination, transparency and predictability, help set the framework for members to design and implement measures to address environmental concerns. Further, WTO rules, including specialized agreements such as the Agreement on TBT (which deals with product regulations), and the Agreement on Sanitary and Phytosanitary Measures (which concerns food safety and animal and plant health), provide scope for environmental objectives to be followed and for necessary trade-related measures to be adopted. WTO rules set up the appropriate balance between the right of members to take regulatory measures, including trade restrictions, to achieve legitimate policy objectives (e.g., protection of human, animal or plant life or health, and natural resources) and the rights of other members under basic trade disciplines. For example, GATT Article XX on General Exceptions lays out a number of specific instances in which members may be exempted from GATT rules. The provision seeks, among other things, to ensure that environmental measures are not applied arbitrarily and are not used as disguised protectionism.

74. Nordstrom and Vaughan, p. 67.

## V. Other Trade Agreements

*146.* Numerous regional and bilateral free trade agreements (FTAs) have been negotiated and signed by a number of countries of the world. Several of these agreements have included environmental provisions either as part of the main agreement or as side agreements or annexes to the main document. The U.S. and Canada, for example, have both negotiated agreements which include provisions dealing with environment. Examination of trade agreements indicates that typically specific environmental provisions are not included in their texts; those that do tend to have provisions similar to GATT's Article XX allowing exceptions for the protection of human, animal and plant health and life as well as environment.

*147.* New Zealand, for example, gives a set of environmental objectives in documents setting out its negotiating positions, but its agreement with Singapore does not contain environmental provisions. An exception is the European Free Trade Area's (Norway, Iceland, Switzerland, and Liechtenstein) European Economic Area Agreement with the EU which contains a brief chapter on the environment.[75] This chapter gives objectives of preserving, protecting, and improving the quality of the environment, protection of human health, and assuring prudent utilization of natural resources with specific measures given in an annex to the agreement. The agreements between the EU and Latin American entities (Chile and Mercosur) have brief provisions for environmental cooperation. The purposes of these include promoting sustainable development, protecting natural resources and preventing environmental degradation. Procedures incorporate the possible exchanges of information, environmental education, and providing technical assistance.

## §3. The Concern of DC and Issues

*148.* DC had a number of concerns about the role of the environment in trade agreements and had opposed their inclusion and expansion beyond those included in the Doha Ministerial Declaration.[76] Primarily, DC's view the inclusion of environmental issues in trade agreements as just another way the industrialized countries imposed trade barriers to the goods produced by the developing and low-income countries, not having the resources or expertise to undertake the costly environmental programs, and which they fear might be imposed as conditions to export products to those industrialized nations (da Motta Veiga, 2003; Hoekman and Anderson, 2000; Huff, 2000). A second concern is the costs imposed on those who attempt to comply with environmental regulations of developed countries, costs which are difficult to meet by smaller countries with limited resources in the presence of many other competing needs. Furthermore, many lack the expertise, skilled manpower and institutions needed to develop and enforce strong environmental regulations.

75. Part IV, Ch. 3; Arts. 73, 74 and 75.
76. M.D. Ingco & J.D. Nash, *What's at Stake? Developing Country Interest in the Doha Development Round* (The World Bank, 2004).

*149.* GATT/WTO rules require that the same regulations must apply to domestic and imported products. Furthermore, it is the final product that matters, not the process and production methods (PPMs). This was the situation faced by countries which contested the tuna/dolphin and shrimp/sea turtle cases, since the final product is not distinguishable by the method used to catch the fish or shrimp. However, the processes are important in both cases, and Article XX of GATT allows regulations to protect animal life, which includes endangered animal species. Such provisions can be interpreted in different ways and, thus, developing nations continue to be concerned that their products produced by methods not acceptable in the industrialized countries for environmental reasons, will be banned.

*150.* Environmental issues affect and are affected by international trade and, following NAFTA and the Uruguay Round of GATT negotiations, have become integrated into trade agreements. However, many agreements, especially those with DC, either lack or minimize environmental provisions. The U.S. is required to include environmental objectives in trade agreements under the 2002 Trade Promotion Act, and Canada generally includes environmental cooperation activities via side agreements to its main agreements.

*151.* Environmental concerns were explicitly included in the Doha round of WTO negotiations under the Doha Ministerial Declaration. However, environmental issues remain controversial and progress has been slow, as it has for many of the other issues, as reflected in the failure and abrupt ending of the Cancun meetings in 2003. With some 135 members of the WTO, it was difficult to arrive at a consensus. One factor in this has been a better organization of the DC and articulation of their concerns in the negotiations, although strong and divergent views among the more developed nations also have delayed the process as has the involvement of NGOs and others with an interest in the outcomes of trade negotiations.

## §4. Environmental Clauses in Trade Agreements

*152.* Environmental issues have become a permanent part of many trade agreements and the negotiating process, especially at the multilateral level although many bilateral and regional agreements and negotiations ignore environmental issues or have given them only a minimal or cursory treatment. None have developed the extensive institutional framework developed by NAFTA and its environmental side agreement. The international environmental concerns continue to be addressed primarily by the several MEAs that have been negotiated and implemented by the international community. These, however, lack the coordination that the GATT/WTO has provided to trade issues. Some of the provisions relating to environment given in Trade Agreements are given below.

*153.* Inter-regional Framework Cooperation Agreement between the EC and its Member States and the Southern Common Market and its Party States in Article 17 contains the following clause relating to environment:

Article 17. Cooperation regarding environmental protection

(1) With the aim of achieving sustainable development, the Parties shall encourage awareness of the issues of environmental protection and the rational use of natural resources in all fields of interregional cooperation.
(2) The Parties shall agree to devote special attention to measures connected with the international dimension of environmental problems.
(3) Cooperation could cover the following in particular:
  (a) exchanges of information and know-how regarding matters including regulations and standards;
  (b) training and education regarding the environment;
  (c) technical assistance, the implementation of joint research projects and, where appropriate, institutional assistance.[77]

*154.* The agreement between the U.S. and Hashemite Kingdom of Jordan on the Establishment of a Free Trade Area contains the following provision:

ARTICLE 5: ENVIRONMENT

(1) The Parties recognize that it is inappropriate to encourage trade by relaxing domestic environmental laws. Accordingly, each Party shall strive to ensure that it does not waive or otherwise derogate from, or offer to waive or otherwise derogate from, such laws as an encouragement for trade with the other Party.
(2) Recognizing the right of each Party to establish its own levels of domestic environmental protection and environmental development policies and priorities, and to adopt or modify accordingly its environmental laws, each Party shall strive to ensure that its laws provide for high levels of environmental protection and shall strive to continue to improve those laws.
(3) (a) A Party shall not fail to effectively enforce its environmental laws, through a sustained or recurring course of action or inaction, in a manner affecting trade between the Parties, after the date of entry into force of this Agreement.
  (b) The Parties recognize that each Party retains the right to exercise discretion with respect to investigatory, prosecutorial, regulatory, and compliance matters and to make decisions regarding the allocation of resources to enforcement with respect to other environmental matters determined to have higher priorities. Accordingly, the parties understand that a Party is in compliance with subparagraph (a) where a course of action or inaction reflects a reasonable exercise of such discretion, or results from a bona fide decision regarding the allocation of resources.
(4) For purposes of this article, "environmental laws" mean any statutes or regulations of a Party, or provision thereof, the primary purpose of which

77. http://www.sice.oas.org/trade/mrcsr/merco%5Feu/M_EU_e2.asp.

is the protection of the environment, or the prevention of a danger to human, animal, or plant life or health, through:

(a) the prevention, abatement or control of the release, discharge, or emission of pollutants or environmental contaminants;

(b) the control of environmentally hazardous or toxic chemicals, substances, materials and wastes, and the dissemination of information related thereto; or

(c) the protection or conservation of wild flora or fauna, including endangered species, their habitat, and specially protected natural areas in the Party's territory, but does not include any statutes or regulations, or provision thereof, directly related to worker safety or health.

# Part II. Pollution and Climate Change

## Chapter 1. Environmental Pollution/Climate Change

*155.* The term "pollution" can be defined as reference to substances or intangible factors, which through the pathways of water or air have an effect on the environment or on human health. For instance, Article 1 of the UNECE Long-Range Trans-boundary Air Pollution Convention defines air pollution as the introduction by man, directly or indirectly, of substances or energy into the air resulting in deleterious effects of such a nature as to endanger human health, harm living resources, ecosystems, and material property, and impair or interfere with amenities and other legitimate uses of the environment, "air pollutants" shall be construed accordingly. Article 1(1)(4) of UNCLOS and Article 2 of Helsinki Convention (1992) define "pollution" of the environment to include the introduction of energy into the sea environment. What constitutes pollution is, however, subject to being determined by international law, depending on the priorities of the international community and its regional configuration. Beyond pollution from traditional industrial activity, innovative technologies and related industrial activity can also be covered.

*156.* International environmental problems have a physical and technological basis. Most problems addressed by international law are political in nature like war, human rights abuses, and trade protectionism resulting in failures of human behavior, which is addressed through the development of rules, institutions, and other means of international governance. Environmental issues involve impacts, often technology-driven, on extremely complicated physical processes, which can be understood only with the aid of science. The ozone problem, for example, results from the incidental release of synthetic compounds such as CFCs, which migrate to the upper atmosphere and catalytically react with ozone, thereby breaking down the ozone layer. The problem was created by technology, diagnosed through Nobel Prize-winning science, and, ultimately, addressed through the development of new technologies.

### §1. Nature of Environmental Problems

*157.* The environmental problems relating to climate change have various peculiar features, which are described below.

## I. Environmental Problems and Scientific Uncertainties

*158.* International environmental problems involve significant scientific uncertainties. Although environmental disputes are often attributable to differences in interests and values among states, they are complicated by uncertainties concerning the facts. Many modern environmental problems have effects that are widely dispersed and long term, with long latency periods. Given the complexity of the physical, economic, and social processes involved, it is not known for sure how serious a problem is, what its causes are, how expensive it will be to address, whether it is even a problem at all, and, if it is, whether it is still possible to address. On these and many other questions, scientists cannot provide conclusive answers. Some argue, for example, that we do not know enough about climate change to justify potentially costly preventive policies; others predict dangerous levels of warming and argue that, if we delay action in order to get better scientific information, it will be too late to act. No matter what choice we make, it may have serious consequences. Decisions must be made in the face of uncertainty.

## II. Problems Are Dynamic

*159.* International environmental problems are extremely dynamic and present a moving target. In part, this fact results from changes in scientific knowledge. When the Montreal Protocol on Substances That Deplete the Ozone Layer (Montreal Protocol) was adopted in 1987, the Antarctic ozone hole had just been discovered, and its significance was not fully understood. By 1990, it had become clear that the Montreal Protocol's requirement to reduce the production and consumption of ODS by 50% was inadequate and that stronger controls were needed. In response, the parties adopted the London Amendments, which provided for the complete phase-out of the principal ODS. Since then, the ozone regime has continued to evolve with the development of scientific understanding of the problem. Moreover, not only does scientific understanding develop, environmental problems themselves change as human behavior and technology change. For example, economies grow, consuming more resources and producing more wastes; new chemicals are created, sometimes replacing more harmful substances but sometimes creating new risks; a fish stock becomes depleted, so fishermen move on to other fisheries and begin to overfish them.

## III. Environmental Problems: Interconnected

*160.* International environmental problems are interconnected and need to be addressed holistically. Further, everything is interconnected and addressing one problem individually may contribute to another. In the early twentieth century, for example, factories built taller smokestacks in order to disperse pollutants more widely and thereby reduce local air pollution. But this "solution" merely converted air pollution from a local to a regional concern. Similar kinds of interconnections characterize a wide variety of environmental issues. Some of the leading replacements for ODS are GHGs, which contribute to global warming. The protection of one species may allow it to multiply, with adverse effects for other species. The limitations on nuclear energy may result in greater use of fossil fuels and higher emissions of $CO_2$.

### IV. Interdependence

*161.* With respect to many environmental issues, states and people around the world are interdependent. For example, the earth has only one ozone layer and one climate system, so that no state can immunize itself against harmful effects or address ozone depletion and climate change without cooperating with other states. Likewise, states benefit from preventive steps taken by other states. Relationships of interdependence and the need for cooperation exist with respect to regional and trans-boundary environmental concerns. Increasing human interference with the climate system poses risks for human and natural systems. The impacts and risks related to climate change can be reduced and managed through adaptation and mitigation. Climate change involves complex interactions and changing likelihoods of diverse impacts. People and societies may perceive or rank risks and potential benefits differently, given diverse values and goals.

## §2. Climate Change

*162.* Climate change refers to a change in the state of the climate that can be identified by changes in the mean and/or the variability of its properties, and that persists for an extended period, typically decades or longer. Climate change may be due to natural internal processes or external forces such as modulations of the solar cycles, volcanic eruptions, and persistent anthropogenic changes in the composition of the atmosphere or in land use. The UNFCCC, in Article 1, defines climate change as: "a change of climate which is attributed directly or indirectly to human activity that alters the composition of the global atmosphere and which is in addition to natural climate variability observed over comparable time periods." The UNFCCC thus makes a distinction between climate change attributable to human activities altering the atmospheric composition, and climate variability attributable to natural causes.

*163.* The changes in climate have caused impacts on natural and human systems everywhere in the world. Evidence of climate-change impacts is strongest and most comprehensive for natural systems. Some impacts on human systems have also been attributed to climate change, with a major or minor contribution of climate change distinguishable from other influences. In many regions, changing precipitation or melting snow and ice are altering hydrological systems, affecting water resources in terms of quantity and quality. Glaciers continue to shrink almost worldwide due to climate change, affecting runoff and water resources downstream. Many terrestrial, freshwater, and marine species have shifted their geographic ranges, seasonal activities, migration patterns, abundances, and species interactions in response to ongoing climate change.

*164.* International environmental law has also placed a significant focus on the protection of the environment during warfare. Armed conflict on an international level is a destructive activity for the environment, causing large-scale pollution and damages. The concerned countries are generally sacrificing their "freedom of action" in the context of war. In response, international environmental law has tried minimization of destruction, rather than the complete elimination of destruction.

*165.* The Convention on the Prohibition of Military or any Other Hostile Use of Environmental Modification Techniques,1976 (ENMOD) sought to protect the states of the environment and natural resources by prohibiting the use of techniques that would have "widespread, long-lasting or severe effects as the means of destruction, damage or injury to any other state party". This Convention followed the American War in Vietnam where massive amounts of herbicides and weather-changing techniques were used. However, these guidelines are far from adequate to efficiently ensure the protection of the environment during warfare. Recognizing the need for clearer guidelines, the UN Environment and the Environmental Law Institute released a report to identify the weaknesses of international environmental law in the regulation of wartime environmental protection in 2009.

## I. Climate Extremes

*166.* Several periods of rapid food and cereal price increases following climate extremes in key producing regions indicate a sensitivity of current markets to climate extremes among other factors. However, there has been increased heat-related mortality and decreased cold-related mortality in some regions as a result of global warming. Local changes in temperature and rainfall have altered the distribution of some waterborne illnesses and disease vectors as well as affected crop patterns. Differences in vulnerability and exposure arise from non-climatic factors and multidimensional inequalities produced by uneven development processes. These differences create different risks from climate change. Climate variability and extremes have also been important in decision-making contexts. Climate-related risks have evolved over time due to both climate change and development. Key risks of climate change are severe impacts relevant to Article 2 of the UNFCCC, which refers to "dangerous anthropogenic interference with the climate system." Risks are considered key due to high hazard or high vulnerability of societies and systems exposed, or both.

## II. Marginalized People

*167.* People who are socially, economically, culturally, politically, or otherwise backward and marginalized are especially vulnerable to climate change and also to some adaptation and mitigation responses. This heightened vulnerability is the product of intersecting social processes that result in inequalities in socioeconomic status and income, as well as in exposure. Such social processes include, for example, discrimination on the basis of gender, class, ethnicity, age, and disability.

## III. Adaptation

*168.* Throughout history, people and societies have adjusted to and coped with climate, climate variability and its extremity, with varying degrees of success. Adaptation is becoming embedded in some planning processes, with more limited implementation of responses. Engineered and technological options are commonly implemented adaptive responses, often integrated within existing programs such as disaster risk management and water management. There is increasing recognition of the value of social, institutional, and ecosystem-based measures and the extent of constraints to adaptation. Most assessments of adaptation have been restricted to impacts, vulnerability, and adaptation planning, with very few assessing the processes of implementation or the effects of adaptation actions. The overall risks of climate change impact can be reduced by limiting the rate and magnitude of climate change which can also reduce the scale of adaptation that might be required. The climate change is projected to amplify existing climate-related risks and create new risks for natural and human systems. Some of these risks will be limited to a particular sector or region, and others will have cascading effects.

### §3. Freshwater Resources and Climate Change

*169.* Freshwater-related risk of climate change increases significantly with increasing GHG concentrations. The percentage of global population experiencing water scarcity and affected by major river floods increases with the level of warming. Climate change is projected to reduce renewable surface water and groundwater resources significantly in most dry subtropical regions, intensifying competition for water among sectors. Climate change can also reduce raw water quality and drinking-water quality even with conventional treatment, due to interacting factors: increased temperature; increased sediment, nutrient, and pollutant loadings from heavy rainfall; increased concentration of pollutants during droughts; and disruption of treatment facilities during floods.

## I. Terrestrial and Freshwater Ecosystems

*170.* A large fraction of both terrestrial and freshwater species faces increased extinction risk under projected climate change, especially as it interacts with other stressors, such as habitat modification, overexploitation, and pollution. Extinction risk is increased with both magnitude and rate of climate change as many species will be unable to track suitable climates under mid- and high-range rates of climate change. Those that cannot adapt sufficiently fast will decrease in abundance or go extinct in part or all of their ranges. Management actions, such as maintenance of genetic diversity, assisted species migration, and reduction of other stressors, can reduce, but not eliminate, risks of impacts to terrestrial and freshwater ecosystems due to climate change, as well as an increase in the inherent capacity of ecosystems and their species to adapt to a changing climate.

## II. Coastal Systems and Low-Lying Areas

*171.* Due to sea-level rise projected throughout the twenty-first century and beyond, coastal systems and low-lying areas will increasingly experience adverse impacts such as submergence, coastal flooding, and coastal erosion. The population and assets projected to be exposed to coastal risks as well as human pressures on coastal ecosystems will increase significantly in the coming decades due to population growth, economic development, and urbanization. The relative costs of coastal adaptation vary among and within regions and countries. Some low-lying DC and small island states are expected to face very high impacts in future that, in some cases, could have associated damage and adaptation costs of several percentage points of their GDP.

## III. Marine Systems

*172.* Due to projected climate change by the mid-twenty-first century and beyond, global marine-species redistribution and marine-biodiversity reduction in sensitive regions will challenge the sustained provision of fisheries productivity and other ecosystem services. Spatial shifts of marine species due to projected warming will cause high-latitude invasions and high local-extinction rates in the tropics and semi-enclosed seas. Species richness and fisheries catch potential are projected to increase, on average, at mid and high latitudes and decrease at tropical latitudes. The progressive expansion of oxygen minimum zones and anoxic "dead zones" is projected to further constrain fish habitat. Open-ocean net primary production is projected to redistribute and, by 2100, fall globally. Climate change adds to the threats of overfishing and other non-climatic stressors, thus complicating marine management regimes.

*173.* For medium- to high-emission scenarios, ocean acidification poses other substantial risks to marine ecosystems, especially polar ecosystems and coral reefs, associated with impacts on the physiology, behavior, and population dynamics of individual species from phytoplankton to animals. Highly calcified mollusks, echinoderms, and reef-building corals are more sensitive than crustaceans and fishes, with potentially detrimental consequences for fisheries and livelihoods. Ocean acidification acts together with other global changes and with local changes. Simultaneous drivers, such as warming and ocean acidification, can lead to interactive, complex, and amplified impacts for species and ecosystems.

## §4. Food Security and Food Production Systems

*174.* For the major crops (wheat, rice, and maize) in tropical and temperate regions, climate change without adaptation is projected to negatively impact production for local temperature increases of 2°C or more above late-twentieth-century levels, although individual locations may benefit. After 2050, the risk of more severe yield impacts increases and depends on the level of warming. Climate change is projected to progressively increase inter-annual variability of crop yields in many regions. All aspects of food security are potentially affected by climate change, including food access, utilization, and price stability. Redistribution of marine fisheries catch potential toward higher latitudes poses risk of reduced supplies, income, and employment in tropical countries, with potential implications for food security. Global temperature increases of -4°C or more above late-twentieth-century levels, combined with increasing food demand, would pose large risks to food security globally and regionally. Risks to food security are generally greater in low-latitude areas.

## §5. Impact on Urban areas

*175.* Many global risks of climate change are concentrated in urban areas. Steps that build resilience and enable sustainable development can accelerate successful climate-change adaptation globally. Heat stress, extreme precipitation, inland and coastal flooding, landslides, air pollution, drought, and water scarcity pose risks in urban areas for people, assets, economies, and ecosystems. Risks are amplified for those lacking essential infrastructure and services or living in poor-quality housing and exposed areas. Reducing basic service deficits, improving housing, and building resilient infrastructure systems could reduce vulnerability and exposure in urban areas.

## §6. Impact on Rural Areas

*176.* Major future rural impacts are expected and can be understood through impacts on water availability and supply, food security, and agricultural incomes, including shifts in production areas of food and non-food crops across the world. These impacts disproportionately affect the welfare of the poor people in rural areas, such as female-headed households and those with limited access to land, modern agricultural inputs, infrastructure, and education. Further adaptations for agriculture, water, forestry, and biodiversity can occur through policies taking account of rural decision-making contexts.

## §7. Impact on Human Health

*177.* Throughout the twenty-first century, climate change is expected to lead to increase in ill-health in many regions and especially in DC with low income, as compared to a baseline without climate change. Examples include greater likelihood of injury, disease, and death due to more intense heat waves and fires; increased likelihood of under-nutrition resulting from diminished food production in poor regions; risks from lost work capacity and reduced labor productivity in vulnerable populations; and increased risks from food- and waterborne diseases. Climate change over the twenty-first century will increase the displacement of people, the risk of which increases when populations that lack the resources for planned migration experience higher exposure to extreme weather conditions, in rural and urban areas, particularly in DC with low income. Expanding opportunities for mobility can reduce vulnerability for such populations. Changes in migration patterns can be responsible for both extreme weather conditions and longer-term climate variability and change, and migration can also be an effective adaptation strategy. Climate change can indirectly increase risks of violent conflicts in the form of civil war and intergroup violence by amplifying well-documented drivers of these conflicts such as poverty and economic shocks.

*178.* The climate-change impacts are projected to slow down economic growth, make poverty reduction more difficult, further erode food security, and prolong existing and even create new poverty traps. Climate-change impacts are expected to exacerbate poverty in most DC and create new poverty pockets in countries with increasing inequality, in both developed countries and DC. In urban and rural areas, wage-labor-dependent poor households that are net buyers of food are expected to be particularly affected due to food price increases, including in regions with high food insecurity and high inequality, although the agricultural self-employed could benefit. Insurance programs, social protection measures, and disaster risk management may enhance long-term livelihood resilience among poor and marginalized people, if policies address poverty and multidimensional inequalities. Managing the risks of climate change involves adaptation and mitigation decisions with implications for future generations, economies, and environments. This section evaluates adaptation as a means to build resilience and to adjust to climate-change impacts. It also considers limits to adaptation, climate-resilient pathways, and the role of transformation.

*179.* Effective risk reduction and adaptation strategies consider the dynamics of vulnerability and exposure and their linkages with socioeconomic processes, sustainable development, and climate change. Adaptation planning and implementation can be enhanced through complementary actions across levels, from individuals to governments. National governments can coordinate adaptation efforts of local and subnational governments, for example, by protecting vulnerable groups, by supporting economic diversification, and by providing information, policy and legal frameworks, and financial support. A first step toward adaptation to future climate change is reducing vulnerability and exposure to present climate variability. Strategies include actions with co-benefits for other objectives. Available strategies and actions can increase resilience across a range of possible future climates while helping to improve human health, livelihoods, social, and economic well-being.

# Part III. Law Relating to Air and Atmospheric Pollution

## Chapter 1. Air Pollution

*180.* Air pollution kills an estimated 7 million people every year and is the biggest environmental health risk. Airborne pollutants are responsible for about one-third of deaths from stroke, chronic respiratory disease, and lung cancer, as well as one-quarter of deaths from heart attack. Air pollution is also fundamentally altering our climate, with profound impacts on the health of the planet. The problem is most acute in urban areas, particularly in Africa and Asia. In low- and middle-income countries, 98% of cities with more than 100,000 inhabitants fail to meet the WHO's air quality guidelines. Human health and the environment are adversely affected by atmospheric pollution caused by introduction of harmful substances into the atmosphere. Many substances can cause air pollution, including acids, $NO_2$, $NO_x$ and sulfur oxides ($SO_x$), hydrocarbon emissions, particulate matter (PM), and heavy metals, particularly mercury and lead. Moreover, strong horizontal winds can spread pollutants. A number of substances like CFCs and halons, when emitted into the atmosphere, cause depletion of the ozone layer, which filters out ultraviolet radiation from the sun. When such radiation passes to the earth's surface unfiltered it can damage human health, particularly by causing skin cancer, threatening vision, and damages biodiversity. Also the changes in the composition of the atmosphere can cause climate change.

### §1. Multilateral Agreements and Atmosphere

*181.* A significant contribution to climate change can be anthropogenic emissions of GHGs, including $CO_2$, $N_2O$, methane ($CH_4$), CFCs, and tropospheric ozone ($O_3$). A significant number of MEAs relate to the atmosphere. For example, there is the 1979 LRTAP. The 1985 Vienna Convention for the Protection of the Ozone Layer, the 1987 Montreal Protocol on Substances That Deplete the Ozone Layer, and the 1992 UNFCCC and the 1997 Kyoto Protocol which relate to climate change.

*182.* Strengthening the role of the UNEP in promoting air quality, the UNEA encouraged governments to take action across sectors to improve air quality; to formulate action plans and establish and implement nationally determined ambient air quality standards; to make air quality data more easily accessible and understandable to the public; and to share with the UNEP Secretariat and other states the results and experiences of their efforts.

## §2. Laws to Promote Air Quality

*183.* Poor air quality can have a significant impact on human health, the environment, and the economy. Many different types of national legislation address air pollution. U.N. Resolution 1/7 focuses, in particular, on air quality standards and access to information. But there can also be local air quality management, which provides for local governments to take measures to address local problems, the regulation of road transport, domestic fires, and nuisances. Most states have extensive industrial air pollution regimes, and many integrate air pollution regulations with other pollution controls. Voluntary instruments like negotiated agreements, or covenants, with industry can improve air pollution provided that they have measurable objectives, clear rules for monitoring and reporting, and are backed up with a regulatory regime.

## §3. Air Quality Standards

*184.* WHO has formulated certain guidelines on ambient air pollution levels, which are used as reference by policymakers across the world to set standards and goals for air quality management. The guidelines contain health-based standards for specific air pollutants that are to be adopted as air quality targets. The WHO's air quality guidelines provide thresholds and limits for key air pollutants that pose health risks. The guidelines apply worldwide and are based on expert evaluation of current scientific evidence for PM, $O_3$, $NO_2$ and $SO_2$. Once major air pollutants are identified, governments may establish national and regional standards, which will set maximum allowable levels for major air pollutants; this defines a required air quality. It is often necessary to set emission limits for particular pollutants and/or to ban particular activities in order to achieve that air quality standard. Making air quality data more easily accessible and understandable to the public: Involvement of the public in the regulation and management of air quality can bring significant benefits. The availability of information to stakeholders will enhance their ability to contribute during collection and analysis of information, prioritization of issues, review, and assessment of existing strategies, working up new strategies, planning actions, investment, and organization. The public will include people who possess relevant expertise; whose interests are directly affected by air quality; who have relevant control or influence; and whose activities have an impact on air quality. Policymakers and regulators may overlook key considerations if they fail fully to involve and inform the public.

§4. AIR QUALITY INFORMATION

*185.* There are a number of ways in which air quality data may be made more accessible and understandable to the public. There may be a requirement on public authorities to make environmental information, including information relating to air quality, available to the public on request. There may be requirements on public authorities to publish air quality information regularly. There may be requirements on public authorities to disseminate environmental information using electronic means. Air quality information may be made available in Pollutant Release and Transfer Registers, which provide easily accessible key environmental data about potentially polluting activities.

§5. ROLE OF UNITED NATIONS

## I. United Nations Environment Assembly (UNEA)

*186.* The UNEA is the world's highest-level decision-making body on the environment, with a membership of all 193 Member States of the U.N. The Assembly meets twice in a year in Nairobi, Kenya to set priorities for global environmental policies and develop international environmental law. Through its ministerial declaration and resolutions, the Assembly provides leadership, catalyzes intergovernmental action on the environment, and contributes to the implementation of the U.N. 2030 Agenda for Sustainable Development. The UNEA is also the governing body of the UNEP.

UNEA at its third sitting adopted resolution 3/8 on Preventing Air Pollution and requested UNEP to regularly undertake an assessment of progress being made by the Member States to adopt and implement key actions that can improve air quality, in time for UNEA-5 and thereafter, synchronized with the Global Environment Outlook cycle. In response to this request, UNEP is providing an update to the 2016 report "Actions on Air Quality" and a comprehensive global picture of national efforts toward improved air quality in time for UNEA-5. The global report update is to be complemented by regional reports led by UNEP regional offices and supported by country-specific case studies. By doing so, the report will identify key actions that cover the range of interventions and policy options at three levels namely global, regional and national. UNEP has been working closely with partners and stakeholders from U.N. Agencies, governments, research institutions, private sector, civil society and relevant NGOs. UNEA is working around the world to tackle air pollution—by supporting cleaner fuels and vehicles, inspiring individuals and city leaders to act, strengthening laws and institutions, and developing affordable technologies to monitor air quality.

## II. United Nations Environment Programme

*187.* Under paragraph 5(a) of Resolution 1/7, the mandate of UNEP is "to undertake strengthened capacity-building activities on air quality, such as workshops and policy development assistance, to support Governments in their efforts to implement" the paragraphs in the resolution that provides for governments' action to improve air quality, national air quality standards, and availability of air quality data. Air pollution has an adverse effect on health as well as other economic and social costs such as lost productivity and missed educational and other human development opportunities. Degradation of air quality not only causes economic damage by imposing costs on business, industry, households, and public services; it also causes damage to the quality of urban life. Similarly, air pollution causes deterioration of buildings and historical monuments. Air pollution can deter investment and so cause further economic damage.

*188.* UNEP assists Member States and other stakeholders to achieve relevant SDGs on cities including SDG 11 (sustainable cities and human settlements) with specific focus on sustainable transport system, sustainable urbanization, access to public spaces, sustainable buildings, per capita environmental impact of cities, and policies toward climate change, resource efficiency, disaster risk reduction, etc. UNEP is promoting sustainable consumption and production practices across Asia and the Pacific to address inefficient resource-use patterns, and cities are the centerpiece where such issues need to be addressed. Since 80% of the GDP comes from its urban areas, the quality and efficiency of Asian and Pacific cities will determine the region's long-term productivity and overall stability. However, inefficiencies, such as unmet demand for urban services (water, energy, and transport), and huge financing requirements hamper economic growth and impede inclusive development, trapping the poor in slums. Air pollution and in-effective wastewater treatment and solid-waste management remain constant problems in cities.

## III. Montevideo Programme Mandate

*189.* Pursuant to the Montevideo Programme mandate, UNEP and U.N.-HABITAT jointly run the Sustainable Cities Programme (SCP), which promotes good environmental governance at all levels to support local and national partners in their adoption of environmental planning management processes and the integration of good practice into national policy and legal frameworks. The UNEP and U.N.-HABITAT are working together with respect to sustainable urban planning and management, analyzing the state of the environment in cities, *inter alia*, considering air pollution, and climate change. The two organizations collaborate within a Partnership Framework with a view to mainstreaming environmental considerations into global urban policymaking, and ensuring that urban issues are included in environmental programs and decision-making at the national and international levels.

*190.* EIA may be used to control urban air pollution by controlling the location of sources of air pollution and by ensuring that adequate control measures are in place. Moreover, transport policies can have a marked effect by increasing the use of public transport and encouraging walking and cycling. Urban air pollution will not necessarily be caused by urban sources. For example, haze pollution may be caused by fires, and slash and burn farm and forest clearance. Dust and sand resulting from desertification may contaminate the urban environment.

# Part IV. Law Relating to Water Pollution

## Chapter 1. Water Pollution

*191.* A key concern for international community is to ensure that both people and the natural environment have adequate freshwater to sustain and nourish their existence. In many parts of the world, communities actually compete with nature for dwindling supplies of fresh water. One of the main legal challenges for governments is to overcome the need for human demand-side competition and to find ways to harmonize the water requirements of people with those of the natural environment. Potentially, the most effective means for achieving such harmonization is to integrate environmental concerns into national and international water laws and policies.

### §1. Fresh Water Availability and Pollution

*192.* Scarcity of freshwater is an increasingly critical public health problem which contributes to waterborne disease, malnutrition, poverty, economic and political instability, and conflict—potentially violent conflict—between countries or groups within countries. Approximately 97.5% of all water is either saltwater or water that has become polluted. Of the remaining 2.5%, nearly 70% is frozen in glaciers and the polar ice caps. Less than 0.01% of all water worldwide is available for human use in lakes, rivers, reservoirs, and easily accessible aquifers. About three-fifths of water flowing in all rivers is shared by two or more countries—in 263 river basins in 145 countries, where two-fifths of the world's population lives. As a result, many countries are highly dependent on water resources that originate from outside their national territory. For example, 34% of water resources in India and 76% of water resources in Pakistan originate from outside these countries. The Nile River Basin is shared by eleven countries that are mutually dependent for their water resources. One billion people do not have access to safe water. The problem will deepen as the world population grows from 7.9 billion people in 2021 to about 9.0 billion by 2050, particularly in countries with high population growth rates that share a major source of freshwater with other countries.

§2. TRANS-BOUNDARY WATERS

*193.* The aquifers and lake and river basins shared by two or more countries form the trans-boundary waters. These support the lives and livelihoods of vast numbers of people across the world. In an era of increasing water stress, how we manage these critical resources is vital to promoting peaceful cooperation and sustainable development. Depleted and degraded trans-boundary water supplies have the potential to cause social unrest and spark conflict within and between countries. To deal with the impacts of climate change combined with the demands of increasing populations and economic growth requires a supranational, integrated approach to trans-boundary water resource management. The 263 trans-boundary lake and river basins cover almost half the Earth's surface. A total of 145 States have territory in these basins, and 30 countries lie entirely within them. There are approximately 300 trans-boundary aquifers, helping to serve the 2 billion people who depend on groundwater. Cooperation is essential, especially in areas vulnerable to the impacts of climate change and where water is already scarce. Wetlands around lakes and floodplains that straddle national boundaries provide essential ecosystem services to the surrounding populations, such as food provision, barriers against flooding and the natural processing of pollution.

Overexploitation of lakes, rivers and aquifers can jeopardize these ecosystem services and have dire consequences for the reliability and sustainability of water supplies, which can cause international tension if those impacts are felt adversely on the other side of a border. Depleted aquifers can also allow saltwater intrusion in coastal areas and increase the concentration of arsenic and fluoride and other toxic substances. Even a positive action can have a negative reaction. For instance, a unilateral move by one country to adapt to climate change by building a dam may drastically reduce a river's flow downstream in another country. The way in which trans-boundary waters are managed affects sustainable development within and beyond a country's borders. Therefore, the various heavily water-dependent sectors—agriculture, industry, energy, navigation and water supply and sanitation—need to cooperate on a supranational level.

## I. Trans-boundary Water Convention

*194.* Since 1948, there have been 37 incidents of acute conflict over water, while approximately 295 international water agreements were negotiated and signed during this period. The Convention on the Protection and Use of Trans-boundary Watercourses and International Lakes (Water Convention) was adopted in Helsinki in 1992 and entered into force in 1996. The Convention is a legally binding instrument promoting the sustainable management of shared water resources, the implementation of the SDGs, the prevention of conflicts, and the promotion of peace and regional integration. The Convention requires parties to prevent, control and reduce trans-boundary impact; use trans-boundary waters in a reasonable and equitable way and ensure their sustainable management. Parties bordering the same trans-boundary waters have to cooperate by entering into specific agreements and establishing joint bodies. As a framework agreement, the Convention does not affect bilateral and multilateral agreements for specific basins or aquifers but fosters their establishment and implementation, as well as further development.

*195.* The Convention was originally negotiated as a regional framework for the pan-European region. Following an amendment procedure, since March 2016, all U.N. Member States can accede to it. Chad and Senegal became the first African Parties in 2018, and Ghana acceded in 2020. The Water Convention is a powerful tool to promote and operationalize the achievement of the 2030 Agenda for Sustainable Development and its SDGs. It directly supports implementation of target 6.5, which requests all countries to implement integrated water resources management, including through trans-boundary cooperation. The Convention and its program of work are also relevant for other SDGs. In 2020, only twenty-four countries reported that all their trans-boundary basins are covered by cooperation arrangements (U.N.-Water 2021).

## II. Trans-boundary Cooperation

*196.* The cooperation among nations can help resolve conflicts over water and maintain public health, food security, and social, environmental, and economic stability. Two examples of such cooperation in the Middle East have been the Good Water Neighbors Project and the Nile Basin Initiative. The Good Water Neighbors Project, established in 2001, has brought together Israeli, Jordanian, and Palestinian communities to protect shared water resources and has improved the local water sector and helped to build peace at the local level. The Nile Basin Initiative, which began in 1999, is an international venture in which nine countries have developed the Nile in a cooperative manner, shared substantial socioeconomic benefits, and promoted regional peace and security.

*197.* Much cooperation over water use also exists in other parts of the world. For example, the Autonomous Water Authority created by Bolivia and Peru, which share Lake Titicaca, has enabled these countries to work together on the management of water resources. Another example of cooperative water use is the situation of the freshwater basin of the Aral Sea, which is shared by six countries. The surface of the sea had shrunk between the 1960s and 2007 to 10% of its original size by diversion of water, which drained two rivers feeding it and devastated the environment. With the completion of the Kok-Aral Dam, the Aral Sea has now begun to fill again. In India, 2900-km long river, the Brahmaputra, is reeling under water pollution in the form of sewage waste and oil discharge. Rapid urbanization and lack of efficient waste disposal systems have rendered it lifeless and polluted. However, efforts to clean up the river are mired in diplomatic issues with China. The state governments of Assam and Arunachal Pradesh have accused China's dam-building activities on the border of polluting the Siang waters, which flow through southern Tibet and is known as the Brahmaputra in India.

## §3. Precautionary Principle and Protection of Rivers

*198.* The Precautionary Principle has been enshrined in a number of agreements related to the protection of river ecosystems, among them are:

(a) Helsinki Convention on the Protection and Use of Trans-boundary Water-courses and International Lakes of 1992 (Article 2(5)).
(b) Charleville-Mezieres Agreement, 1994 concerning the Protection of the Scheldt and Meuse Rivers (Articles 2(a) and 3(2)(a)).
(c) Sofia Convention on Cooperation for the Protection and Sustainable Use of the Danube, 1994 (Article 2(4)), and Rotterdam Convention on the Protection of the Rhine, 1998 (Article 4).

The principle has been framed rather differently in these different agreements. For example, the 1992 Helsinki Convention as well as the 1998 Rotterdam Convention on the Protection of the Rhine state that "The Parties shall be guided by … the precautionary principle," the 1994 Convention on Cooperation for the Protection and Sustainable Use of the Danube River sets out that "the Precautionary principle constitute a basis for all measures aiming at the protection of the Danube River." The principle has been invoked in international litigation as regards river protection. For instance, in the *Gabcíkovo-Nagymaros* case brought before the ICJ, Hungary, the precautionary principle was invoked to support the existence of an environmental state of necessity as a ground for justifying the breach of its obligations toward Slovakia.[78] While recognizing the seriousness of the environmental concerns put forward by Hungary to justify its refusal to observe the treaty it had concluded with the former Czechoslovakia, the ICJ refused to accept the existence of a "grave and imminent peril" justifying a state of necessity because of the uncertain nature of the dangers invoked by the Hungarian authorities.

Therefore, a state of necessity can only be invoked under international law of state responsibility in the event of a sufficient degree of certainty and inevitability that a peril will materialize. In so doing, the ICJ eschewed addressing the issue of precaution. However, in a separate opinion, Judge Weeramantry saw the precautionary principle as a constituent of the wider legal principle of sustainable development.

## §4. Water Quality and Treatment Standards

*199.* Water quality and treatment standards usually come in one of the three following forms.

78. Unilateral suspension of works on its section of a dam on the Danube) (*Gabcíkovo-Nagymaros* Case, 1997).

## I. Technological Standards

*200.* The technical standards specify that the treatment must include certain technologies or processes. Frequently, this standard is expressed in the form that "secondary treatment" or "biological treatment" is required without identifying either the water quality of the effluent to be produced or the exact details of the technical process to be used.

## II. Effluent Standards

*201.* These are specifications of the physical, biological, and chemical quality of the effluent to be produced by the treatment. These usually include allowable concentrations of Biochemical Oxygen Demand (BOD), Chemical Oxygen Demand (COD), Suspended Solids (SS), Nitrogen, Phosphorus. Most such concentrations are expressed in mg/l (milligrams/liter).

## III. Uniform Effluent Standards

*202.* The uniform effluent standards target concentrations of pollutants in the effluent and standardize them across the entire country. This approach has the advantage of simplicity, ease of implementation, and the appearance of "fairness" for all to whom it is applicable. Ambient or Stream Quality Standards, by contrast, seek to fix standards for the quality of the water body receiving the waste. Where the receiving water is used for drinking, bathing, fishing, or reuse, the standards for the receiving water are relatively high. If however natural processes of dilution and biodegradation can improve the quality sufficiently before there is significant use of the resource, then the standards can be lower. WHO came up with drinking-water quality guidelines which may be used as the international reference points for drinking-water quality. Although the WHO provides thorough guidelines and recommendations for best management strategies (e.g., water-safety plans, applications for management strategies), it does fall short in recommending numerical benchmarks for acceptable parameters for microbial and chemical concentrations in drinking water compared to the developed countries like U.S. Many of the acceptable concentrations the WHO recommend for individual contaminants are significantly higher than what is set by the U.S. So, it is open to question whether the WHO guidelines should be used as a standard for drinking-water quality.

### §5. Maximum Allowable Pollutants

*203.* The maximum allowable pollutants are determined by environmental scientists, once the desired stream quality is known. These concentrations become the standards for that discharge. Under this arrangement, different discharges in different environmental contexts must meet different effluent standards. Ambient standards have the advantage that they ensure that resources are efficiently allocated to address local environmental conditions. The major disadvantages are that the approach requires considerable planning and environmental science. The ambient standards offer more efficient and cost-effective approach to improving the environment if properly developed and enforced. Where rigorous water quality modeling is not possible or practical, the establishment of watershed or river basin management boards can still help to prioritize investment in treatment in a systematic fashion. It makes no sense to invest large amounts of money in wastewater treatment for a single city if pollution from other cities or agricultural runoff can nullify the beneficial impact. It will make sense to concentrate efforts where they can make a difference by adopting a holistic approach.

# Part V. Law Relating to Pollution of Sea

*204.* At present, the oceans are in the state of declining health because of increasing marine pollution. The Global Ocean Commission, a group including former heads of state, private sector leaders, and scientific and economic advisors, has identified five main drivers namely rising demand for resources, technological advances, decline of fish stocks, climate change, biodiversity and habitat loss, and weak high seas governance. Thirty-six percent of the world's oceans lay within the sovereign territory and under the governance of coastal nation-states. As physical boundaries and barriers do not exist between marine zones governed under various political regimes, happenings in one area have varying degrees of effect or ramifications in other areas.

# Chapter 1. Law of Sea

*205.* The U.N. has made efforts to ensure the peaceful, cooperative, legally defined uses of the seas and oceans for the individual and common benefit of mankind and to prevent pollution. Its groundbreaking work in adopting the 1982 Law of the Sea Convention stands as a defining moment in the extension of international law to the vast, shared seawater resources. The U.N. Office of Legal Affairs, through its Division of Ocean Affairs and the Law of the Sea, plays a major role in supporting those efforts.

## §1. Conventions and Programs

*206.* The UNEP, particularly through its Regional Seas Programme, protects oceans and seas and promotes the environmentally sound use of marine resources. The UNESCO, through its Intergovernmental Oceanographic Commission, coordinates programs in marine research, observation systems, hazard mitigation, and better managing ocean and coastal areas. The IMO has developed and administers a wide range of treaties, focusing, in particular, on preventing the pollution of the oceans and seas. These include the MARPOL of 1973, as modified by the 1978 Protocol (MARPOL), and the 1954 International Convention for the Prevention of Pollution of the Sea by Oil (the "OILPOL Convention"). Further, since the adoption of the Law of the Sea Convention, additional agreements have further expanded the legal regime governing the oceans and seas. Among these is the 1995 U.N. Agreement on Straddling Fish Stocks and Highly Migratory Fish Stocks, which provides a regime for the conservation and management of these stocks, with a view to ensuring their long-term conservation and sustainable use.

## §2. Law of Sea Convention

*207.* The provisions of the Law of the Sea Convention are implemented with the assistance of several bodies. Among these, the International Seabed Authority (ISA) enables states parties to organize and control activities relating to mineral resources in the international seabed area. The ITLOS adjudicates disputes on the interpretation and application of the Convention. And the Commission on the Limits of the Continental Shelf (CLCS) applies scientific and technical formulas to delineate the outer limits of the continental shelf when that submerged portion of the land territory of a coastal state extends farther than 200 nmi beyond its coastline.

## §3. Law of Sea: U.N. and Related Bodies

*208.* The international law of the sea comprises all the legal norms pertaining to the sea and is applicable to regulations of relations between states pertaining to oceans and seas. It contains rules on the delimitation and exploitation of maritime areas as well as provisions on the protection and exploration of the oceans. However, some fields fall outside its scope; these include matters covered by national legislation, such as regulations on port and harbor operations, and maritime law. Earlier the sea was simply a source of food and was only of interest to people to that extent. With the rise of the great seafaring nations such as the Netherlands, Portugal, and Spain from the fifteenth century onward, however, these kingdoms increasingly sought to expand their spheres of influence. Access to mineral resources and other new commodities aroused ambitions and triggered a race to conquer the oceans, faraway islands, and coastlines and dominate the world. This led to numerous wars and sea battles.

Early on, scholars sought answers to one important question: who does the sea actually belong to? It is a question which the international law of the sea has been unable to resolve satisfactorily to this day. From the outset, the quest for an answer was dominated by the tension between the concept of the freedom of the seas, or *mare liberum* (the free sea), formulated by the Dutch philosopher and jurist Hugo Grotius (1583–1645), and the concept of *mare clausum* (closed sea) developed by the English scholar and polymath John Selden (1584–1654). The pivotal issue was—and is—whether the sea is an international territory and all nations are free to use it, or whether it can be claimed by individual states. Neither of these two positions has ultimately prevailed, and the conflict between these positions is still apparent in the present structure of the international law of the sea.

## §4. United Nations Convention on Law of Sea

*209.* At present, the primary instrument of governance for the seas is the UNCLOS, adopted in 1982 as the outcome of the Third United Nations Conference on the Law of the Sea (UNCLOS III). Various norms of CIL may supplement UNCLOS. The Convention is the most comprehensive international treaty. It is based on the four Geneva Conventions on the Law of the Sea adopted in 1958: these are the Convention on the Territorial Sea and the Contiguous Zone; the Convention on the High Seas; the Convention on Fishing and Conservation of the Living Resources of the High Seas; and the Convention on the Continental Shelf. These treaties codified the—unwritten—customary law which had previously applied. For example, since the mid-seventeenth century, countries had generally accepted that national rights applied to a specified belt of water, known as the territorial sea, extending from a nation's coastlines, usually for 3 nmi—roughly equivalent to the distance traveled by a cannon shot.

*210.* From the mid-twentieth century, the seas became matter of increasing interest for the countries as a source of natural resources such as oil and gas. Many coastal states attempted to extend their national jurisdiction over ever-larger areas of the sea and the seabed, some laying claim to a 200 nmi zone. The concept of "mare liberum" appeared to have been consigned to history. After an initial attempt to regulate the maximum permissible extent of the territorial sea in an international treaty failed in 1930, the four Geneva Conventions were finally adopted under U.N. auspices in 1958. The aim of these international agreements was to prevent the sea from being divided up among various countries. However, this aim was not achieved in full. For example, the discovery of major deep seabed deposits of manganese nodules in the eastern and central Pacific Ocean, at a considerable distance from the coast, in the 1960s sparked new ambitions among the industrial countries. Similarly, there is debate as to which nations can lay claim to the wealth of mineral resources located in the Arctic. These resources will become easier to access as the sea ice retreats in future. In the exclusive economic zone (EEZ), which extends for up to 200 nmi, the coastal state has sovereign rights for the purpose of exploring and exploiting the natural resources of the waters, whether living or non-living. On the continental shelf, which may extend beyond the EEZ, the coastal state has sovereign rights for the purpose of exploring and exploiting the natural resources, whether living or non-living, on or under the seabed.

## I. UNCLOS and Rights of Coastal States

*211.* The UNCLOS draws together the four Geneva Conventions—the "old" law of the sea—in a single unified treaty. In substantive terms, however, it actually goes further than the four. For example, under the "new" law of the sea, the rights of the coastal states are expanded, in some cases substantially, in both qualitative and quantitative terms. For example, each coastal state has exclusive rights to exploit the fish stocks in the EEZ which extends to a distance of 200 nmi from the coastal baseline. Under the Geneva Conventions, the EEZ did not exist. UNCLOS also provides the legal basis for the ITLOS, which commenced its work in Hamburg in 1996. However, the tribunal is not the only judicial institution responsible for safeguarding compliance with UNCLOS. The states parties to UNCLOS are free to choose whether they wish to submit disputes concerning the interpretation and application of UNCLOS to ITLOS, or whether they prefer to apply to the ICJ in The Hague. It took some years for UNCLOS to be accepted: most industrialized countries rejected it at first due to a number of highly contentious provisions on deep-sea mining. For example, UNCLOS initially required these nations to share their deep-sea mining know-how with the DC. Once the provisions had been watered down, reinforcing the position of the industrial nations, UNCLOS entered into force in 1994.

*212.* The international law of the sea establishes a framework for conduct, especially in relation to economic interests, the compliance of which is mandatory. It regulated fishing and navigation and the extraction of oil and gas at sea. Also, the exploitation of other resources of the deep seabed and the protection of the marine environment are regulated. The law divides the sea into various legal zones. It defines the legal status and extent of these zones and establishes norms governing the rights and jurisdictions of the coastal and flag states in respect of these zones. Jurisdiction ranges from full territorial sovereignty (in internal waters) to limited "aquitorial" sovereignty (in the territorial sea) and limited jurisdiction (in the EEZ and continental shelf). The reference for the calculation of the various maritime zones is known as the baseline. The normal baseline is the mean low-water line along the coast as marked on charts officially recognized by the coastal state.

### *A. Jurisdiction*

*213.* A state enjoys exclusive rights to make use of certain resources of the EEZ and the continental shelf, such as the right to fish and to extract minerals. Waters on the landward side of the baseline belong to the state's internal waters. They form part of the national territory of the coastal state, which has complete jurisdiction over them. In some cases, however, it is not the low-water line which delimits the internal waters; this applies in cases where straight baselines or closing lines across a bay are drawn. The law of the sea permits this approach if the coast is characterized by deep indentations and inlets (as in Norway), if a chain of islands stretches along and immediately adjacent to the coast (as with the North Frisian Islands) or if the coast has a bay. For example, the Wadden Sea, to the extent that it lies landwards of the outermost points of the North Frisian Islands, is just as much part of Germany's internal waters as the ports of Kiel, Hamburg, and Bremen. The territorial sea extends seawards of the baseline to a limit not exceeding 12 nmi. It is here that international law begins to restrict the sovereignty of the coastal state: ships of all states enjoy the right of innocent passage through the territorial sea. The passage through the territorial sea cannot be made subject to permission or imposition of similar restrictions by the coastal states. Under certain circumstances, however, it may channel ships in transit, e.g., by creating shipping lanes, in order to ensure the safety of navigation.

### *B. Rights in Different Zones*

*214.* Coastal states have different rights in different coastal zones of the sea. This subject has also been dealt with under UNCLOS. Depending on the distance from the shoreline and depth of water, the sea has been divided into territorial waters, contiguous zone, EEZ, and continental shelf.

### *C. Territorial Waters*

*215.* UNCLOS divides the sea into various legal zones, with the state's sovereignty decreasing with increasing distance from the coast. Every state has the right to territorial sea, not exceeding 12 nmi, in addition to its internal waters. In the territorial sea, the sovereignty of the coastal state is already restricted under international law, as ships of all states enjoy the right of innocent passage through it.

### *D. Contiguous Zone*

*216.* The contiguous zone is the sea adjacent to territorial waters and extends up to 24 nmi seawards from the baseline. In the contiguous zone, the coastal state may merely exercise rights of control. In this area, which partly overlaps with the territorial sea, the coastal state may verify compliance with or infringement of its national laws and regulations, including customs, fiscal, immigration or sanitary laws and regulations, within its territorial sea.

### *E. Exclusive Economic Zone*

*217.* Further out to sea, there is the EEZ, which stretches to 200 nmi seawards of the baseline. Unlike the internal waters and the territorial sea, the EEZ does not form part of the national territory. The coastal state has limited rights which apply not to the maritime area itself but only to the resources existing within it. A coastal state may not assert territorial claims to any part of the Exclusive EEZ. All states enjoy freedom of navigation in the EEZ and have the right to lay submarine cables and pipelines there. As the term "Exclusive Economic Zone" implies, that only the coastal state may erect and utilize structures such as oil platforms and wind turbines here, or engage in fishing. The third countries are excluded from such activities in EEZ of a particular country. This is significant from an economic perspective. For example, around 90% of all commercially exploitable fish species occur in the coastal states' EEZs. This figure is even more striking given that these economic zones make up just 35% of the sea's total area. The coastal states also have jurisdiction over marine scientific research. The conduct of marine research activities by third countries in the EEZ generally requires the authorization of the coastal state. In matters pertaining to the protection and preservation of the marine environment, the coastal state enjoys specific rights in the EEZ. It alone may propose the designation of a marine protected area within its EEZ to the IMO in order to protect the area concerned against pollution from ships.

*218.* Denmark, Germany, Poland, and Sweden lie so close together that their EEZs are limited to a narrow belt of water. In some areas, e.g., east of Flensburg, the limits actually lie within the 12 mi zone. In densely populated Europe with its many borders, the EEZ often extends for less than 200 nmi. This applies to the Adriatic, the North Sea, and the Mediterranean. Nonetheless, worldwide, around 90% of all commercially relevant fish species are caught in the relatively narrow belt of water which forms the EEZs. This applies to the Adriatic, the North Sea, and the Mediterranean.

### *F. Continental Shelf*

*219.* There is a legal and a geological definition of the term "continental shelf." Legally speaking, the term denotes the zone which extends out to a maximum limit of 200 nmi seawards from the baseline. Geologically, the term is applied to the broad, relatively shallow submarine platform adjacent to the coast, which slopes gradually to an average depth of 130 m. The steep continental slope with a gradient of up to 90 degrees adjoins it on the seaward side. UNCLOS also contains specific provisions relating to the continental shelf, of which parts may lie well beneath the EEZ. Like the EEZ, this is an area of jurisdiction where only the coastal state has the right to explore and exploit natural resources. Nature and law dictate that every coastal state in the world has a continental shelf, but the width of that shelf varies considerably, according to geological conditions. As the law stands, however, each coastal state may claim a continental shelf of up to 200 nmi. If the natural continental shelf extends beyond 200 nmi, an even larger area can be designated as the continental shelf. In that case, under international law, the maximum outer limit may not exceed 350 nmi from the baseline or, alternatively, 100 nmi seawards from the 2,500 m isobath.

*220.* In cases where a coastal state intends to establish the outer limits of its continental shelf beyond 200 nmi, it is required to provide evidence to the U.N. CLCS that the submarine area concerned is genuinely a natural prolongation of its territory. The Commission scrutinizes the geological and hydrographic data submitted and finally makes a recommendation. The outer limits of the shelf established by a coastal state on the basis of these recommendations are final and binding. However, there is still disagreement within the international community concerning the legal implications of a Commission recommendation. The Commission has no powers of judicial control. The scrutiny by the CLCS is merely intended to ensure that the limits of the continental shelf are established in compliance with scientific standards. However, the CLCS is not a paper tiger, because a recommendation by the Commission, once published, puts a coastal state under considerable political pressure. Any deviation must be justified, and not once has a recommendation by the CLCS been disregarded. The outer limits of the EEZ mark the start of international waters (the high seas). This term applies to the water column beyond the EEZ rather than to the seabed. The high seas are open to all states. No state may subject any part of the high seas to its sovereignty. The "freedom of the high seas"—just as Hugo Grotius envisaged—comprises, in particular, freedom of navigation, freedom of fishing, and freedom of marine scientific research. Mining operations are monitored by the ISA based in Kingston, Jamaica, which was established specifically for this purpose by the states parties to UNCLOS. The ISA is responsible, in particular, for ensuring the equitable sharing of the benefits arising from deep seabed mining activities.

## *G. Ocean Pollution*

*221.* There are six main sources of ocean pollution addressed in the UNCLOS (1982): land-based and coastal activities; continental-shelf drilling; potential seabed mining; ocean dumping; vessel-source pollution; and pollution from or through the atmosphere. With regard to marine pollution from foreign vessels, coastal states can exercise jurisdiction only for the enforcement of laws and regulations adopted in accordance with the Convention or for "generally accepted international rules and standards." Such rules and standards, many of which are already in place, are adopted through a competent international organization, namely the IMO. On the other hand, it is the duty of the "flag state," the state where a ship is registered and whose flag it flies, to enforce the rules adopted for the control of marine pollution from vessels, irrespective of where a violation occurs. This serves as a safeguard for the enforcement of international rules, particularly in waters beyond the national jurisdiction of the coastal state, i.e., on the high seas.

### *H. Port State*

*222.* The UNCLOS gives enforcement powers to the "port state" or the state where a ship is destined. In doing so, it has incorporated a method developed in other conventions for the enforcement of treaty obligations dealing with shipping standards, marine safety, and pollution prevention. The port state can enforce any type of international rule or national regulations adopted in accordance with the Convention or applicable international rules as a condition for the entry of foreign vessels into their ports or internal waters or for a call at their offshore terminals. This has already become a significant factor in the strengthening of international standards.

*223.* UNCLOS is the main convention which regulates maritime issues in a comprehensive way. These include rights of civil and naval navigation; the protection of coasts and the marine environment; rights to living and non-living resources; and marine scientific research.[79] Agreement relating to the Implementation of Part XI of the UNCLOS has removed certain obstacles relating to the seabed area that had prevented mainly industrialized countries from signing the Convention.

### *I. International Seabed Authority*

*224.* ISA is the organization through which states parties to the UNCLOS organize and control activities relating to the deep seabed's mineral resources in the international seabed area, beyond the limits of national jurisdiction. ISA located in Kingston, Jamaica, was inaugurated in 1994. The ISA has been given broad discretionary powers to assess the potential environmental impact of a deep seabed mining operation, recommend changes, formulate rules and regulations, establish a monitoring program, and recommend issuance of emergency orders by the council to prevent serious environmental damage. States are to be held liable for any damage caused by either their own enterprise or contractors under their jurisdiction.

*225.* The 1992 UNCED held in Rio de Janeiro, Brazil, placed a great deal of emphasis on the protection and preservation of the oceans' environment in harmony with the rational use and development of their living resources, thus establishing the concept of "sustainable development" embodied in Agenda 21, the program of action adopted at the Conference. A recurring topic in implementing the program of action adopted in Rio De Janeiro is the necessity to combat the degradation and depletion of fish stocks, both in the zones under national jurisdiction and in the high seas. A second recurring topic is addressing fish stock depletion causes, such as overfishing and excess fishing capacity, by-catch, and discards.

79. Division for Ocean Affairs and the Law of the Sea of the United Nations Office of Legal Affairs website.

*J. International Tribunal for the Law of the Sea*

*226.* This tribunal is operational since 1996 and was established to settle disputes relating to the interpretation or application of the UNCLOS. It is composed of twenty-one judges elected by the states parties; it is located in the German seaport of Hamburg. It received its first application instituting a case in 2001.

## §5. Commission on the Limits of the Continental Shelf

*227.* This Commission facilitates implementation of the UNCLOS with respect to delineation of the outer limits of the continental shelf when that submerged portion of the land territory of a coastal state extends beyond the 200 nmi from its coastline which is established as the minimal legal distance under the Convention. Under Article 76 of the Convention, the coastal state may establish the outer limits of its juridical continental shelf, in such cases, through the application of specified scientific and technical formulas.

## §6. Intergovernmental Oceanographic Commission of the UNESCO

*228.* Intergovernmental Oceanographic Commission of the UNESCO promotes international cooperation and coordinates programs in marine research, services, observation systems, hazard mitigation, and capacity development in order to learn more and better manage the nature and resources of the ocean and coastal areas. UNEP's Regional Seas Programme aims to protect oceans and seas and promote the environmentally sound use of marine resources.

## §7. UNEP's Global Programme of Action for the Protection of the Marine Environment from Land-Based Activities

*229.* UNEP's Global Programme of Action for the Protection of the Marine Environment from Land-based Activities was adopted in 1995 under UNEP auspices. This is a milestone in international efforts to protect oceans, estuaries, and coastal waters from pollution caused by human activities on land. It addresses what might be the most serious threat to the marine environment: the flow of chemicals, pollutants, and sewage into the sea. UNCBD (1992) aims at the protection and conservation of the diverse range of species of animal and plant life and their habitats.

## §8. United Nations Agreement on Straddling Fish Stocks and Highly Migratory Fish Stocks, 1995

*230.* The 1995 U.N. Agreement on Straddling Fish Stocks and Highly Migratory Fish Stocks provides a regime for the conservation and management of these stocks, with a view to ensuring their long-term conservation and sustainable use.

Entered into force in 2001, IMO is the U.N. specialized agency responsible for measures to prevent marine pollution from ships and to improve the safety of international shipping. UNEP's Global Marine Oil Pollution Information Gateway provides a clearing-house mechanism under the Global Programme of Action for the Protection of the Marine Environment from Land-Based Activities. A clearing-house for information on the global, regional, and local problems caused by marine oil pollution, the international community's efforts to address the problem, and the quest for ways to take preventive action.

## §9. Agreement on the Conservation of Small Cetaceans of the Baltic and North Seas, 1991

*231.* Agreement on the Conservation of Small Cetaceans of the Baltic, North-East Atlantic, Irish and North entered into force on March 29, 1994. The agreement was approved at Geneva on September 13, 1991, during the Third Meeting of the COP to the Convention on the Conservation of Migratory Species of Wild Animals pursuant to Article IV (4) of the said Convention, which was done at Bonn on June 23, 1979 ("Bonn Convention"). The amendment to the agreement, which entered into force on February 3, 2008, changed the name of the agreement. The agreement was previously known as "Agreement on the Conservation of Small Cetaceans of the Baltic and North Seas."

This agreement aims to promote close cooperation among state parties to achieve and maintain a favorable conservation status for small cetaceans. The parties are obligated to engage in habitat conservation and management, surveys and research, pollution mitigation, and public information. The Agreement on the Conservation of Cetaceans in the Black Sea, the Mediterranean Sea and Contiguous Atlantic Area, 1996, seeks to reduce the threat to cetaceans in the Mediterranean and the Black Sea waters. It requires that states implement a detailed conservation plan for cetaceans, including legislation banning the deliberate capture of cetaceans; measures to minimize their incidental capture; and the creation of protected zones. The 1970 Declaration of Principles Governing the Seabed and the Ocean Floor, and the Subsoil Thereof, beyond the Limits of National Jurisdiction 1971 Treaty on the Prohibition of the Emplacement of Nuclear Weapons on the Sea-bed and the Ocean Floor and in the Subsoil Thereof (Sea-Bed Treaty) ban the emplacement of nuclear weapons, or any weapon of mass destruction, on the sea-bed or ocean floor.

## §10. Treaties Developed by IMO Dealing with Marine Pollution

*232.* The International Convention Relating to Intervention on the High Seas in Cases of Oil Pollution Casualties (1969); the Convention on the Prevention of Marine Pollution by Dumping of Wastes and Other Matters (1972); and the International Convention on Oil Pollution Preparedness, Response and Cooperation (1990); Additional IMO treaties: the International Convention on Civil Liability for Oil Pollution Damage (CLC) (1969) and the International Convention on the Establishment of an International Fund for Oil Pollution Damage (FUND) (1971) all together establish a system for providing compensation to those who have suffered financially as a result of pollution. As revised in 1992, they enable victims of oil pollution to obtain compensation much more simply and quickly than had been possible before this revision. In the disarmament sphere, a major U.N. initiative for protecting the oceans took shape in 1971. Treaty on the Prohibition of the Emplacement of Nuclear Weapons on the Sea-bed and the Ocean Floor and in the Subsoil Thereof (Sea-Bed Treaty) bans the emplacement of nuclear weapons, or any weapon of mass destruction, on the seabed or ocean floor.

## §11. The High Seas Treaty 2023

*233.* The High Seas Treaty 2023, also known as the agreement on Biodiversity Beyond National Jurisdiction (BBNJ) was signed in New York on September 20, 2023. Eighty-four countries have signed the treaty marking their commitment to ratify the treaty. For the treaty to enter into force, fifty-nine other countries are needed to ratify the treaty by 2025. The treaty is applicable to High Seas and the seabed beyond national jurisdiction. High Seas contain marine resources and biodiversity and provide invaluable ecological, economic, social, cultural, scientific and food security benefits to humanity. However, they are under mounting pressure from pollution, overexploitation, climate change and biodiversity loss. For better addressing these challenges, and in view of future increasing demands for marine resources, it appeared necessary to establish a new treaty.

The treaty provides for the common governance of about half of the Earth's surface and 95% of the ocean's volume, the largest habitat on the planet, to:

- promote equity and fairness
- tackle environmental degradation
- fight climate change, and
- prevent biodiversity loss in the high seas

*234.* The adoption of the treaty is a historic achievement marking the successful end of more than a decade of work. It complements the UNCLOS, which provided the legal framework under which all human activities in the ocean takes place. The text of the treaty was agreed in March 2023 and formally adopted on June 19, 2023, by consensus, at UN Headquarters in New York. The treaty will allow the establishment of marine protected areas in the high seas at global level, safeguarding the ocean from human pressures in a major contribution to reducing climate change, to protecting biodiversity and protect at least 30% of the planet by 2030. The treaty addresses a glaring gap in ocean protection, as only about 1% of the high seas is currently protected. The treaty also sets a framework for a fair and equitable sharing of monetary and non-monetary benefits from marine genetic resources, and for capacity building and transfer of marine technologies to developing countries, as well as a voluntary fund to support developing countries to achieve UN SDG.

# Chapter 2. The Regulation of Oil Spills from Ships and Offshore Installations

## §1. Introduction

*235.* It is the fundamental duty of companies involved in offshore petroleum exploration and production to prevent oil spills caused by blowouts or otherwise so as to ensure the integrity of oil and/or gas wells. The blowouts from offshore oil wells can have long-term and major effects like loss of human life, pollution of marine and shoreline ecosystems, substantial commercial losses by companies directly involved and third parties affected by the spill.

## §2. Treaties and Conventions

### I. The MARPOL Convention

*236.* The MARPOL Convention is the main international convention covering prevention of pollution of the marine environment by ships. The Convention includes regulations aimed at preventing and minimizing pollution from ships both accidental pollution and routine marine operations. The problem with marine pollution is that vast areas of the oceans are not under control of any one country. While conventions such as the Basel Convention prevent trans-boundary movement of hazardous wastes, in case of maritime issues, it is difficult to demarcate clear-cut boundaries. One of the earliest attempts for maritime protection is the UNCLOS which also has a number of environmental measures including prevention of oil pollution and prevents deliberate dumping of harmful materials. But to provide more specific pollution prevention and protection measures even beyond national maritime boundaries, MARPOL was evolved. It can trace its origin to the U.N. convention on human environment. Under MARPOL, all ships carrying flags of countries that are parties to the convention must adhere to its requirements.

*237.* There are annexures in MARPOL dealing with specific pollution. A brief overview is as follows:

> Annex I—for the Prevention of Pollution by Oil covers areas such as oil spills, double hulls made mandatory for oil tankers. Annex II—for the Control of Pollution by Noxious Liquid Substances in Bulk covers the criterion for discharge, not permitted in case of 12 mi within land. Annex III—for prevention of Pollution by Harmful Substances Carried by Sea in Packaged Form Covers areas such as detailed standards on packaging, lists substances that are regarded as harmful.
>
> Annex IV—for Prevention of Pollution by Sewage from Ships covers sewage pollution. Also, categorizes special areas such as Baltic sea. More requirements for special areas under the convention. Annex V—for the Prevention of Pollution by Garbage from Ships covers pollution from disposal of garbage. Plastic disposal is completely banned. Annex VI—for the Prevention of Air

Pollution from Ships prescribes limits for sulfur oxide and nitrogen oxide emissions from ship exhausts. Emissions of ODS have been banned. Annex 1 and 2 are mandatory while the rest are voluntary in nature.

*238.* Maritime boundaries are much vast than land boundaries, and oceans almost cover 70% of our planet. There is an abundance of biodiversity in these marine areas which sustain a number of food chains. Marine resources provide direct food, oxygen and also play a moderating effect on the global climate change. Accidental spillage of oil from ship tankers is perhaps the most visible source of pollution and for long, a need has been felt to tackle it effectively. While there are a number of treaties as far as river waters sharing by riparian parties is concerned, the same in case of oceanic waterways is not very comprehensive. This is why MARPOL is significant as it is a global effort in reducing pollution and provides protection to our marine resources.

## II. International Convention for the Safety of Life at Sea, 1974

*239.* The objective of the Safety of Life at Sea (SOLAS) Convention is to specify minimum standards of SOLAS. It came into force on May 25, 1980 and provides parameters for the construction, equipment, and operation of ships, compatible with their safety. Flag States are responsible for ensuring that ships under their flag comply with its requirements, and a number of certificates are prescribed in the Convention as proof that this has been done. This Convention makes mandatory the International Safety Management (ISM) code and the International Ship Port Facility Security (ISPS) code.

## III. International Convention on Standards of Training Certification and Watch Keeping for Seafarers, 1978 (STCW)

*240.* This Convention was the first step in establishing basic requirements on training, certification, and keeping a watch for and on seafarers at international level. The Convention prescribes minimum standards with respect to training, certification and watchkeeping for seafarers which countries are obliged to meet in shipping business.

## IV. Convention on the International Regulations for Preventing Collisions at Sea, 1972 (COLREG)

*241.* This Convention outlines the requirements of ships to provide clear navigation signaling equipment and to abide by international rules of navigation.

## V. Loadline International Convention, 1966

*242.* This Convention provides limitations on the draught to which a ship may be loaded and thus makes a significant contribution to her safety. These limits are given in the form of freeboards, which constitute, besides external weather tight and watertight integrity.

## VI. OPRC International Convention on Oil

*243.* Parties to the International Convention on Oil Pollution Preparedness, Response and Co-operation Convention (OPRC) are required to establish measures for dealing with pollution preparedness, pollution incidents, either nationally or in cooperation with other countries and are required to provide assistance to others in case of pollution emergency. Provision has been made for the reimbursement of any assistance so provided. The Convention provides for IMO to play an important coordinating role.

## VII. International Convention Relating to Intervention on the High Seas in Cases of Oil Pollution Casualties, 1969

*244.* The Convention affirms the right of a coastal state to take such measures on the high seas as may be necessary to prevent, mitigate, or eliminate danger to its coastline or related interests from pollution by oil or the threat thereof, following upon a maritime casualty. The 1973 Protocol extended the Convention to cover substances other than oil.

## VIII. The International Convention on Salvage

*245.* The Convention makes provision for an enhanced salvage award taking into account the skill and efforts of the salvors in preventing or minimizing damage to the environment. It replaced a convention on the law of salvage adopted in Brussels in 1910 which incorporated the "no cure, no pay" principle under which a salvor is only rewarded for services if the operation is successful.

## IX. CLC International Conventions on Civil Liability for Oil Pollution Damage, 1969 and 1992

*246.* The Civil Liability Conventions (CLCs) were adopted to ensure that adequate compensation is available to persons who suffer oil pollution damage resulting from maritime casualties involving oil-carrying ships. The Conventions place the liability for such damage on the owner of the ship from which the polluting oil escaped or was discharged. The Convention applies to all seagoing vessels actually carrying oil in bulk as cargo. Ships carrying more than 2,000 tons of oil are required to maintain insurance in respect of oil pollution damage. This does not apply to warships or other vessels owned or operated by a state and used for the time being for government non-commercial services. The Convention, however, applies in respect of the liability and jurisdiction provisions, to ships owned by a state and used for commercial purposes. The Convention covers pollution damage resulting from spills of persistent oils suffered in the territory (including the territorial sea) of a state party to the Convention. The Protocol of 1976, which entered into force in 1981, provided for the applicable unit of account used under the Convention to be based on the Special Drawing Rights (SDR) as used by the International Monetary Fund (IMF), replacing the "Poincaré franc," based on the "official" value of gold, as the applicable unit of account. The liability under this Convention is strict, and it is the duty of the owner to prove in each case that any of the available exceptions should in fact operate. However, except where the owner has been guilty of actual fault, they may limit liability in respect of any one incident.

*247.* The Protocol of 1992 changed the entry into force requirements by reducing from six to four the number of large tanker-owning countries that were needed for entry into force. The 1992 Protocol also widened the scope of the Convention to cover pollution damage caused in the EEZ or equivalent area of a state party. The Protocol covers pollution damage as before, but environmental damage compensation is limited to costs incurred for reasonable measures to reinstate the contaminated environment. From May 16, 1998, parties to the 1992 Protocol ceased to be parties to the 1969 CLC due to a mechanism for compulsory denunciation of the "old" regime established in the 1992 Protocol. However, there are a number of states which are party to the 1969 CLC and have not yet ratified the 1992 regime—which is intended to eventually replace the 1969 CLC. The 1992 Protocol allows states party to the 1992 Protocol to issue certificates to ships registered in states which are not party to the 1992 Protocol, so that a shipowner can obtain certificates to both the 1969 and 1992 CLC, even when the ship is registered in a country which has not yet ratified the 1992 Protocol. This is important because a ship which has only a 1969 CLC may find it difficult to trade to a country which has ratified the 1992 Protocol, since it establishes higher limits of liability.

*248.* The 2000 Amendments were adopted on October 18, 2000 and came into force from November 1, 2003. This amendment raised the compensation limits by 50% compared to the limits set in the 1992 Protocol, as follows: (i) for a ship not exceeding 5,000 gross tonnage, liability is limited to 4.51 million SDR (USD 5.78 million); (ii) for a ship of 5,000–140,000 gross tonnage, liability is limited to 4.51 million SDR plus 631 SDR for each additional gross ton over 5; and (iii) for a ship over 140,000 gross tonnage, liability is limited to 89.77 million SDR.

## X. FUND, 1971 and 1992, and the Supplementary Fund Protocol, 2003

*249.* The liability of the shipowner under CLC is limited according to the size of the ship. The purpose of the Fund Conventions is to provide "top-up" compensation for pollution damage when the limited liability of the shipowner is inadequate. The 1971 Fund Convention was superseded by the 1992 Fund Convention, which came into force on May 30, 1996, and the Supplementary Fund Protocol which took effect on March 3, 2005. The Fund Conventions are administered by an intergovernmental organization, the International Oil Pollution Compensation Funds (IOPC funds), and financed by the oil industry.

## §3. Quality and Risk Assessment Study

*250.* The companies while chartering ships operate a ship vetting process to get a quality and risk assessment study for the ship they want to hire. This quality and risk assessment assists the company in deciding whether or not to charter a particular ship. Ship vetting or ship screening is a complex quality and risk assessment process taking into consideration many factors affecting the tanker management and operational standards of the ship in question. For the safe transport by sea, the ship has to comply with applicable legislation and regulatory standards and, in some cases, shipping industry's guidance and criteria. All vetting systems employ different methods for determining the acceptability of a ship for charter, and some factors influence charterers in different ways. However, some of the key factors normally considered include assessing seaworthiness and other relevant aspects: shipowner/operator performance assessment and rating; incidents and casualty history; ship inspections and condition assessment data; Port State inspection performance and history; terminal performance and feedback, etc. Usually an accredited surveyor physically inspects a vessel, and other information is gathered from various other sources and databases collected on the historical performance of the vessel and operator. When accredited inspectors carry out inspections, copies of their reports are filed with industry databases. This information collectively is used to determine the ship's suitability for the charter. Databases have been established such as that used by the Oil Companies International Marine Forum's (OCIMF's) global Ship Inspection Report (SIRE) Programme, the European Barge Inspection Scheme (EBIS), the Chemical Distribution Institute (CDI), and the international EQUASIS ship information system. Part of the vetting program is meant for a due diligence check that the ship complies with legislative and regulatory requirements.

*251.* Before the business of transporting the cargo can commence, the vessel and the charterer need to complete the chartering agreement (called the Charter Party). As the ship requires loading, it will proceed to the loading port where it must comply with a number of rules, regulations, and industry practices. It may be subjected to a Port State Control inspection which will verify whether the vessel is in compliance with the various international conventions and national legislation, relating to environment and otherwise. When the ship reaches the off-loading port, it could be subjected to the same Port State Control inspections as at the loading port and may have to comply with similar oil spill response arrangements as that experienced at the loading port, depending on the status of conventions in that country.

## §4. IMO Conventions/Port State Requirements/Local, National, and Regional Response Plans

*252.* While the priority for all marine operations is the prevention of oil spills, it is recognized that marine spills are a risk for which industry and coastal state governments must prepare plans. A cooperative approach by all parties concerned is essential to ensure an effective response. When developing plans, companies should seek the cooperation of those who share the risk and those who will participate in the response, by integrating their plans with those of national authorities, industry partners, and response resources. In 1990, the IMO adopted an important Convention which promotes the spirit of bilateral cooperation between countries and between governments and industry. By November 2018, a total number of 112 were state parties to the OPRC 1990 Convention. A significant amount of work has been, and continues to be, carried out by the oil industry in conjunction with the IMO to encourage the spirit of cooperation between national governments and the oil industry. This Global Initiative assists DC in preparing for major oil spills by direct assistance and also runs workshops and conferences for educational purposes. The cooperation between IMO and the industry has resulted in internationally accepted guidelines on a range of oil spill matters being jointly published by the IMO and the International Petroleum Industry Environmental Conservation Association (IPIECA).

## §5. Blowout and Oil Spill Liability

*253.* Exploration and production takes place on the continental shelf, and/or within the Territorial Sea of each nation-state, where international law recognizes the right of the "host" state to regulate resources. National petroleum laws, workplace safety laws, and/or environmental laws contained in legislations and subordinate laws protect human health, their safety, and the environment from offshore oil spills. Legal issues related to these aspects can be grouped into three broad topic areas which are: the prevention of spills including but not limited to laws and regulations directed at maintaining the integrity of wells, emergency response, and clean-up requirements, and liability and compensation for loss and damage once an incident has occurred. The most important are provisions that exist for monitoring, compliance, enforcement, and roles and responsibilities of regulators.

*254.* Regulation of offshore oil and gas industry is primarily the task of national governments, still the offshore oil industry is a very much global industry, and this brings international influence to bear on national legal systems. Major international oil companies work around the world, as do independent companies specializing in operations such as drilling and cementing, regularly moving personnel and equipment from one country to another. So, integrated operations tend to cross national boundaries. Companies with international operations may spread good local domestic oilfield practices nationally, regionally, and globally. National laws may specifically refer to the technical standards, guidelines, and recommendations produced and/or endorsed by industry and standards associations. These standards are often the benchmarks for good oilfields practice, not only in terms of technical procedures such as drilling but also in relation to safety and EA, auditing and reporting procedures.

## I. Piper Alpha Disaster

*255.* Piper Alpha oil rig explosion off the coast of the U.K. on July 6, 1988 caused 167 deaths and significant oil pollution. In August 2009, thirty-one years later, the blowout of the Montara oil well off the coastline of Australia caused one of the worst maritime oil spill disasters. Within one year, the blowout in the Gulf of Mexico, in April 2010, of the Deepwater Macondo well took the lives of eleven workers and cost the company many billions of dollars for individual compensation claims, clean-up costs along with criminal liability for billions of dollars.

*256.* These offshore catastrophes generate global publicity, and their impacts are felt throughout the international community. A catastrophic incident in one country may not only lead to legal reviews into offshore regulations in that nation but internationally. Examples include the reviews into offshore safety and regulation in Australia after the Piper Alpha explosion and in the U.K. in response to the Deepwater Horizon incident. These reviews examine the actions of the companies involved and adequacy of laws and regulatory systems. Thus, the Piper Alpha explosion saw a major reorientation of safety regulation from a prescriptive to a goals-based model in many countries. The Montara and Macondo well blowouts caused a major shift in attitudes and requirements relating to safety and environmental protection. The Macondo blowout, in particular, has exposed offshore petroleum laws and models of regulation to assessment and review.

## II. Macondo Blowout

*257.* In the history of offshore oil and gas exploration particularly of deep sea, the blow out in the Macondo well on April 20, 2010 will be remembered for many reasons, more particularly for the liability toward containment, removal and restoration of environment as well as huge liabilities toward other service providers, third parties and the government. As per reports at Macondo well, an explosion caused by a blowout on the Deepwater Horizon Rig killed eleven crewman and ignited a fireball visible from 56 km away. The fire could not be contained or extinguished and eventually burning after thirty-six hours—rig sank on April 22, 2010 leaving the well gushing at the sea floor. The Ownership of Macondo Prospect (as available on net) was British Petroleum (BP)—the operator owned 65%, Anandarko Petroleum (APC) 25%, and Mitsui (MITSY) 10%. Transocean—provided Deepwater Horizon Drilling Rig that exploded. Cameron International (CAM) provided blowout preventer which was to control the blowout. When the blowout took place, Halliburton (HAL) was cementing the well to stabilize its walls.

*258.* This blow out caused the largest offshore oil spill in the history of the U.S. A U.S. federal judge ruled in 2014 that BP had acted with "gross negligence" in its actions leading up to the accident. A large number of claims for compensation were filed under the settlement for businesses and individuals. Almost immediately after the incident, private parties and governmental entities began filing lawsuits, eventually totaling over 3,000 cases with more than 100,000 plaintiffs. On August 10, 2010, the Judicial Panel on Multidistrict Litigation (MDL) consolidated pretrial proceedings in the U.S. District Court for the Eastern District of Louisiana for most federal cases. In addition, a group of Transocean companies, constituting the owner, operator and employer of the Deepwater Horizon rig and crew, filed an action under admiralty law to seek to limit their liability. The admiralty limitations action was consolidated with other cases in the MDL proceedings, and other primary defendants, including BP and its cement contractor, HAL, were joined as parties.

*259.* The lawsuits filed resulted in a number of settlements, penalties, and costs paid by BP, totaling approximately USD 69 billion. This included USD 18.7 billion settlement with the federal and state governments of U.S. to resolve civil claims and environmental restoration costs, and a settlement with private plaintiffs that involved the establishment of a claims fund estimated to have resulted in the payout of over USD 12 billion for economic and property damage losses. Other defendants in the case, including but not limited to Transocean and HAL, also paid billions to settle their respective liabilities to governments, private plaintiffs, and other defendants. So, the total liability for Macondo disaster for cleanup, claims, punitive damages awards, or fines has been in billions of dollars.

## A. *Likely Consequences*

### 1. Huge Liability

*260.* Macondo blowout has brought a new dimension so far as quantum of liability is concerned. The huge nature of liability has created challenges for small companies and countries with undeveloped or underdeveloped legislation on offshore disaster liabilities. This incident will certainly lead to emphasis and protracted negotiation in future on exclusion of liability clauses for such disaster on the part of the operators and rig contractors. There can also be problems in enforcement of judgments and awards in view of huge liability arising out of environmental cleanup and restoration. It will also force evolution of more stringent safety regime, and one unfortunate result would be small rig operators will find it difficult to operate in the areas where liability is unrestricted or with large cap. Macondo well blowout has also brought in focus the inadequacies of legislation at international as well as national front to deal with disaster of big magnitude and capability and capacity of small contractors to meet the same. The proper realization of liability may result in shooting up of costs. There will also be problems in availability of insurance and underwriters for offshore operations. Even at present, insurances are not available against terrorism and in case it is available, it is at a very high cost.

*261.* Huge liability with a cap or without cap will certainly hit offshore drilling companies. On the other hand, companies may not get insurance to pay unlimited or large capped liabilities and costs for environmental cleanup and restoration or third-party claims or fines imposed by the Host Government. Small companies will ultimately be out of business from areas of uncapped or area with large-cap liabilities likes Gulf of Mexico. All these developments will ultimately result in an increased business cost for oil companies. The offshore drilling activity is even otherwise determined by liability considerations. All these factors will increase the cost of oil, and in the present low-prices scenario, this aspect will bring disastrous consequences to fiscal aspects. In this background, there can also be a review of cost recovery aspects in Production Sharing Contracts (PSC). In PSC regime, allowing full oil spill liability as cost recoverable, may cut in the profit oil of the host governments. On the other hand, limitation on cost recovery of such costs including insurances will adversely hit profit margins of operators.

## 2. Exclusion of Liability

*262.* The district court was to apply a proper definition to the term "gross negligence" contained in the Clean Water Act (CWA). The district court found that the discharge of oil was a result of BP's gross negligence and "willful misconduct." In doing so, the court undertook long discussion about the definitions of those two terms, since they are not defined by the CWA or the Oil Pollution Act (OPA). The court found that gross negligence is "an extreme departure from the care required under the circumstances or a failure to exercise even slight care," and that willful misconduct is "an act, intentionally done, with knowledge that the performance will probably result in injury, or done in such a way as to allow an inference of a reckless disregard of the probable consequences." The court rejected the argument that the company, or "managerial agents" of the company, needed to ratify the reckless behavior of employees in order for the company to be found grossly negligent. The court concluded that a corporation is "vicariously liable under the CWA's enhanced penalty provision for the gross negligence and/or willful misconduct of its employees." However, the district court found that contractual indemnities that purport to indemnify parties for liabilities caused by that party's own gross negligence are enforceable, except with respect to punitive damages or civil penalties. Part of the justification for allowing contractual indemnities to survive was the commercial nature of the arrangement and the division of risks and rewards among the parties to the agreement.

*263.* In the light of this decision, some offshore agreements for the Gulf of Mexico have sought to define the specific personnel or job titles within an organization whose conduct can be imputed to the company, for purposes of private indemnities excluding the operator's gross negligence or willful misconduct. While these contractual provisions will not necessarily protect operators from future CWA liabilities, they may help clarify contractual indemnity obligations between contractors or partners that involve allegations of the gross negligence or willful misconduct of particular employees.

*B. Responses in U.S.*

1. Administrative Reforms

*264.* At the time of the Deepwater Horizon incident, the Minerals Management Service (MMS) had responsibility for three interrelated functions: (1) maximizing revenues from operations; (2) promoting resource development; and (3) enforcing safety regulations. After the incident, efforts were initiated to reorganize these functions. On June 21, 2010, the MMS was renamed the Bureau of Ocean Energy Management, Regulation and Enforcement (the BOEMRE). On October 1, 2010, the BOEMRE division responsible for revenue collection was separated out and became the Office of Natural Resources Revenues (ONRR) under the jurisdiction of the Department of the Interior's Office of Policy, Management and Budget. Then, in October 1, 2011, BOEMRE was divided into the Bureau of Ocean Energy Management (BOEM) and the Bureau of Safety and Environmental Enforcement (BSEE). BOEM is responsible for, among other things, environmental and economic studies and analyzes, while BSEE is responsible for, among other things, permitting, offshore regulatory programs, training, environmental compliance, inspections, and oil spill response. BSEE published several final rules that increased oversight, training and reporting requirements for offshore operators, including the Drilling Safety Rule, the Safety and Environmental Management Systems (SEMS) I & II rules, and the Blowout Preventer and Well Control Rule (WCR). The overall regulatory approach changed from being primarily prescriptive in nature to being goal-oriented. In July 2019, changes to the WCR were made as certain rules imposed undue burdens on industry without significantly enhancing safety or environmental protection.

2. Clean Water Act

*265.* In the U.S., in case of oil spill, fines are imposed under CWA for coastal restoration. If operator is found grossly negligent, his liability is calculated at the rate of USD 4,300 per barrel. Absent a finding of gross negligence, the liability of operator will be at the rate of USD 1,100 per barrel. Besides, there is also Oil Spill Liability Trust Fund (OSLTF) which is funded by a tax of 8 cents per barrel of oil. The removal costs and damages not covered by a responsible party are covered by this fund. The maximum payment from this fund for any single incident is USD 1 billion.

3. Oil Pollution Act

*266.* The OPA of 1990 was enacted in the wake of the EXXON VALDEZ oil spill for the prevention of oil spills on navigable waters, the adjoining shorelines, and the EEZ. It provided federal response to spills, increased the liability of polluters for such spills, and provided compensation to those that incurred removal costs and damages as a result of these spills. The OPA provides that polluters are strictly liable for removal costs and damages resulting from a discharge up to statutory liability limits. In general, polluters are liable without limit when the discharge results from gross negligence or willful misconduct or a violation of operation, safety, or construction regulations.

### *C. Liability in Some Other Countries*

#### 1. Canada

*267.* In 2018, Canada took a significant step to improve the system for compensating victims of ship-source oil pollution. This included changes to the Marine Liability Act to make sure compensation is available for victims and responders of ship-source oil pollution caused by any type of oil from any type of ship. The Government of Canada has announced that as part of the Energy Safety and Security Act, companies working in the Atlantic as well as in the Arctic offshore will have to provide the government with unfettered access to USD 1 billion via a promissory note or letter of credit, so the money can be accessed immediately in the event of a spill. However, if the operator is found to be at fault or negligent, the liability will be unlimited.

#### 2. United Kingdom

*268.* In the U.K, operator is fully responsible for any costs for controlling oil spill, but a provision for backup fund underwritten by all rig operators has been evolved and is in operation. This fund is administered by the Offshore Pollution Liability Association (OPLA). The member operators accept strict liability for pollution damage and remedial measures, up to USD 120 million per incident and USD 240 million in the annual aggregate. In December 2012, the U.K. government published its final report on the adequacy of the present regulatory regime for offshore oil and gas operations on the UK Continental Shelf (UKCS) in the post-Macondo era. Responsibility for offshore oil and gas regulation in the U.K. is split between three authorities: (1) the Health & Safety Executive (HSE), which is responsible for the safety integrity of E&P operations; (2) the Department of Energy and Climate Change (DECC), which is responsible for licensing and drilling consents as well as environmental protection and response; and (3) the Maritime and Coastguard Agency (MCA), which is responsible for responding to oil spills.

*269.* In 1988, the U.K. suffered its own "Macondo" when the Occidental-operated Piper Alpha production platform exploded, resulting in 167 deaths. The subsequent regulatory review led to a raft of safety legislation, with the effect that the U.K.'s offshore regulatory regime is now regarded as one of the most robust in the world and acknowledged as a "gold standard." Nevertheless, Macondo provided a poignant reminder of the importance of maintaining and developing a regulatory regime of the highest standard, capable of managing incidents in increasingly complex and remote drilling scenarios. In 2011, DECC has been reviewing the systems and processes in place with the aim of improving and strengthening procedures, including those demonstrating financial responsibility, with regard to exploration and production activity. One of the areas scrutinized was the financial capability of licensees following a blowout from drilling operations on the UKCS.

*270.* In respect to drilling activity, Oil Pollution Emergency Plans (OPEPs) contain worst-case scenario information, and details are provided of the incident response actions to be implemented should such a scenario occur, including loss of well containment/ well blow out. These actions can include deployment of a capping/containment device or the drilling of a relief well with the related logistical and time-frame factors. All the response mechanisms to be used by the operators during any such incidents will be expensive (first-party costs), as may the compensation costs for pollution damage (third-party costs). For an OPEP to be credible and for DECC to have sufficient assurance that the OPEP will be implemented when required, DECC requires operators to provide sufficient evidence that the risks of the operation have been appropriately estimated and that the financial mechanisms are in place to meet those risks. The level of financial responsibility that companies need to demonstrate for any particular well should be calculated by establishing the combined: cost of well control; cost of financial remediation and compensation from pollution, and this should accompany the relevant OPEP at the time it is submitted to DECC for approval, unless otherwise agreed with DECC. Financial responsibility can be verified by means of: reliance on credit/financial strength rating of the operator or co-venturer; insurance; parent company guarantee/affiliate undertaking; any combination of the above.

*271.* DECC is aware through the auspices of Oil & Gas UK (OGUK), an Indemnities and Insurance Review Group was established under a forum to provide assistance to a review of what and how to demonstrate financial responsibility with regard to both first- and third-party costs, including the OPOL limit. The outcome of this working group was the production of OGUK Guidelines. These guidelines contain five appendices setting out certificates that, depending on particular circumstances, OGUK recommends should be submitted to DECC. This guidance has effect on and from January 1, 2013.

### 3. Position in Norway

*272.* Norwegian offshore activities in the Barents and Norwegian Seas generally take place quite far offshore. An important tool in this regard is the system of EIA. Norway is not an EU member, but as a member of the European Economic Area, it has incorporated the EIA Directive of the EU into its domestic legal system. The system consists of three separate processes, one of them being offshore projects. Onshore projects, which meet specified criteria, are governed by the Planning and Building Act. Offshore oil and gas projects are regulated by the Petroleum Act.

The Petroleum Safety Authority (PSA) Norway has the regulatory responsibility for safety, emergency preparedness, and the working environment for all offshore and onshore petroleum-related activities in Norway. Permission from the PSA to start drilling a new well depends on the applicant's ability to handle a potential blowout. The PSA report of assessments and recommendations after the Macondo incident was finally issued on June 16, 2011. Part one of the report focuses on lessons for safety and emergency preparedness in connection with drilling and well operations on the Norwegian Continental Shelf, and part two contains guidance on the prevention of major accidents, in general, for the whole Norwegian petroleum industry.

## III. Countries with Underdeveloped or No Legislation

*273.* If care is not taken in the contracts and a specific provision dealing with environmental liability is not included, operator cannot be made liable in the absence of clear-cut legislation on oil spill liability. It would also be difficult to take any insurance, as there will be uncertainty as to the extent of compensation or fines. Such uncertainty about the magnitude of liability will lead to high operating costs. In PSC regimes, cost-recovery provisions are to be revisited if a new system is developed to tackle offshore oil spill liability. The complex nature of liability questions will arise and require settlement as operator works along with many other service providers. If not resolved to the satisfaction of all the stakeholders, it will result in prolonged and costly litigation/arbitration—say for twenty years. Further, even if aggrieved party gets an award out of arbitration or judgment of the court in its favor, assets of operator may not be adequate to meet huge direct and special damages arising out of oil/gas spills. Which will lead to a situation where you have a remedy but it cannot be implemented!

*274.* There is a strong and pressing need for creation of OSLTF as implemented in U.K. Second, the issue of liability should be raised on international forums, and the U.N. may come up with some scheme or suggestions to deal with it effectively. The World Oil Regimes, particularly PSC, and cost recovery aspect of offshore oil spill costs to be reviewed keeping in view this new factor of huge uncertain liabilities. On domestic front, the concerned host governments must bring clear and unambiguous legislation with respect to offshore oil spill liability so that operators, rig operators and insurance companies level of confidence is increased.

# Part VI. Chemical and Radiological Pollution

## Chapter 1. Chemical Pollutants

*275.* Chemical pollutants have been released since the Industrial Revolution, but their dispersal has accelerated in the last half-century. Emissions of $CO_2$, with their long-term effects on the climate, atmosphere and oceans, are a striking example, but many other substances have been released in the form of industrial and agricultural emissions. Trillions of tons of chemically active material are discharged into the environment by mining, mineral processing, farming, construction and energy production. In addition to this, humans have synthesized more than 140,000 chemicals and mixtures of chemicals (UNEP 2019). As per a recent analysis of global inventories of chemicals estimates, this figure could be over 350,000, which is many times larger than previously reported (Wang et al., 2020). New synthetic chemicals are constantly being developed. Recently, the U.S.A. alone produced an average of 1,500 new substances a year (GAO, 2019). Many of these substances are known to be toxic in small doses, sometimes in combination with other pollutants, or as breakdown products after release into the biosphere and geosphere.

*276.* The chemical signature of humans has been detected in the upper atmosphere, on the highest mountains, in the deepest oceans, from pole to pole and in the most remote, uninhabited regions, in soil, water, air, and in the human food chain (Gruber, 2018). There are more than 700 known "dead zones" in oceans and lakes, and pollution by fertilizers, agrochemicals and sediments is one of the factors most strongly associated with these habitat collapses (Diaz and Rosenberg, 2008, Laffoley and Baxter, 2019). Industrial chemicals, including known carcinogens and their residues, have been detected in the blood and tissues of all populations, including the unborn and infants (Mathiesen et al., 2021, Soleman et al., 2020), and in mother's milk (Hu et al., 2021, van den Berg et al., 2017). They are found in aquatic biota, plants and wild animals, as well as foodstuffs (Gruber, 2018). The chemical toxicity can impair life functions and the combined and cumulative effects of all anthropogenic chemicals, acting together, can potentially impair human life itself.

*277.* The industrial wastes containing poisonous chemicals contaminate vegetation, surface water, as well as groundwater supplies. With the passage of time, these chemicals find way into all those organisms that eat the plants or grass or drink water contaminated with these chemicals. Heavy metals such as lead, mercury, manganese, cadmium, and chromium are generally toxic to life forms in greater than allowable trace quantities. In many countries, various surface water bodies have already been heavily contaminated with poisonous chemicals posing a serious danger to aquatic life. Fishes living in several highly polluted water bodies such as rivers, lakes, and along seashores where untreated chemical effluents are released are found to be so contaminated with poisonous chemicals that their consumption is harmful to health.

## §1. Accidental Release of Toxic Chemicals

*278.* The chemical pollution is also caused by the accidental release of toxic chemicals. Such accident had taken place in the Union Carbide Plant at Bhopal in December 1984. In this incidence, highly toxic Methyl Isocyanate (MIC) gas leaked from the plant resulting in the death of thousands of people and animals in the surrounding localities. Many more suffered from different types of ailments. The exact impact of the chemical on the health of future generations cannot be assessed. The excessive use of chemical fertilizers to boost the production also contaminates water bodies and groundwater. Contamination of water with fertilizers leads to very undesirable effects such as eutrophication. This is due to this reason that phosphate and nitrate encourage the growth of algae, which depletes the water body of its oxygen content. As a result, fishes and other aquatic life forms are adversely affected. Moreover, it is well established that nitrate in sufficient concentration is toxic to higher organisms including human beings.

## §2. Use of Pesticides

*279.* The use of pesticides has increased enormously in the recent past. These pesticides find their way into, water bodies, lakes, rivers and contaminate them. Most of these chemicals are toxic in nature. These chemicals get progressively concentrated in the food chain and can cause long-term damage to the health of human beings. The pesticides also enter into our bodies directly if the food particles to which these chemicals are sticking are not thoroughly washed before consumption. Dichlorodiphenyltrichloroethane (DDT) and other chlorinated hydrocarbons, which have long been used as pesticides, have been found to be toxic. DDT is a highly stable compound and is not easily metabolized or broken down by animals. It is deposited and stored in the fatty tissues. Since DDT is not easily biodegradable, there is a resultant build-up of this toxic chemical within the animals, soil, and water over a period. Investigations have revealed that people living in some of the urban areas have alarming amounts of DDT in their bodies. DDT and other nonbiodegradable pesticides are now being replaced with biodegradable pesticides.

## §3. Persistent Organic Pollutants

*280.* POPs are toxic chemicals that adversely affect human health and the environment throughout the world. Because they can be transported by wind and water, most POPs generated in one country may affect people and wildlife far from where they are used and released. They persist for long periods of time in the environment and can accumulate and pass from one species to the next through the food chain. To address this global concern, the U.S. joined forces with ninety other countries and the EC to sign a groundbreaking U.N. treaty Exit in Stockholm, Sweden, in May 2001. Under the treaty, known as the Stockholm Convention, countries agreed to reduce or eliminate the production, use, and/or release of twelve key POPs, and specified under the Convention a scientific review process that has led to the addition of other POPs chemicals of global concern.

## §4. International Efforts for Regulation

*281.* International attempts to regulate the release and flow of toxic chemicals began with agreements, such as the Vienna Convention for the Protection of the Ozone Layer (March 22, 1985) and the Basel Convention on the Control of Transboundary Movements of Hazardous Wastes and their Disposal (March 22, 1989). These were followed by the adoption of the Stockholm Convention on POPs in 2001, and the Minamata Convention on Mercury in 2013. There are success stories of preventing or cleaning up chemical pollution using international, national and regional initiatives and instruments, such as those of the Montreal Protocol amendments for controlling ODS (e.g., chlorofluorocarbons, carbon tetrachloride) (U.S.-EPA 2018), the United States Environmental Protection Agency (U.S.-EPA 2018), and the European Chemicals Agency (ECHA 2016). However, at current rate of progress, it will take over 100,000 years to evaluate all existing synthetic chemicals for human and environmental safety, and an additional 2,000 years to evaluate each year's new products (Cribb, 2017). These estimates strongly suggest that current international regulation of the worldwide effusion of toxic chemicals has failed.

*282.* Furthermore, it is far from clear whether international bans are being universally observed, especially in countries where regulation of the manufacture, use and disposal of chemicals is weak or corrupt (UNEP, 2019). The U.N.'s SDGs specified seventeen key issues, among which at least four highlighted environmental pollution as one of the factors causing critical global problems. The long-range transport of many chemicals via air, groundwater, soil or international trade, and the constant introduction of novel chemicals are also challenging the capacity of the biosphere to absorb and deal with the present and future impact of chemical pollution. The UNEP tentatively calls for "a comprehensive multi-stakeholder preventative strategy" in its Global Chemical Outlook Report (UNEP, 2019). Key aspects of their strategies are a set of responses to address identified challenges related to chemical exposure and sound chemical management at "country and regional level," "corporate level and civil society" and "international level."

### I. Impact of Stockholm Convention

*283.* The Stockholm Convention has added an important global dimension to national and regional efforts to control POPs. The U.S. and Canada signed an agreement for the Virtual Elimination of Persistent Toxic Substances in the Great Lakes to reduce emissions from toxic substances. The U.S. has also signed the regional protocol of the UNECE on POPs under the LRTAP Exit which addresses the Stockholm Convention POPs and other chemicals. The U.S. has also provided ample financial and technical support to countries across the globe supporting POPs reduction. A few of these initiatives include dioxin and furan release inventories in Asia and Russia and the reduction of Polychlorinated Biphenyls (PCBs) sources in Russia.

## §5. Commercial Use

*284.* Many POPs were widely used during the boom in industrial production after World War II, when thousands of synthetic chemicals were introduced into commercial use. Many of these chemicals proved beneficial in pest and disease control, crop production, and industry. These same chemicals, however, have had unforeseen effects on human health and the environment. Many people are familiar with some of the most well-known intentionally produced POPs, such as PCBs, DDT, and dioxins. POPs include a range of substances. Chemicals have been used in agriculture, disease control, manufacturing, or industrial processes, e.g., PCBs, which have been useful in a variety of industrial applications (e.g., in electrical transformers and large capacitors, as hydraulic and heat exchange fluids, and as additives to paints and lubricants) and DDT, which is still used to control mosquitoes that carry malaria in some parts of the world. Unintentionally produced chemicals, such as dioxins, that result from some industrial processes and from combustion like from municipal and medical waste incineration and backyard burning of trash.

### I. Use of DDT

*285.* DDT is one of the most famous and controversial pesticides ever made. An estimated 4 billion pounds of this inexpensive and historically effective chemical has been produced and applied worldwide since 1940. DDT has been used extensively on agricultural crops, particularly cotton. It was also used to protect soldiers from insect-borne diseases such as malaria and typhus during World War II, and it remains a valuable public health tool in parts of the tropics. The heavy use of this highly persistent chemical, however, led to widespread environmental contamination and the accumulation of DDT in humans and wildlife.[80] A wealth of scientific laboratory and field data have now confirmed research from the 1960s that suggested, among other effects, that high levels of Dichlorodiphenyldichloroethylene

80. A phenomenon brought to public attention by Rachel Carson in her 1962 book, *Silent Spring*.

(DDE) (a metabolite of DDT) in certain birds of prey caused their eggshells to thin so dramatically that they could not produce live offspring. One bird species especially sensitive to DDE was the bald eagle. Public concern about the eagles' decline and the possibility of other long-term harmful effects of DDT exposure to both humans and wildlife prompted the U.S.-EPA to cancel the registration of DDT in 1972.

### §6. Long-Range Transport

*286.* A major impetus for the Stockholm Convention was the finding of POPs contamination in relatively pristine Arctic regions—thousands of miles from any known source. Much of the evidence for long-range transport of airborne gaseous and particulate substances to the U.S. focuses on dust or smoke because they are visible in satellite images. Tracing the movement of most POPs in the environment is complex because these compounds can exist in different phases (e.g., as a gas or attached to airborne particles) and can be exchanged among environmental media. For example, some POPs can be carried for many miles when they evaporate from water or land surfaces into the air, or when they adsorb to airborne particles. Then, they can return to Earth on particles or in snow, rain, or mist. POPs also travel through oceans, rivers, lakes, and, to a lesser extent, with the help of animal carriers, such as migratory species.

### §7. POP and the Stockholm Convention

*287.* The Stockholm Convention on POP, which was adopted in 2001 and entered into force in 2004, is a global treaty for safeguarding human health and the environment from highly harmful chemicals that persist in the environment and affect the well-being of humans as well as wildlife. The Convention requires parties to eliminate and/or reduce POPs, which may cause cancer and diminished intelligence and have the ability to travel over great distances. The Stockholm Convention is managed by the U.N. Environment Program Exit, and its Secretariat is based in Geneva, Switzerland. UNEP is the leading international environmental entity that supports the agenda and implementation of environmental sustainability for the U.N.

## I. Role of the Parties

*288.* The role of parties is to implement the obligations of the Convention, including eliminating or restricting the production and use of the intentionally produced POPs, prohibiting and eliminating production and use or import of POPs, conducting research, identifying areas contaminated with POPs, and providing financial support and incentives for the Convention. The process of becoming a party begins with a state or regional economic integration organization submitting a means of ratification, acceptance, approval, or accession to the depositary. Official contact points and national focal points are nominated to carry out administrative, communications, and information exchange procedures.

## II. Intentionally and Unintentionally Produced Chemicals

*289.* The Stockholm Convention initially focused on twelve intentionally and unintentionally produced chemicals, the additional substances have also been added to the agreement in May 2009 and will continue to do so. In the U.S., the treaty is of particular importance for the people and environment of Alaska, which are impacted by POPs transported by air and water from outside the state. This is particularly true for Alaskan Natives, who rely heavily on traditional diets consisting of fish and wildlife. The Convention requires parties to eliminate or restrict the production and use of the intentionally produced POPs, subject to specified exemptions, with special provisions for DDT and PCBs. DDT is placed in the restriction annex, which means that its production and use are restricted to disease-vector control. The Convention also establishes a public DDT registry of users and producers, and it encourages the development of safe, effective, affordable, and environmentally friendly alternatives.

*290.* For PCBs, the Convention prohibits new PCB production and envisages phasing out electrical equipment that contains high concentrations of PCBs by 2025. The Convention also prohibits trade in POPs chemicals for which parties have eliminated production and use. Such POPs may be exported only for environmentally sound disposal. For those POPs that one or more parties continue to produce or use pursuant to specific exemptions, the Convention allows export of such POPs only to those parties that have an allowed use exemption under the Convention and those non-parties that provide certification that they will minimize or prevent environmental releases and destroy or dispose of the POPs in an environmentally sound manner.

### *A. Unintentionally Produced POPs*

*291.* The Stockholm Convention calls upon parties to take certain specified measures to reduce releases of unintentionally produced POPs with the goal of their continuing minimization and, where feasible, ultimate elimination. It specifically requires parties to develop national action plans to address the release of these POPs; promote the development of preventative measures; apply best available techniques (BAT) for certain new pollution sources, e.g., municipal, hospital, and hazardous waste incinerators, within four years after the Convention enters into force. Parties must also promote BAT and best environmental practices for other new and existing sources. The Convention requires parties to develop strategies for identifying stockpiles consisting of or containing intentionally produced POPs chemicals; products and articles in use and wastes consisting of, containing, or contaminated with any POPs chemical.

*B. Exemptions/Exceptions for Intentionally Produced POPs*

*292.* The Stockholm Convention generally exempts those quantities of intentionally produced POPs that are used for laboratory-scale research or as a reference standard, which occur as unintentional trace contaminants in products and articles. POPs which are used in closed-system and site-limited processes are also exempt or exist in articles manufactured or already in use on the date that the Convention enters into force for that party. The Convention also allows parties to register for specific exemptions on a country-by-country basis. These exemptions are subject to review and expire after five years, unless extended by the COP.

## III. Sites Contaminated with POPs

*293.* As per the Convention, parties are to take appropriate measures so that POPs wastes are managed in an environmentally sound manner. This includes both destruction and disposal techniques. Although remediation of contaminated sites is not required, any such remediation must be performed in an environmentally sound manner. The Convention provides for an effectiveness evaluation, based on a POPs monitoring and data collection effort that will use existing monitoring programs and mechanisms to the extent possible.

## IV. Financial and Technical Assistance

*294.* The Convention creates a flexible system of technical and financial aid to help DC and countries with economies in transition to meet their obligations. Although the Convention does not create a new fund or establish specific assessments, developed countries are to collectively provide new and additional financial resources. These funds will enable developing country parties to meet the agreed full incremental costs of implementing measures to fulfill their obligations under the Convention. On an interim basis, the Convention designates the GEF as the primary, but not exclusive, component of the financial mechanism. The GEF is a financial mechanism established to address global environmental threats. The Convention also specifies that developed countries provide technical assistance and capacity building to help DC and countries with economies in transition to meet their obligations.

## V. Process for Adding New Chemicals

*295.* New chemicals can be added to the treaty based on a scientific review procedure that involves parties and interested observers. For addition, a party nominates a chemical, and proposal is sent to a scientific review committee comprised of government-designated experts, who apply the Convention's screening criteria (for persistence, bioaccumulation, toxicity, and long-range transport). If the chemical meets the screening criteria, the committee prepares a risk profile for the chemical.

If, on the basis of the risk profile, the committee finds that the "chemical is likely, as a result of its long-range environmental transport to lead to significant adverse human health and/or environmental effects such that global action is warranted," the committee prepares a risk management evaluation that considers socioeconomic factors. Based on the risk profile and the risk management evaluation, the review committee makes a recommendation to the COP whether the chemical should be listed or not listed under the Convention. The COP makes the final decision by a three-fourths majority as to whether the chemical will be listed under the Convention. The decision of the COP to add a chemical to the treaty is binding on all parties one year later, except for (a) parties that "opt out" of this decision within the one-year period, or (b) parties that choose to invoke a separate "opt in" procedure under which they are not bound until they affirmatively accept a new obligation. The COP began adding new chemicals to the agreement in May 2009.

## Chapter 2. Radiological Pollution

*296.* The radiological pollution is the physical pollution of air, water, and other items by radioactive materials. The ability of certain materials to emit the proton, gamma rays and electrons by their nuclei is known as the radioactivity. The protons are known as the alpha particles, and the electrons are the beta particles. These materials are known as the radioactive elements. The environmental radiations can be from different sources and can be natural or manmade. The natural radiations are also known as the background radiations, e.g., cosmic rays which reach the surface of the earth from space. It includes the radioactive elements like radium, uranium, thorium, radon, potassium, and carbon. These occur in the rock, soil, and water. The man-made radiations include the mining and refining of plutonium (Pu) and thorium. This production and explosion of nuclear weapons include the nuclear fuels, power plants, and radioactive isotopes.

*297.* In 1945, the first atom bomb was exploded in Japan, devastating the Hiroshima and Nagasaki cities annihilating the whole population. It affected the flora, fauna and humans of that area. Despite this devastation, the nuclear race is still going on at full speed between different nations. The radioactive elements namely strontium, radium and iodine are produced in the environment and affect other materials. The gases and particles, which are produced by the radioactive material are carried by the wind. The rain brings down the radioactive particles to the ground known as nuclear fallout. The soil transfers these radioactive substances to the plants, and ultimately, they reach the human body and cause many ill effects. The iodine may affect the white blood cells, bone marrow, spleen, lymph, cause skin cancer, affect sterility, and cause damage to the lung. The strontium has the ability to aggregate in the bones and cause bone cancer and also leads to tissue degeneration.

*298.* The radioactive materials are passed through the land to water and adversely affect aquatic animals. They reach human beings through the food chain. The nuclear power generates a lot of energy, which is used to run turbines and produces electricity. The fuel and the coolant in an atomic reactor used for producing electricity create pollution in the environment. The atomic reactors are also rich in the radioactive materials, and real problem is in their disposal. If not properly disposed, they can cause potential harm to the living organisms. If they escape, they can cause unchecked harm. The gases escape as vapor and cause pollution on the land and water. The use of radioactive isotopes is multipurpose and is of a great scientific value, but some residue may be present in the wastewater coming out from atomic reactors and may reach the human body via the food chain. The people who work in power plants have more chances of exposure to harmful radiations. The human beings also receive radiation and radiotherapy from x-rays.

§1. NUCLEAR PROLIFERATION

*299.* Most countries participate in international initiatives designed to limit the proliferation of nuclear weapons which in a way save the world from hazards of pollution emanating from the use of nuclear energy. The international safeguards system has since 1970 successfully prevented the diversion of fissile materials into weapons, and scope of the safeguard has been widened to cover undeclared nuclear activities. The International Atomic Energy Agency (IAEA) undertakes regular inspections of civil nuclear facilities and audits the movement of nuclear materials through them. The initial development of nuclear technology was military, during World War II. Two nuclear bombs made from uranium-235 and Pu-239 were dropped on Japan's Hiroshima and Nagasaki, respectively, in August 1945, and these brought the long war to a sudden end. The immense and previously unimaginable power of the atom had been demonstrated.

## I. Non-Proliferation Treaty

*300.* In the course of half a century, nuclear technology has enabled access to a virtually unlimited source of energy at a time when constraints are arising on the use of fossil fuels. In the 1960s, it was widely assumed that there would be thirty to thirty-five nuclear weapons states (NWS) by the turn of the century. In fact, there were eight—a tremendous testimony to the effectiveness of the Nuclear Non-Proliferation Treaty (NPT) and its incentives both against weapons and for civil nuclear power, despite the influence of the Cold War (1950s to 1980s) which saw a massive build-up of nuclear weapons particularly by the U.S. and the Soviet Union. The nuclear non-proliferation regime is much more than the NPT, although this is the preeminent international treaty on the subject. The regime includes treaties, conventions, and common arrangements covering security and physical protection, export controls, nuclear test-bans and, potentially, fissile material production cut-offs. The international community can apply pressure to states outside the NPT to make every possible effort to conform to the full range of international norms and safeguards on nuclear non-proliferation that make up this regime.

### *A. The NPT Origins and Objectives*

*301.* The IAEA's safeguards system under the NPT has been a conspicuous international success in curbing the diversion of civil uranium into military uses. It has involved cooperation in developing nuclear energy while ensuring that civil uranium, Pu, and associated plants are used only for peaceful purposes and do not contribute in any way to a proliferation of nuclear weapons programs. In 1995, the NPT was extended indefinitely. Its scope widened to include undeclared nuclear activities. Most countries have renounced nuclear weapons, recognizing that possession of them would threaten rather than enhance national security. They have therefore embraced the NPT as a public commitment to use nuclear materials and technology only for peaceful purposes. The successful conclusion, in 1968, of negotiations on the NPT was a landmark in the history of non-proliferation. After coming into force in 1970, it was indefinitely extended in May 1995. The NPT was essentially an agreement among the five NWS and the other countries interested in nuclear technology. The deal was that assistance and cooperation would be traded for pledges, backed by international scrutiny, that no plant or material would be diverted to weapons use. Those who refused to be part of the deal would be excluded from international cooperation or trade involving nuclear technology.

### *B. Parties to NPT*

*302.* In 2020, there were 191 states parties to the NPT including the five declared NWS which had manufactured and exploded a nuclear weapon before 1967 namely China, France, Russia, the U.K., and the U.S. The main countries remaining outside the NPT are Israel, India, and Pakistan, though North Korea has moved to join. These all have weapons programs which have come to maturity since 1970, so these countries cannot join without renouncing and dismantling their weapon programs. In 2008, special arrangements were agreed for India, bringing in a way in the NPT structure. The ratification of the Additional Protocol by India in 2014 put it on a similar footing to the five NWS. Till May 2023, 182 states had in force safeguard agreements with IAEA. The Tenth Review Conference was held in August 2022 and the Eleventh Review Conference will be held in 2026.

### *C. Objectives of NPT*

*303.* The main objectives of NPT are to stop the further spread of nuclear weapons, to provide security for nonnuclear-weapon states which have given up the nuclear option, to encourage international cooperation in the peaceful uses of nuclear energy, and to pursue negotiations in good faith toward nuclear disarmament leading to the elimination of nuclear weapons. The most important factor underpinning the safeguards regime is international political pressure and how particular nations perceive their long-term security interests in relation to their immediate neighbors. International pressure not to acquire weapons is enough to deter most states from developing a weapons program. The major risk of nuclear weapons proliferation will always lay with countries which have not joined the NPT and which have significant unsafeguarded nuclear activities, and those which have joined but disregard their treaty commitments.

## §2. Nuclear Energy for Peaceful Purposes

*304.* For ensuring that nuclear energy is used for peaceful purposes, various steps have been taken by the international community one of which was the establishment of IAEA.

## I. International Atomic Energy Agency

*305.* The IAEA was set up by unanimous resolution of the U.N. in 1957 to help nations develop nuclear energy for peaceful purposes. Allied to this role is the administration of safeguards arrangements. This provides assurance to the international community that individual countries are honoring their treaty commitments to use nuclear materials and facilities exclusively for peaceful purposes. The IAEA therefore undertakes regular inspections of civil nuclear facilities to verify the accuracy of documentation supplied to it. The agency checks inventories and undertakes sampling and analysis of materials. Safeguards are designed to deter diversion of nuclear material by increasing the risk of early detection. They are complemented by controls on the export of sensitive technology from countries such as the U.K. and the U.S. through voluntary bodies such as the Nuclear Suppliers Group (NSG). Safeguards are backed up by the threat of international sanctions.

*306.* The nuclear safeguards are a means of reassurance whereby non-NWS demonstrate to others that they are abiding by their peaceful commitments. Their specific objective is to verify whether declared (usually traded) nuclear material remains within the civil nuclear fuel cycle and is being used solely for peaceful purposes or not. Non-NWS parties to the NPT agree to accept technical safeguards measures applied by the IAEA. These require that operators of nuclear facilities maintain and declare detailed accounting records of all movements and transactions involving nuclear material.

### *A. Inspection*

*307.* IAEA carries out design information verifications and physical inventory verifications once a year in most of the facilities that are under IAEA safeguards worldwide. Inspections are also carried out in a selected number of almost locations outside facilities every year. Their records and the actual nuclear material are audited. Inspections by the IAEA are complemented by other measures such as surveillance cameras and instrumentation. The aim of traditional IAEA safeguards is to deter the diversion of nuclear material from peaceful use by maximizing the chances of early detection. At a broader level, they provide assurance to the international community that countries are honoring their treaty commitments to use nuclear materials and facilities exclusively for peaceful purposes. In this way, safeguards are a service both to the international community and to individual states, who recognize that it is in their own interest to demonstrate compliance with these commitments. The inspections act as an alert system providing a warning of the possible diversion of nuclear material from peaceful activities.

*308.* In 2022, the IAEA conducted almost 3000 in-field verification activities at more than 1300 nuclear facilities and 'locations outside facilities' around the world. (According to the Safeguards Statement and Background for 2022, published on June 14, 2023). As a result of this verification, the IAEA drew safeguards conclusions for 188 States with safeguards agreements in force.

*B. Nuclear Material Accountability*

*309.* The nuclear material accountability is ensured by tracking all transfers and the flow of materials in any nuclear facility. This includes sampling and analysis of nuclear material, on-site inspections, review, and verification of operating records. Physical Security restricts access to nuclear materials at the site of use. Through Containment and Surveillance, the use of seals, automatic cameras and other instruments is resorted to detect unreported movement or tampering with nuclear materials, as well as spot-checks on-site. All NPT non-weapon states are required to accept these "full-scope" safeguards, which apply to all nuclear facilities in the country. In the five weapons states plus the non-NPT states (India, Pakistan, and Israel), facility-specific safeguards apply to relevant plants. IAEA inspectors regularly visit these facilities to verify completeness and accuracy of records.

*310.* Under the NPT, the uranium supplied to NWS is not covered by safeguards. However, normally there is at least a "peaceful use" clause in the supply contract. Neither the peaceful use clause nor the bilateral treaty means that materials are restricted to facilities on the state's list of facilities eligible for IAEA inspection. The NPT is supplemented by other safeguards systems such as those among certain European nations (Euratom Safeguards) and between individual countries (bilateral agreements) such as Australia and customer countries for its uranium, or Japan and the U.S. The terms of the NPT cannot be enforced by the IAEA itself, nor can nations be forced to sign the treaty. In reality, as shown in Iran and North Korea, safeguards are backed up by diplomatic, political, and economic measures.

*C. Safeguards Problems*

*311.* Iraq, Iran and North Korea illustrate both the strengths and weaknesses of international safeguards. While accepting safeguards at declared facilities, Iraq and Iran had set up elaborate equipment in an attempt to enrich uranium, in Iraq's case, to weapons grade. North Korea used research reactors (not commercial electricity-generating reactors) and a reprocessing plant to produce some weapons-grade Pu. The uranium used as fuel probably came from indigenous sources, and the key nuclear facilities concerned were built by the countries themselves without being declared to the IAEA and placing any safeguards arrangements. In North Korea, the activities concerned took place before the conclusion of its NPT safeguards agreement, using a Russian research reactor and a reprocessing plant. Nevertheless, the activities were detected in Iraq and North Korea and brought under control using international diplomacy.

## II. Undeclared Nuclear Activities: The Additional Protocol

*312.* Following discovery of Iraq's clandestine program, in 1993 a program was initiated to strengthen and extend the classical safeguards system, and a model protocol was agreed by the IAEA Board of Governors in 1997. This was to boost the IAEA's ability to detect undeclared nuclear activities. Innovations were of two kinds, and some could be implemented on the basis of IAEA's existing legal authority through safeguards agreements and inspections, while others required further legal authority through an Additional Protocol. This was to be agreed by each non-weapon state with IAEA, as a supplement to their existing comprehensive safeguards agreement. NPT weapons states have also agreed to accept the principles of the Model Additional Protocol.

### *A. Model Additional Protocol*

*313.* The IAEA is given considerably more information on nuclear and nuclear-related activities, including research and development, production of uranium and thorium and nuclear-related imports and exports. IAEA inspectors have greater rights of access that includes any suspect location, at short notice (e.g., two hours). The IAEA can deploy environmental sampling and remote monitoring techniques to detect illicit activities. States are to streamline administrative procedures, so that IAEA inspectors get automatic visa renewal and can communicate more readily with IAEA headquarters. All these elements enhance the IAEA's ability to provide assurances that all nuclear activities and material in the country concerned has been declared for safeguards purposes.

*314.* As of August 2014, 124 states plus Taiwan, Greenland, and Euratom had Additional Protocols in force, and 20 more including Belarus and Iran had approved it and signed but are not yet in force. There are seventy states plus Taiwan with significant nuclear activities. Those remaining without an Additional Protocol include Israel, Pakistan, and North Korea—all outside the NPT. The evolution of safeguards is linked with evaluation of each state, taking account of its particular situation and the kind of nuclear materials it has, involving greater judgment on the part of IAEA and the development of effective methodologies, which reassure NPT States. Where non-weapon states have a safeguards agreement with the IAEA and an Additional Protocol in force, the IAEA is able to say each year not only that declared nuclear material remains in peaceful activities, but also that there are no undeclared nuclear materials or activities.

## III. Limitations of Safeguards

*315.* Apart from situations addressed by the Additional Protocol, the greatest risk of nuclear weapons proliferation lies with countries which have not joined the NPT and which have significant unsafeguarded nuclear activities. While safeguards apply to some of their activities, others remain beyond scrutiny. A further concern is that countries may develop various sensitive nuclear fuel cycle facilities and research reactors under full safeguards and then subsequently opt out of the NPT. Bilateral agreements insisted upon by Australia and Canada for sale of uranium address this by including fallback provisions, but many countries are outside the scope of these agreements. If a nuclear-capable country does leave the NPT, it is likely to be reported by the IAEA to the U.N. Security Council, just as if it were in breach of its safeguards agreement. Trade sanctions would then be likely to be imposed on such country.

*316.* IAEA safeguards together with bilateral safeguards applied under the NPT ensure that supplied uranium do not contribute to nuclear weapons proliferation. In fact, the worldwide application of the safeguards and the substantial world trade in uranium for nuclear electricity make the proliferation of nuclear weapons much less likely. The Additional Protocol, once it is widely in force will provide credible assurance that there are no undeclared nuclear materials or activities in the states concerned. This will be a major step forward in preventing nuclear proliferation.

## IV. Safeguards in Countries with Nuclear Weapons

*317.* In NWS, IAEA safeguards apply under a "voluntary offer agreement." Where offered, facilities are put on each state's "list of facilities that are eligible for IAEA safeguards," and it is up to IAEA to decide which facilities are to be inspected. However, all these facilities must maintain IAEA-standard accounting:

| *S. No.* | *Country* | *First Weapon Test* | *Safeguards Situation for Nuclear Power* |
|---|---|---|---|
| 1 | U.S. | 1945 | All civil nuclear facilities are subject to IAEA safeguards. The National Nuclear Safety Administration (NNSA) applies some materials accounting to all fuel cycle facilities and communicates with IAEA. |
| 2 | U.K. | 1952 | All civil nuclear facilities are subject to IAEA safeguards. |
| 3 | Russia | 1949 | IAEA safeguards not generally applied, though this is changing. |
| 4 | France | 1960 | All civil nuclear facilities are under Euratom safeguards, all civil facilities containing safeguards-obligated nuclear material are subject to IAEA safeguards. |

| *S. No.* | *Country* | *First Weapon Test* | *Safeguards Situation for Nuclear Power* |
|---|---|---|---|
| 5 | China | 1964 | All imported nuclear power plants are under IAEA safeguards, as is the Russian-supplied Shaanxi centrifuge enrichment plant. |
| 6 | India | 1974 | Fourteen civil power reactors are under IAEA safeguards, along with all future civil facilities, pursuant to 2008 U.S.-India agreement and 2014 Additional Protocol. |
| 7 | Pakistan | 1998 | Civil power reactors under item-specific IAEA safeguards. |

## V. Other IAEA Developments

*318.* In May 1995, NPT parties reaffirmed their commitment to a Fissile Materials Cut-off Treaty to prohibit the production of any further fissile material for weapons. This aims to complement the Comprehensive Test Ban Treaty agreed in 1996 and to codify commitments made by the U.S., U.K., France, and Russia to cease production of weapons material, as well as putting a similar ban on China. This treaty has also put more pressure on Israel, India, and Pakistan to agree to international verification. Another initiative relates to Pu and spent fuel. For uranium, safeguards take account of its nature, e.g., natural, depleted, low-enriched or high-enriched (above 20% U-235), and the corresponding degree of concern regarding proliferation. A similarly differentiated approach is being considered for Pu. Two or three categories are possible namely degraded Pu, low-grade Pu, and high-grade Pu. The first two correspond to what is generally known as a reactor-grade Pu, sometimes defined as having more than 19% non-fissile isotopes. There are also several other treaties and arrangements designed to reduce the risk of civil nuclear power's contributing to weapons proliferation.

## VI. EURATOM and the IAEA

*319.* Activities regarding safeguards are carried out jointly by the IAEA and EURATOM, and a 1992 agreement enables the IAEA itself to deploy more of its resources in Member States where independent regional safeguards systems are not in place. Shortly after entry into force of the NPT, multilateral consultations on nuclear export controls led to the establishment of two separate mechanisms for dealing with nuclear exports namely the Zangger Committee in 1971 and the NSG in 1975. The Zangger Committee, also known as the Non-Proliferation Treaty Exporters Committee, was set up to consider procedures for exports of nuclear material and equipment related to NPT commitments. In August 1974, the committee came up with a trigger list of items which would require the application of IAEA safeguards if exported to a non-NWS which was not party to the NPT. The trigger list is regularly updated. The Zangger Committee now has thirty-nine Member States.

### §3. Sensitive Nuclear Technologies

*320.* The nuclear power reactors themselves are not a proliferation concern, but enrichment and reprocessing technologies are open to misuse and have been the cause of proliferation through illicit or unsafeguarded use. This problem is largely addressed in the Additional Protocol, and in fact, such Sensitive Nuclear Technologies (SNT) are largely confined to NPT weapons states plus Japan. For most countries, they would make no economic sense, and several recent initiatives focus on how to create conditions which make them unattractive propositions. The NPT itself refers to the "inalienable" right to use nuclear energy, but it does not guarantee the right to develop SNT. Nor, however, does it explicitly limit the development of SNT, other than by the fundamental obligations of non-NWS not to acquire or seek to acquire nuclear weapons, and to place all their nuclear material under IAEA safeguards.

*321.* The current approaches to control the spread of SNT have focused on measures against the transfer of equipment, components, special materials, and technology, through national export controls and multilateral coordination within the NSG. Further, any enrichment or reprocessing plant in an NPT non-NWS must be fully safeguarded. While safeguards are an essential part of international confidence building, they cannot alone provide assurance about a country's future intent. The concern is that an enrichment or reprocessing facility under safeguards today could be used as the basis for breakout from non-proliferation commitments in the future. In the case of enrichment, a centrifuge plant could produce sufficient fuel for a nuclear weapon in a relatively short time. Hence there is some diplomatic pressure to limit the countries with SNT facilities to those regarded as presenting a low proliferation risk. One initiative to this end is the International Framework for Nuclear Energy Cooperation (IFNEC), formerly known as the Global Nuclear Energy Partnership (GNEP).

*322.* The NSG (formerly known as the London Group or London Suppliers Group) was set up in 1974 after India exploded its first nuclear device. The main reason for the group's formation was to bring in France, a major nuclear supplier nation which was not then party to the NPT. It included both members and nonmembers of the Zangger Committee. The group communicated its guidelines, essentially a set of export rules, to the IAEA in 1978. The NSG Guidelines ensure that transfers of nuclear material or equipment would not be diverted to unsafeguarded nuclear fuel cycle or nuclear explosive activities, and formal government assurances to this effect were required from recipients. The guidelines also recognized the need for physical protection measures in the transfer of sensitive facilities, technology and weapons-usable materials, and strengthened retransfer provisions. The NSG began with seven members—the U.S., the former U.S.S.R., the U.K., France, Germany, Canada, and Japan—but now it includes forty-six countries.

*323.* Civil nuclear power has not been the cause of or route to nuclear weapons in any country that has nuclear weapons, and no uranium traded for electricity production has ever been diverted for military use. All nuclear weapons programs have either preceded or risen independently of civil nuclear power. As little as five tons of natural uranium are required to produce a nuclear weapon. Uranium could be recovered in such quantities from most granites, or from seawater—sources which would be quite uneconomic for commercial use. In contrast, world trade for electricity production is almost 70,000 tons of uranium per year, all of which can be accounted for. There is no chance that the resurgent problem of nuclear weapons proliferation tackled by turning away from nuclear power or ceasing trade in the tens of thousands of tons each year needed for it.

### §4. Responsibility for Wastes

*324.* Each country is ethically and legally responsible for its own wastes, therefore the default position is that all nuclear wastes will be disposed of in each of the fifty or so countries concerned. The main ingredients of high-level nuclear wastes are created in the nuclear reactors which make the electricity. There is thus no moral obligation on uranium suppliers in respect to the wastes, other than that involved in safeguards procedures. For instance, Australian uranium is supplied under safeguards, which are essentially accounting and inspection procedures to ensure that neither the uranium nor any product of it (e.g., Pu) contributes to fulfilling the aspirations of anyone wanting to build weapons. With the IAEA, the Australian Safeguards and Non-Proliferation Office tracks "Australian Obligated Nuclear Materials" all the way through to used fuel, reprocessing, and recycling of Pu in mixed oxide fuels. Thus, any international waste repository has implications under the NPT. The trustworthiness and standing of the host country are fundamental to the project's acceptability to NPT states, which comprise virtually every country but India, Pakistan, Israel, and North Korea. Also, the international treaty produced by IAEA and signed by most nations of the world in 1997 covering the management and disposal of used fuel and high-level wastes requires that the host facility or system meets the highest national and international standards.

## I. International Repositories

*325.* Over fifty countries currently have spent fuel stored in temporary locations, awaiting reprocessing or disposal. Not all countries have the appropriate geological conditions for such disposal—and, for many countries with small nuclear programs, the financial and human resources required for the construction and operation of a geological disposal facility are daunting. In 1980, the IAEA-sponsored International Nuclear Fuel Cycle Evaluation (INFCE) waste management and disposal report had firmly recommended that proposals "for establishing multinational and international repositories should be elaborated" due to their non-proliferation advantages. Centralized facilities for disposal of spent fuel and/or vitrified high-level wastes would reduce the diversion risk and be more economical. Individual waste repositories for spent nuclear fuel and other high-level wastes must be reliably safe and secure.

*326.* There have been several proposals for regional and international repositories for disposal of high-level nuclear wastes, and in 2003, the concept received strong endorsement from the head of IAEA. The European Commission funded the studies to assess the feasibility of European regional waste repositories. Arising from these studies, fourteen EU countries resolved to set up a European Repository Development Organization (ERDO) to collaborate on nuclear waste disposal. Since 2009, the IFNEC has focused on possible multinational repositories for their safety, security and environmental benefits. In May 2016, a high-level commission in South Australia recommended the establishment of an international repository. In 2019, IFNEC suggested that it was not timely to develop a multinational repository until national repository projects were more advanced.

## II. Achieving High-Security Means

*327.* A vital contribution can be made to global environmental safety by ensuring that radioactive substances are permanently removed from the human environment. They can greatly enhance global security in the broader sense by preventing malicious use of fissile and radiological materials. Insofar as these functions are less than fully assured in any of the fifty countries concerned with radioactive wastes, there is a justification for some kind of international collaboration and facilities, possibly on a regional basis. Certainly, geological disposal is the only foreseeable way of ensuring adequate safety and security in the long-term management of used fuel which is treated as waste, and also of separated high-level radioactive wastes which, if recycling of actinides becomes established, eventually will be mainly fission products. While acknowledging each county's responsibility for its own wastes, the limits to the logic on indigenous disposal can be seen from the changing national borders within Europe over the last century.

# Part VII. Trans-boundary Pollution

*328.* The international law tries to regulate the interactions of states by defining their respective rights and obligations. Despite its tremendous development, international environmental law remains rooted in the interstate system and can be understood as an effort to reconcile the differing and often competing concerns of states. The intrastate environmental problems become legally relevant when activities within one state inflict significant harm in the territory of another. Under classical principles of international law, the concept of state sovereignty gives rise to two potentially contradictory notions. One is the principle of territorial integrity, which recognizes the right of states to be free of interference from others, and the principle of territorial sovereignty which recognizes the freedom of states to do as they like within their own territory. International environmental law strikes a balance between territorial integrity and territorial sovereignty and harmonizes it. This goal is reflected in the obligation not to cause significant trans-boundary harm, which is the core of international environmental law. The need to balance the competing sovereign interests involved is even more clearly reflected in the principle of "equitable utilization," which is set forth in the U.N. Convention on the Law of Non-Navigational Uses of International Watercourses (Watercourses Convention), and reflected in the ILC's 2001 Draft Articles on the Prevention of Trans-boundary Harm from Hazardous Activities, requiring that solutions must be based on "an equitable balance of interests."

From an economic point of view, the no-harm rule can be understood as an effort to "internalize" significant trans-boundary external factors. Externalities are the costs of an activity that are not borne by the actor but that fall on others. For example, one country emits $SO_2$ that causes acid rain to fall on its neighbor downwind or it discharges pollution into a river, causing damage to lower riparian states. To the extent that a country is able to "externalize" the costs of polluting, it has no economic incentive to stop. The no-harm rule is meant to address this problem, by prohibiting one state from imposing significant environmental costs on another.

*329.* Although the no-harm principle has achieved canonical status, in practice, it is not consistently applied to resolve specific environmental disputes by courts or tribunals. Despite efforts to codify the rules of state responsibility for trans-boundary pollution, the *Trail Smelter* case, which arose between the U.S. and Canada in the 1920s,[81] remains the singular case where a state has been found

81. *Trail Smelter* Case (*United States v. Canada*), Award, 1941, 3 U.N.R.I.A.A. 1905.

legally responsible for failure to prevent trans-boundary pollution. Even the massive trans-boundary pollution caused by the Chernobyl and Sandoz accidents did not lead to legal claims by the victim states.[82] The *Sandoz Chemical Fire* case involved a fire at a Sandoz corporation warehouse in Switzerland. The fire resulted in thousands of cubic meters of chemically contaminated water seeping into the Rhine and constituted one of the worst environmental disasters ever in Western Europe. None of the states affected brought claims against Switzerland. In the case of Chernobyl, nuclear accident where Ukraine refused to acknowledge liability, the international community paid for the costs of withdrawing from active service of the reactors.

*330.* A pragmatic way to control trans-boundary pollution is through negotiations among the states concerned to reach a mutually satisfactory outcome and, in some cases, to establish institutional arrangements that can manage the externalities on an ongoing basis. Examples include the International Joint Commission, which has been operating for close to a century under the 1909 U.S.–Canada Boundary Waters Treaty, and the Long-Range Trans-boundary Air Pollution (LRTAP) regime in Europe. To some degree, the no-harm rule and the equitable utilization principle form part of the legal context in which these are negotiated and implemented.

*331.* The principles of international environmental law on the existence of trans-boundary institutions guarantee the expeditious resolution of trans-boundary pollution problems. There is some irony in the fact that the Trail Smelter itself is subject of disagreement between Canada and the U.S. and that the no-harm rule, which the first *Trail Smelter* case crystallized, has not played a significant role in the resolution of the other disputes. Nor the International Joint Commission was able to resolve the matter, notwithstanding the fact that the issue is one of trans-boundary water pollution, and that the commission is a well-established institution. Indeed, the interstate level and international environmental law have been bypassed through efforts by governmental and nongovernmental actors within the U.S. to apply U.S. law to the Smelter's activities and its alleged trans-boundary impacts.[83]

---

82. Bodansky Daniel, Brunnée Jutta & Hey Allen, *The Oxford Handbook of International Environmental Law*, Law, International Law, Environment and Energy Law (August 2008), Online Publication Date: September 2012, DOI: 10.1093/oxfordhb/9780199552153.013.0001.
83. A.L. Parrish, *Trail Smelter Dejà Vu: Extraterritoriality, International Environmental Law, and the Search for Solutions to Canadian-U.S. Trans-boundary Water Pollution Disputes*, 85 B.U. L. Rev. 363 (2005).

# Chapter 1. Trans-boundary Air Pollution

*332.* Pollution is trans-boundary when it occurs between states whether or not the states concerned share a common border and polluted air from one country crosses to another and spread pollution in another country. The state from where pollution originates is designated as the "state of origin" and the state affected by such pollution as "affected State"(s). It is not limited to land borders, but it may also extend to maritime boundaries and zones as well.

*333.* MVP IV gave a mandate to the international law community to develop legal measures to address trans-boundary air pollution. The program envisaged the promotion of agreements to combat trans-boundary air pollution, the assistance of DC to strengthen their national legislation and institutions to prevent, reduce, and control trans-boundary air pollution, and the development of national laws in this regard. The policy initiatives by the international law community resonate with the trans-boundary air pollution mandate given by MVP IV, for example, paragraph 5(c) of Resolution 1/77 provides for the UNEP Executive Director to explore opportunities for strengthened trans-boundary air pollution cooperation. The most comprehensive international agreement relating to trans-boundary pollution is the 1979 Convention and its Protocols. This Convention extends to the Economic Commission for Europe (ECE) region and is a framework agreement to address the major concerns about acid rain and other dispersed pollutants. The Convention provided a framework for cooperation and the development of further MEAs relating to control of trans-boundary air pollution.

## §1. Agreements on Trans-boundary Air Pollution

*334.* There are a number of bilateral and multilateral regional agreements on trans-boundary air pollution, and substantial regional efforts have been made to deal with the issue and address the concerns. Some MEAs limit pollution by individual substances and in the process address air pollution. There has been development of sub-regional and regional agreements to combat trans-boundary pollution, in particular, trans-boundary air pollution, including haze, dust, and brown clouds, and examine the feasibility of developing agreements at the global level. These have assisted DC and countries with economies in transition to strengthen their national legislation and institutions to prevent, reduce, and control at source trans-boundary air pollution and develop and promote laws and practices to address and avoid trans-boundary air and water pollution.

## §2. International Efforts

*335.* The Stockholm Convention on POPs identifies the POPs that fall within its scope. The production and use of nine POPs are prohibited. Further, the production and release into the environment of other POPs are required to be minimized. As POPs are particularly harmful to human health and the environment, and can be transported, *inter alia*, by air so the control measures introduced by the Stockholm Convention help in mitigating trans-boundary air pollution. There have been efforts to build on the comprehensive 1979 Convention (extending to ECE) in order to create a global agreement to reduce trans-boundary air pollution. The Convention, although regional, provides a basis to address trans-boundary air pollution on a global scale. There can also be an umbrella organization or agreement under which the 1979 Convention would fall, and such organization oversees the development of other regional treaties to address trans-boundary air pollution. The emission of gaseous substances and PM into the air has the capacity to spread and cause trans-boundary pollution. That, in turn, can lead to disputes between states. For example, the influential and seminal *Trail Smelter* case dealt with the settlement of damages incurred because of the trans-boundary discharge of $SO_2$ emission.

### I. Trans-boundary Damage

*336.* The issue of trans-boundary damage, including trans-boundary damage by air pollution, is addressed by Principle 2 of 1992 of the Rio Declaration and the earlier and near identical Principle 21 of the 1972 Stockholm Declaration of the U.N. Conference on the Human Environment (the Stockholm Declaration). Both express the common conviction that states have, in accordance with the Charter of the U.N. and the principles of international law, the sovereign right to exploit their resources pursuant to their environmental policies with the responsibility to ensure that activities within their jurisdiction do not cause damage to the environment of other states or of areas beyond the limits of national jurisdiction. That responsibility has led to binding legal instruments to control trans-boundary pollution.

*337.* There are MEAs that address the issue of climate change and ozone depletion. In 2011, the COP of the UNFCCC decided to establish the Ad Hoc Working Group on the Durban Platform for Enhanced Action (ADP) as a subsidiary body. The mandate of the ADP was to develop a protocol, another legal instrument, or an agreed outcome with legal force under the Convention applicable to all parties.

## §3. Trans-boundary Air Pollution and Law

*338.* The international law of trans-boundary pollution is part of international environmental law and is also part of the still-emerging international energy law. It is among the historically oldest parts of international environmental law, which has its roots in the *Trail Smelter Arbitration* case and indirectly, the *Corfu Channel* Case. The focus of the law has moved from repairing the effects of such pollution after it is caused to their preventive control. The sources of the legal control of trans-boundary pollution have diversified. In addition to territorial integrity and sovereignty, the Rio Environmental Principles are relevant for trans-boundary pollution regulation. There is the customary law of hazardous activity-related pollution and on pollution within shared resources, a range of treaty regimes dealing with specific aspects of trans-boundary pollution, and, finally, the customary law of state responsibility for unlawful acts in this context.

## §4. LEGAL YARDSTICKS

*339.* The international legal standards on trans-boundary pollution have evolved considerably. Placed on the foundation of territorial integrity and the law of the sea, there is a set of specific customary principles and rules, and also of treaty law for certain segments within the overall scope of trans-boundary pollution.

### I. Territorial Integrity and States Rights

*340.* Trans-boundary pollution involves two sovereigns, the state from which the pollution originates and the state that is affected by it. The territorial integrity of the affected state is the international legal yardstick that governs trans-boundary pollution. The state of origin then is under a negative duty not to cause trans-boundary pollution itself, through its organs, or any controlled entities. It also has a positive duty to regulate private activities that are likely to cause trans-boundary pollution. This is a due diligence obligation and thus obligation of conduct, rather than result, that evolves in light of changing circumstances and technological innovation. The question is as to which type of pollution falls under these obligations arising from territorial integrity, in particular, whether it must be capable of causing physical harm to the environment or the population of the affected state. The customary *sic utere tuo* principle addresses significant physical harm. But that does necessarily mean that territorial integrity cannot be a residual yardstick to be opposed to such trans-boundary pollution that does not cause harm or is likely to do so, but which nevertheless impairs the affected state's ability to govern its territory's environment without external interference. However, the obligation is to the extent of any pollution beyond a de minimis threshold. This issue has arisen particularly with regard to the emission of radioactive substances in the atmosphere or the sea.

*341.* In the Nuclear Tests Cases, it was argued that the decisional sovereignty of the affected sovereign would be affected by any pollution, regardless of its harmful effects. There, the ICJ did not pronounce explicitly on that suggestion. However, in its Legality of the Threat or Use of Nuclear Weapons Advisory Opinion, in determining the applicable legal standard, the court opined that "respect of the environment of other States" was required, not just the doing of no harm to it. In the *MOX Plant* case before ITLOS, the tribunal considered that the Convention's prohibitions to pollute the marine environment were triggered by Ireland's contention that there would be a discharge of radioactive substances, regardless of its detrimental effect.

## §5. Principles of Environmental Law and Trans-boundary Pollution

*342.* Since 1992, sustainable development has been the universal norm for combining economic and environmental concerns that also underlie the law on trans-boundary pollution. This norm is concretized in the Rio Declaration's Principles. Most of these principles direct action in regard to both state-internal and trans-boundary matters, although some only apply to the latter. The principles offer a coherent set of regulations for controlling trans-boundary pollution. The Rio Principles have a directional effect on the control of trans-boundary pollution. The Rio Principles have been affirmed and further concretized through international legalization, such as treaties, infra-treaty rule making. Some principles have now become customary law and as such are directly applicable legal yardsticks for trans-boundary pollution control.

### I. *Sic utere tuo ut alienum non laedas*

*343.* The foundational Rio Principle 2 provides that states have the responsibility to ensure that activities within their jurisdiction or control do not cause damage to the environment of other states. This emanates from the overarching idea of the responsibility of every state toward the international community, of the established customary principle of *sic utere tuo ut alienum non laedas*. This principle is directly applicable to trans-boundary pollution control. It provides that a state must not use its territory, or knowingly allow it to be used, in such a way that causes significant harm to another state's environment. In the Legality of the Threat or Use of Nuclear Weapons Advisory Opinion, the ICJ stated its status and content as follows: "the general obligation of States to ensure that activities within their jurisdiction and control respect the environment of other States … is now part of the corpus of international law relating to the environment" (at paragraph 29).

*344.* The problem is how to determine which concrete requirements the state of origin faces in order to meet this responsibility. The potential requirements in international law then range from formal permission for any or some polluting activities, the prescription of procedural or substantive standards for that permission, appropriate response measures to eliminate or mitigate harm, to compensation and liability. The measures which the state of origin needs to take depends on the activity and the risks it presents, seen in light of the other Rio Principles.

### II. Environmental Information

*345.* Rio Principal 10 demands that the public be provided with environmental information for ensuring that environmental rules are being effectively applied. This mechanism has been enshrined in regional treaty law, for instance, the UNECE Convention on Access to Information, Public Participation in Decision-Making and Access to Justice in Environmental Matters (Access to Information on Environmental Matters; Access to Justice in Environmental Matters). Such information must also be provided across borders, that is, to actors under the jurisdiction of a state potentially affected by pollution activities in the state of origin without discrimination.

## III. Liability and Compensation

*346.* Rio Principle 13 requires that rules be developed regarding liability and compensation for the victims of pollution and Liability for environmental damage be fixed. This clearly applies to trans-boundary pollution. It dovetails with Rio Principle 16, which demands that the polluter bear, in principle, the cost of pollution (Polluter Pays). This principle has been implemented through customary and treaty law, in regard to states taking measures to provide for compensation of victims of trans-boundary pollution and that the cost of such compensation be borne by operators of the pollution-causing activities, and for that their liability in national law be established.

## IV. Precautionary Principle

*347.* Rio Principle 15 deals with the precautionary approach/principle. Under it, threats of serious damage call for cost-effective preventive measure, even where full scientific uncertainty remains lacking. The principle is still in the process of crystallizing into customary law, as stated by ITLOS in its Responsibilities Advisory Opinion. In its general thrust of favoring preventive action, the principle underlies, however, many if not all of the customary and treaty law on the control of trans-boundary pollution in its various forms.

## V. Environmental Impact Assessment

*348.* Rio Principle 17 demands that an EIA be carried out for proposed activities that are likely to have a significant adverse impact on the environment. This principle considers carrying on of EIA as an instrument of national law. The principle of a prior EIA for an activity that is likely to cause trans-boundary pollution is established in general international law. It requires specifically the consideration of such environmental impacts, such as pollution, that occur in other states. In Pulp Mills on the River Uruguay, the ICJ has confirmed this customary status. However, this case concerned a shared resource in the sense that the administration of the River Plate is undertaken by Uruguay and Argentina. Nevertheless, this pronouncement that occurred in a borderline case also extends to pure trans-boundary scenarios.

*349.* While the legal status of EIAs has been established, the customary law-determined content remains inadequate. It only requires that some EIA take place, but does not prescribe the precise procedures or its details for carrying it out. The customary EIA principle is, however, concretized through different means. At international level, such concretization of procedure is contained in the UNEP EIA Principles applied to trans-boundary impacts. In Pulp Mills, the ICJ recognized that these are capable of concretizing the customary rule, on the basis that the UNEP is the international body with a universal environmental mandate. Further concretization can be achieved through treaty law. Thus, under UNCLOS, in the *Straits of Johor* case, ITLOS enjoined the carrying out of a public EIA in a trans-boundary context by using expert advice. The regional Convention on EIA in a Trans-boundary Context ("Espoo Convention") applies and has been used for assessing the effects of large trans-boundary projects, such as the North Stream Pipeline. However, it is for national law to provide for detailed impact assessment procedures in a transnational pollution context.

### VI. Prior Information and Consultation

*350.* According to Rio Principle 19, states shall provide prior and timely information to those states which may be potentially affected by activities that may have a significant adverse trans-boundary environmental effect and shall consult with those states. This has established as a principle under customary law. The principle underlies the treaty regimes on trans-boundary pollution control. These regimes strengthen the duty to consult, providing for the need to obtain the consent of the affected state.

### VII. The Effectiveness of Procedure

*351.* The Rio Principles rely essentially on procedure to achieve the objective of sustainable development in regard to trans-boundary pollution. The legal effectiveness of procedural obligations has been considerably strengthened by ICJ's judgment in Pulp Mills on the River Uruguay. In this case, the court deduced from such procedures that states ought not to authorize polluting activities that would render them pointless. While the case directly concerned a shared resource, this rationale may be applied to all instances of trans-boundary pollution for which states are under conventional or customary procedural obligation.

## §6. The Customary Law of Trans-boundary Pollution from Hazardous Activities

*352.* Pollution presents a risk of significant harm where such risk either takes the form of a high probability of causing significant trans-boundary harm or a low probability of causing disastrous trans-boundary harm. Causing such a risk is not prohibited per se by general international law. However, it is specifically controlled by it. The ILC has codified the relevant customary rules in two sets of Draft Articles, which are considered to restate the relevant customary law authoritatively. They comprise prevention as well as the making good of harm where the risk has materialized. The Draft Articles call on states to conclude treaties that implement these customary rules.

*353.* The first set of Draft Articles deals with prevention of trans-boundary pollution. In addition to notification and exchange of information, this includes the important principles that such activities require prior authorization by the territorial state of origin, which needs to balance the interests of all concerned states equitably. There is also a duty on the state of origin to prevent significant trans-boundary harm.

*354.* The second set of Draft Articles provides for the allocation of loss from such pollution.[84] These refer to liability, rather than responsibility, to emphasize the fact that incidents involving hazardous activities may occur despite compliance by the state of origin with its preventive obligations. It is the risk inherent in the activity, where it materializes that triggers certain consequences. There is the duty to promptly and adequately compensate the losses due to trans-boundary pollution that results from the hazardous activity, in the event of both compliance and noncompliance with the preventive duties. The compensation must be available to the victims in the affected state and should include the liability without fault of the operator, in line with the polluter pays principle. The victims must have access to competent courts in the state of origin, on the basis of non-discrimination. In case of a breach of the preventive duties there can be, additionally, state responsibility for unlawful acts where the relevant conditions are met (*see* preamble of the Draft Articles on Allocation of Loss).

## §7. The Customary Law on Trans-boundary Pollution Control Within Shared Resources

*355.* There is also specifically developed customary law on trans-boundary pollution in regard to shared resources. The law of natural resources that are shared by two or more states rests on a foundation of trans-boundary pollution control, to which it adds the cooperation on resource management. The ILC Draft Articles on the Law of Trans-boundary Aquifers emphasize the continuing role of state borders. Draft Article 6 deals with a general obligation not to cause significant harm, and each aquifer state shall, in regard to trans-boundary aquifers or aquifer systems in its territory, take all appropriate measures to prevent the causing of significant harm to other aquifer states or other states in whose territory a discharge zone is located. Where significant harm nevertheless is caused to another aquifer state or a state in whose territory a discharge zone is located, the Aquifer State causing such harm shall take, in consultation with the affected state, all response measures to eliminate or mitigate such harm.

84. "Allocation of Loss in the Case of Trans-boundary Harm Arising out of Hazardous Activities," annexed to UNGA Res 61/36 (2006).

*356.* Article 7 of the Convention on the Law of the Non-navigational Uses of International Watercourses contains a general obligation for Watercourse States not to cause significant harm to other such states, in utilizing an international watercourse in their territories. They shall take measures to prevent the causing of such harm. Where significant harm nevertheless is caused, the state must take all appropriate measures to eliminate or mitigate such harm. Article 21 provides that each watercourse state shall take steps to harmonize its policies with those of the others in this connection. Watercourse states shall, at the request of any of them, consult with a view to arriving at mutually agreeable measures and methods to prevent, reduce, and control pollution of an international watercourse. The procedural obligations imply a substantive prohibition for each state not to allow potentially polluting activities.

## §8. Treaty Regimes and Regulation of Trans-boundary Pollution

*357.* Certain types of trans-boundary pollution are regulated by way of an institutionalized multilateral treaty, or regime, universally or regionally. In their focus on reducing the pollution at its source, these treaties harmonize national law for the respective sector, which is achieved both through the treaty itself and subsequent decisions by the meetings of the parties to the treaty. The Basel Convention protects the territorial integrity of the affected state through the requirement of its prior informed consent. Infra-treaty (secondary) rulemaking by the meeting of the parties of the Convention has established standards for parties in avoiding trans-boundary pollution resulting from the hazardous waste.

*358.* The Basel Protocol on Liability and Compensation provides for liability as well as adequate and prompt compensation for damage resulting from the trans-boundary movement of hazardous wastes and other wastes, including incidents occurring because of illegal traffic in those wastes. It allocates financial responsibility for an incident at any stage of a trans-boundary movement, from the point at which the wastes are loaded on the means of transport to their export, international transit, import, to its final disposal. This model of prior informed consent to the trans-boundary movement of hazardous substances susceptible of polluting the environment in the importing state is also followed by the Rotterdam and the Stockholm Conventions, respectively on pesticides and industrial chemicals that have been banned or severely restricted for health or environmental reasons by parties and on POPs. Thus, multilateral treaty regimes that have a different purpose may become involved in trans-boundary pollution. Thus, a monitoring system operated by the Preparatory Commission for the Comprehensive Nuclear-Test-Ban Treaty Organization (CTBTO) tracked the spread of radioactivity on a global scale after the Fukushima disaster.

*359.* Regionally, and concluded under the auspices of the UNECE, the Long-range Trans-boundary Air Pollution Convention deals with such trans-boundary air pollution that has adverse effects in the area under the jurisdiction of another state at such a distance that it is not generally possible to distinguish the contribution of individual emission sources or groups of sources. In addition to the reduction of such pollution at source, consultations shall be held, upon request, at an early stage between, on the one hand, the state of origin and, on the other, those states that are actually affected by or exposed to a significant risk of long-range trans-boundary air pollution. ASEAN has produced the Agreement on Trans-boundary Haze Pollution. According to its Article 2, the objective of this agreement is to prevent and monitor trans-boundary haze pollution as a result of land and/or forest fires that should be mitigated, through concerted national efforts and intensified regional and international cooperation.

## §9. State Responsibility

*360.* Trans-boundary pollution can trigger the international responsibility of a state for unlawful acts. The relevant customary law is reflected in the ILC's Draft Articles on the International Responsibility of states for Internationally Wrongful Acts. This responsibility has the condition that the state of origin violated a specific obligation incumbent on it in regard to the pollution. CIL as concretized through the UNEP EIA Principles creates an obligation, at least as to the carrying out of impact assessment. The specific preventive and compensatory obligations under the customary law on hazardous activities do so as well.

*361.* It is generally accepted that there is no general requirement of a material or moral damage suffered by the victim state for the acting state to be responsible. Thus, actual harm for the environment of the affected state through pollution needs not to be demonstrated. Where a primary obligation has been violated, this will create a secondary obligation for the acting state, to cease an ongoing violation which allows the potentially affected state to enforce a preventive obligation, by demanding that the required preventive measures be taken by the state of origin. Where cessation is not sufficient, reparation for the causal consequences of the breach is to be made.

*362.* Whether a state that is the victim of the breach of one of the obligations on trans-boundary pollution control by another is entitled to breach the same obligation, as a countermeasure, Article 50 ILC Draft Articles on State Responsibility does not make explicit mention, among the obligations regarding the environment exempted from any countermeasure. The prohibition of causing significant harm to the environment of another state, through trans-boundary pollution, could, however, fall under the residual exemption that is provided for peremptory norms of general international law within the meaning of Article 50(1)(d) which refers to the generally accepted definition of peremptory international law contained in Article 53 VCLT (*Jus cogens*). The environment of each state or, for that matter, the global commons, do not feature in the lists of peremptory norms enunciated by the ILC in its commentaries on the Vienna Convention on the Law of Treaties (VCLT) and on the Draft Articles on State Responsibility or by the ICJ in its jurisprudence. However, if all values of the international community may give rise to peremptory norms, then this could also cover the environment of each state. In that case, at least the rules on hazardous trans-boundary pollution control would lose their materially reciprocal character.

*363.* International law on trans-boundary pollution has developed regulatory instruments comprising prevention, reduction, control and liability, and compensation. This law has its basis in customary law, which is supplemented by bilateral and multilateral treaty regimes. These seek to establish the dynamic regulation of the pollution through the respective meeting of the parties, including the harmonization of the laws of both states of origin of pollution and the affected states. Trans-boundary pollution regulation increasingly involves non-state actors, both in the sense that actors become subject to liability regimes and that the public receives rights, under international law, on the preventive and the remedial side of trans-boundary pollution regulation. The Rio Principles have been directing these developments.

## §10. Problems and Issues

*364.* There is no single institution responsible for overseeing all international legal activity relating to the atmosphere. This has resulted in difficulties concerning the regulation of HFCs, for example—there have been fragmented debates about which body should be responsible for the control of HFCs, without any single international organization empowered to take an authoritative view on the way forward.

### I. Inadequate Geographical Coverage

*365.* Despite extensive activity by the international law community to protect the atmosphere, there are a number of gaps in implementation. Sometimes there is inadequate geographical coverage, for example, the 1979 Convention relates only to the area of the UNECE. And, there may be a failure to regulate some activities and substances outside Europe that are required to be controlled. However, the international community has recognized the necessity to act to strengthen international, regional, and local efforts to tackle degradation of the atmosphere. The Resolution 1/7 recognized that poor air quality is a growing challenge, in particular, to health in cities and urban areas, that air pollution is an impediment to national sustainable development, and that promoting air quality is a priority to protect public health and provide co-benefits for the climate, biodiversity, and food security. The Resolution provides a program for Governments and a strengthened mandate for UNEP to address air pollution.

*366.* There are a number of MEAs protecting air quality and the global atmosphere, but there are problems arising because of inadequate regulation of some activities. Further, there is also failure to cover some substances, and, it has been argued that there is a necessity to clarify what are the applicable principles and rules. Besides, there is no treaty that covers the entire range of atmospheric environmental problems in a comprehensive and systematic manner, which augurs badly because by its very nature the atmosphere knows no boundaries and needs holistic treatment by international environmental law.

## II. Ad Hoc Approach

*367.* So far, the international law community has addressed problems relating to the atmosphere on an ad hoc basis, as the various political mandates have arisen. This has left the landscape filled by a number of different forums and MEAs, and inevitably some topics have overlapped, engaging more than one forum or organization. For example, the UNFCCC COP and the Montreal Protocol MOP have had an extensive discussion about the best way to regulate HFCs, and the 1979 Convention has been discussed globally as a model to regulate trans-boundary air pollution.

*368.* In the process of cooperation for tackling air pollution, there may be opportunities for synergies by tackling the different adverse effects of the same pollutant or activity. For example, reduced air pollution can also reduce impact on the climate. CCAC targets short-lived climate pollutants for reduction e.g., black carbon, $CH_4$ and HFCs. It has been estimated that "fast action" on black carbon and methane would potentially cut the rate of climate change in half for the next several decades, as well as will reduce air pollution-related deaths by as much as 2.4 million per year and avoiding annual crop losses of 50 to more than 100 million tons.

## III. Unregulated Industrial Development

*369.* The industrial development is a major cause of air pollution, through emissions from processes, industrial expansion, and the use of old technologies. Agriculture contributes to climate change, through the emission of methane, from livestock digestion processes and stored animal manure, and $N_2O$ from organic and mineral nitrogen fertilizers. The transport sector is a major contributor to the emission of $CO_2$, particulates, and $NO_2$. There may be synergies to be made like working to mitigate atmospheric pollution by cooperating with other sectors. The international community should be able to reinforce actions that can be taken at the national level to reduce air pollution, for example, the conservation of energy, reforestation, purchasing of energy-efficient products, and the use of green forms of transportation.

# Chapter 2. Trans-boundary Marine Pollution

*370.* The ecological unity of the countries does not and cannot correspond to political boundaries. While carrying out lawful activities within their own areas, states may have impacts on each other particularly in marine area. These mutual impacts, so long as they have not reached the level of "significant," are considered tolerable. The knowledge of the extent and pervasiveness of detrimental effects caused by near-coast harm is less than complete. The protection of the global marine environment depends upon existence of strong, ecosystem-based laws, agreements, principles, and norms that focus on acts that protect, conserve, and sustainably use marine resources. Above all an effective enforcement machinery is fundamental for the success of all the above.

## §1. Legal Protection of Oceans

*371.* As trans-boundary harm is not demonstrable in the traditionally defined material sense and a negotiated agreement may not exist between states relative to marine conservation and/or protection, a void exists for legal protection of the world's oceans. This is the case within states' sovereign waters and in waters where they enjoy sovereign rights i.e., in EEZs and on continental shelves. Even where a legal obligation does exist to protect and preserve the seas, as in the UNCLOS, states are reluctant to invoke the jurisdiction of international tribunals to hold fellow states accountable for breaches of their international obligations on marine conservation. For marine areas beyond the jurisdiction of states (the high seas), CIL provides an obligation to prevent harm, but in the absence of an effective enforcement regime this becomes a moral obligation.

## §2. Precautionary Principles and Marine Pollution

*372.* Ever since, the precautionary principle has been at the forefront in the field of marine pollution, where an abundance of data on pollution yielded little understanding but much concern. Since the beginning of the 1990s, the principle has been set out in a host of agreements which are listed below:

- the 1990 International Convention on Oil Pollution Preparedness, Response, and Cooperation (preamble);
- the 1992 Convention for the Protection of the Marine Environment of the North-East Atlantic (OSPAR) (Article 2(2)(a));
- the 1992 Helsinki Convention on the Protection of the Marine Environment of the Baltic Sea Area (Article 3(2));
- the 1976 Barcelona Convention for the Protection of the Mediterranean Sea against Pollution (as amended in 1995) (Article 4(3)(a));

– the 1980 Athens Protocol for the Protection of the Mediterranean Sea against Pollution from Land-based Sources and Activities (as amended in 1996) (Fifth Recital of the Athens Protocol as amended in Syracuse on March 7, 1996 (not yet in force)).

## §3. The 2003 Framework Convention for the Protection of the Marine Environment of the Caspian Sea (Article 5)

*373.* The scope of precautionary principal varies tremendously from one agreement to another. Some of the marine pollution agreements endorse a rather stringent version of the principle. For example, pursuant to the 1976 Barcelona Convention, OSPAR and The Baltic Marine Environment Protection Commission (HELCOM) agreements, the contracting parties "shall apply the precautionary principle." In other agreements concerning marine pollution, the principle has been framed in general terms rather than in a definitive form. The Preamble of the OPRC convention merely notes the "importance of precautionary measures and prevention in avoiding oil pollution in the first instance." In addition, the OSPAR and HELCOM agreements are the most stringent international agreements relating to the marine environment as regards the level of proof in order to trigger precautionary measures. Both agreements call upon the parties to take precautionary measures "when there are reasonable grounds for concern" (OSPAR) or "where there is reason to assume" (HELCOM) that the marine environment will be impaired. In contrast to the Rio Declaration, which submitted the precautionary principle to "serious or irreversible damage," the OSPAR and HELCOM agreements do not apply any threshold requirements to threats of serious or irreversible damage, and it is sufficient that a substance may give rise to a hazard to human health or harm living resources or marine ecosystem for the principle to be implemented. As to the extent of the damage, thresholds vary significantly. According to some, the principle should only apply to risks entailing non-negligible damage. Thus, the 1992 UNFCCC and the 1976 Barcelona Convention for the Protection of the Mediterranean Sea against Pollution only recognize recourse to the principle in order to avert "threats of serious or irreversible damage."

## §4. OSPAR Convention

*374.* The 1992 OSPAR Convention applies the principle when pollution "may bring about hazards to human health, harm living resources and marine ecosystems," while the 1994 Scheldt-Meuse Agreements require that dangerous substances have "a significant trans-frontier impact" in order for the principle to apply. In a case opposing Malaysia to Singapore as regards the ecological threats entailed by impoldering projects carried out close to the Malaysian territory, ITLOS held that "given the possible implications of land reclamation on the marine environment, prudence and caution require," the parties "establish mechanisms for exchanging information and assessing the risks of land reclamation works" (Case concerning

Land Reclamation by Singapore in and around the Straits of Johor, 2003). The natural resources of the maritime spaces of the EEZ and the continental shelf are subject to functional rights, rather than sovereignty of the coastal state. Nevertheless, these rights are deserving of the same protection as the territorial rights against trans-boundary pollution. This is the implication of the *Straits of Johor* case of ITLOS, even though it directly concerned the environment of the territorial sea only.

## §5. United Nations Convention on Law of Sea

*375.* The Convention lays down the fundamental obligation of all states to protect and preserve the marine environment. All states to cooperate on a global and regional basis in formulating rules and standards and take measures for this purpose. The Coastal states are empowered to enforce their national standards and anti-pollution measures within their territorial sea and granted jurisdiction for the protection and preservation of the marine environment of its EEZs. Such jurisdiction allows coastal states to control, prevent, and reduce marine pollution from dumping, land-based sources, or seabed activities subject to national jurisdiction, or from or through the atmosphere.

*376.* According to Article 1 UNCLOS, maritime pollution is relevant not just when it is likely to cause harm to living resources and marine life, but also where it likely has a range of other effects, such as hazards to human health, hindrance to marine activities, including fishing and other legitimate uses of the sea, impairment of quality for use of seawater, and reduction of amenities. International law does not stipulate an obligation for states to cooperate, which must be provided for specifically in treaty or customary law. So far, this is the case only for trans-boundary pollution resulting from hazardous activity. However, states do cooperate in that matter, and a number of multilateral environmental treaties, both regional and universal have been concluded.

# Part VIII. Forest, Wild Life, and Fisheries

## Chapter 1. Forests, Plants, and Ecosystem

*377.* The importance of forests for the well-being of people and the planet is well known. Some 1.6 billion people worldwide depend directly on forests for food, shelter, energy, medicines and income. Apart from this, a vast majority of terrestrial biodiversity is found in the forests. Together, they contain more than 60,000 different tree species and provide habitats for 80% of amphibian species, 75% of bird species and 68% of mammal species. About 60% of all vascular plants are found in tropical forests. Mangroves provide breeding grounds and nurseries for numerous species of fish and shellfish and help trap sediments. The conservation of the majority of the world's biodiversity is thus dependent on the way in which interaction and use are made of the world's forests. Forests provide clean air and fresh water and help to avert desertification. They regulate in a big way world climate, absorbing one-third of global GHG emissions.

### §1. The United Nations Strategic Plan for Forests 2017–2030

*378.* The United Nations Strategic Plan for Forests 2017–2030 (UNSPF) is a blueprint and outlines a vision for a future where all types of forests and trees are sustainably managed. This plan was created to promote sustainable forest management (SFM) and enhance the contribution of forests and trees to the 2030 Agenda for Sustainable Development. At the heart of the Strategic Plan are six Global Forest Goals and twenty-six associated targets which are voluntary and universal. The goals fully encompass and build on the foundation of the four Global Objectives on Forests of the United Nations Forest Instrument (UNFI) adopted by the UNGA in 2007. The historic agreement on the UNSPF was forged at a special session of the United Nations Forum on Forests (UNFF) in January 2017 and subsequently adopted by the UNGA, through its Resolution 71/285 in April 2017. The Strategic Plan set out, for the first time, a shared U.N. vision and mission on the world's forests.

*379.* The plan recognizes that in order to create a world in which forests could provide, *inter alia*, environmental benefits for present and future generations, more forests will be needed. Accordingly, the first Global Forest Goal provides for increasing forest area by 3% by 2030. It is also well recognized that achieving the

Global Forest Goals and targets by 2030 will require action by all actors at all levels. Given the cross-sectoral nature of forests, the plan highlights the need for strengthened cooperation, coordination, coherence and synergies as being essential in enhancing the contribution of forests to sustainable development.

## §2. International Conventions and Forests

*380.* Many existing international treaties contain provisions that aim to regulate activities related to forests, but there is no exclusive global legal instrument in which forests are in focus. Further, there is also no international treaty in which all environmental, social, and economic aspects of forest ecosystems are included. International negotiations aimed at a global forest convention were initiated in 1990, proposed and endorsed by the G-7, the group of seven major industrialized states. At that time, it was thought that it would be feasible to conclude a forest convention in 1992, when the UNCED would be held in Rio de Janeiro, Brazil. But during the negotiations in Rio, it became apparent that the international community was far from reaching a consensus on the contents of a forest convention agreement. Instead, a "Non-Legally Binding Authoritative Statement of Principles for a Global Consensus on the Management, Conservation and Sustainable Development of all Types of Forests" (Forest Principles) was adopted.

*381.* The most important global conventions indirectly related to forests are the UNFCCC, the CBD and the United Nations Convention to Combat Desertification (UNCCD) in those Countries Experiencing Serious Drought and Desertification, particularly in Africa (UNCCD). Although all have forestry relevance, they all have in common the trait of taking into account only certain aspects, functions and roles of forests. Besides, there are many more agreements aimed at environmental conservation, including habitat protection and protection of particular species of fauna and flora at the regional level.

### I. United Nations Framework Convention on Climate Change

*382.* UNFCCC was adopted as a consequence of the worldwide concern over global warming. The ultimate objective of the convention is to limit human-induced disturbances to the global climate system by seeking to achieve a stable level of GHG in the atmosphere. In 1997, the COP adopted an additional legally binding commitment, the Kyoto Protocol, which sets out emission reduction targets and methods. However, the Kyoto Protocol does not include further operational details that will determine how these cuts are to be achieved and how countries' efforts are to be measured and assessed.

*383.* There is a close relationship between climate and forests. Forests act as reservoirs by storing carbon in biomass and soils and as carbon sinks when their area or productivity is increased, which results in greater uptake of atmospheric $CO_2$, the most important GHG. Various forestry practices have a significant role in helping to slow down the accumulation of $CO_2$ in the atmosphere. Conversely, forests are a source of GHG when biomass burns or decays. Some practices involved in plantation development, forest management and agroforestry, such as tilling and use of natural fertilizers, can release GHG.

## II. Kyoto Protocol and Forests

*384.* UNFCCC mentions forests only briefly, however, the Kyoto Protocol is more explicit. Article 2 states that industrialized parties shall "implement and/or further elaborate policies and measures ... such as ... promotion of sustainable forest management practices, afforestation and reforestation." Under the protocol, certain human-induced activities in the land-use, land-use change and forestry (LULUCF) sector that remove GHGs from the atmosphere, namely afforestation, reforestation and tackling deforestation, may be used by industrialized countries to offset their emission targets. Conversely, changes in these activities that deplete carbon sinks, such as deforestation, will be subtracted from the number of permitted emissions. Many uncertainties and complexities surround this subject, and there is a need for further definition. LULUCF proved to be one of the major breaking points at the COP in November 2000, when the lack of consensus necessitated that the session be resumed at a later date.

## III. Convention on Biological Diversity

*385.* CBD has three goals namely the conservation of biological diversity, the sustainable use of the components of biological diversity, and the fair and equitable sharing of benefits arising from the use of genetic resources. A large part of the world's terrestrial biological diversity is found in forests, and forest ecosystems are estimated to contain 70% of the world's plant and animal species. Since its adoption, CBD has expanded and include forests within its purview. In 1995, COP-2 adopted a statement on biological diversity and forests and stressed that forests have a crucial role in maintaining global biological diversity. In 1996, a Work Programme for Forest Biological Diversity was adopted by COP-3. The Work Programme focused on the research, cooperation, and development of technologies necessary for the conservation and sustainable use of forest biological diversity of all types of forests. In 1998, COP-4 decided to consider forests as one of the three priority themes for COP-6 in 2002. It also established an Ad Hoc Technical Expert Group on Forest Biological Diversity. This group has a mandate to provide advice on scientific research and development, to review available information on status, trends, and threats to forest biological diversity and to suggest actions for the conservation and sustainable use of forest biological diversity. It has had two meetings and has the potential to become an interesting forum for developing an inclusive forest biodiversity policy framework.

*386.* The COP of CBD is supported by a Subsidiary Body on Scientific, Technical and Technological Advice, which works on a wide variety of biological diversity-related concerns including topics such as forest fires and harvesting of non-timber forest resources. CBD has influenced the global dialogue on forests also through its leading role in support of recognition of the traditional forest-related knowledge of indigenous people and forest-dependent people in the Intergovernmental Panel on Forests and Intergovernmental Forum on Forests (IPF/IFF) process. CBD certainly includes articles on indigenous and traditional forest-related knowledge, but at the same time it also presents the risk for indigenous people to be seen as a "resource" for biological diversity, i.e., as people who can provide knowledge on components of biological diversity, rather than as people who hold legal, social, cultural and economic rights in relation to it. Another influential link with forests is provided by the GEF, which provides funding for projects under CBD that support activities related to biological diversity, including forest biological diversity. Furthermore, CBD established in 2000 the Global Taxonomy Initiative, also of relevance to forests.

## §3. UNCCD in Countries Experiencing Serious Drought and/or Desertification, Particularly in Africa

*387.* UNCCD aims at combating desertification, mitigating the effects of drought and contributing to sustainable development. This involves long-term strategies that focus on improved productivity of land and rehabilitation, conservation, and sustainable management of land and water resources, leading to improved living conditions for people. Protection and expansion of forests are important elements in UNCCD, since forests have significant ecological functions that mitigate effects of drought and prevent desertification. Strategies to deal with desertification are likely to mitigate forest loss as well, and vice versa. Intact forest ecosystems help stabilize the soil; consequently, deforestation fosters both desertification and land degradation. Deforestation has serious consequences in terms of water runoff, soil erosion, and loss of soil fertility. In addition to this ecological connection, the underlying socioeconomic conditions and causes of forest loss and desertification are very similar. Deforestation and other unsustainable forestry practices carried out by poor rural communities for economic, commercial or survival purposes have contributed to land degradation and loss of soil fertility in many DC. SFM is an important part of the corrective actions envisaged under UNCCD to tackle land degradation, promote sustainable agricultural and rural development, and reduce rural poverty. The significance of UNCCD for forests is potentially enormous, but the lack of implementation and compliance with the convention and persistent uncertainties regarding funding make it difficult for UNCCD to define its work program more precisely in regard to the inclusion of forests.

## §4. Ramsar Convention on Wetlands of International Importance

*388.* The objective of the Ramsar Convention is the conservation and wise use of wetlands through national action and international cooperation. More than a two thousand four hundred sites, totalling over 2.5 million square kilometres, are designated as wetlands of international importance. Some of these sites contain forest ecosystems, such as mangroves, although the exact number cannot be established, as forests as such are not identified under the convention.

Originally, the Ramsar Convention focused exclusively on preserving wetlands as waterfowl habitat, but it has developed extensively over time to embrace the broader implications of wetland destruction. Its COP has taken several decisions to acknowledge the importance of wetlands for their biological diversity and other ecological and environmental functions. More emphasis has been placed on the concept of sustainable development, including participation of local communities and indigenous peoples. Since 1999, the criteria for designating a wetland to be of international importance have included the following:

(1) it supports vulnerable, endangered or critically endangered species or threatened ecological communities;
(2) it supports populations of plant and/or animal species important for maintaining the biological diversity of a particular biogeographic region.

## §5. Convention for the Protection of the World Cultural and Natural Heritage (World Heritage Convention)

*389.* The World Heritage Convention (WHC) aims to establish a system of collective protection of cultural and natural heritage of outstanding universal value. States recognize their duty to ensure the protection, conservation and transmission to future generations of their cultural and natural heritage. Forests can be considered as natural heritage, defined as "natural sites or precisely delineated areas of outstanding universal value from the point of view of science, conservation or natural beauty" (Article 2). WHC establishes the World Heritage List containing world heritage sites. The Operational Guidelines of the convention, devised to guide in establishing the World Heritage List, represent a flexible mechanism to reflect new concepts. The latest revision (Intergovernmental Committee for the Protection of the World Cultural and Natural Heritage, 1999) requires that the natural heritage sites listed should "be outstanding examples representing significant on-going ecological and biological processes in the evolution and development of terrestrial … ecosystems and communities of plants and animals" or "contain the most important and significant natural habitats for in-situ conservation of biological diversity" (paragraph 44).

*390.* As of September 2023, a total of 1,199 world heritage sites (933 cultural, 227 natural, and 39 mixed cultural and natural properties) exist across 168 countries. With 59 selected areas, Italy is the country with the most sites; followed by China with 57, then France and Germany with 52 each.

## §6. Convention on International Trade in Endangered Species of Wild Fauna and Flora

### I. Protection of Wild Fauna and Flora

*391.* CITES aims at protecting certain endangered species of wild fauna and flora from overexploitation through international trade, via a system of import/export permits. The convention focuses exclusively on trade and is based on the view that the control of international markets will contribute to the preservation of endangered species. CITES operates by listing endangered species in one of its three appendices, which constitute different levels of control in international trade. Numerous forest animal species are included in the appendices, but at present only sixteen tree species which are used for timber have been listed. Listing of timber producing species of major commercial importance has become increasingly controversial in recent years, because some parties think this may have the potential to lead to the introduction of unfair trade restrictions. While listing in CITES appendices will help draw attention to the need to take action for better management and conservation of given species, it is clear that listing, as such, does not conserve species.

*392.* COP-10 of CITES recognized in 1997 "that commercial trade may be beneficial to the conservation of species and ecosystems when carried out at levels that are not detrimental to the survival of the species in question"; however, the COP also noted "that some timber species may be under threat because of detrimental levels of use and international trade." In 1994, CITES formed the Timber Working Group to study implementation problems resulting from the inclusion of timber species in CITES and to review the definition of terms and units used to describe parts and derivatives of timber trees in trade. CITES has also instituted a Mahogany Working Group and a Plants Committee.

### II. COVID-19 and Exploitation of Animals

*393.* The rumours that COVID-19 virus was born in a lab depicts the existing tensions between International and domestic law and policy. This may also be taken as an example of failure to engage meaningfully with environment. The shortcomings of international environmental law seem to have allowed the inception of the virus. Although there is continuing controversy surrounding the origins of COVID-19, the scientific evidence suggests that the virus was incepted via zoonotic transfer. This brings the question of man's relationship with the natural world and the environmental protections that are in place. International environmental law does not seem capable enough in instituting safeguards which can mitigate the spreading of viruses from animals to humans. Such safeguards are meant not only for the protection of human beings but also for the protection of animals. Thus, the relationship with animals and the manner in which they are exploited for economic gain become important.

*394.* The preamble of the CITES recognizes the irreplaceable nature of wild flora and fauna and acknowledges as well the growing value of wild fauna and flora from aesthetic, scientific, cultural and economic points of view. This recognition of the role of wild flora and fauna must be renewed as the world is witnessing the debilitating consequences of interfering with their natural environment. The co-relation between CITES and COVID-19 becomes apparent on considering the aim of the treaty in preventing illegal international trade which leads to habitat destruction removing necessary buffer zones between humans and wild fauna, thereby making it more likely that animal pathogens come into contact with people. Animal specimens traded illegally are also likely to be sold or bought from places where sanitary standards are being properly kept or enforced. It makes the spread of diseases more likely. Many emerging infectious diseases have originated in wild animals. Many of them were not considered illegally traded CITES-listed species. However, illegal wildlife trade flows will only make these episodes worse, by degrading or bringing people too close to animal habitats, and therefore contributing to the spread of diseases.

## §7. Vienna Convention for the Protection of the Ozone Layer (Vienna Convention)

*395.* Human-induced emissions of certain gases—particularly CFCs and halons—react with ozone and thus deplete the ozone layer, causing increased levels of ultraviolet rays which may cause harm to human health and the environment. Through the Vienna Convention, states make a commitment to protect the ozone layer from these destructive gases and to cooperate with each other in research so as to improve scientific understanding of the processes involved. The Vienna Convention is a framework agreement, without targets or timetables for action. The Montreal Protocol on Substances That Deplete the Ozone Layer was agreed in 1987 and has been amended four times since. Many states have not yet ratified these amendments. The protocol contains detailed international standards governing the production and consumption of ozone-depleting chemicals and aims to reduce and eventually eliminate human-induced emissions of ODS.

*396.* The convention establishes a framework for the adoption of measures to protect "human health and the environment against adverse effects … from human activities which modify … the ozone layer" (Article 2). The main relevance of the ozone regime for forests is the link between depletion of the ozone layer and the possible adverse effects this might have on forests (Article 1.2). For commercial forests, tree breeding and genetic engineering may be used to improve tolerance of ultraviolet-B (UV-B) radiation, but for unmanaged or natural forests these methods are not an option. While many forest tree species appear to be UV-B tolerant, there is some evidence that detrimental UV-B effects can slowly accumulate in trees from year to year (UNEP, 1998). While it can be argued that implementation of the ozone regime would be beneficial to forests, the ozone regime does not explicitly consider forests.

## §8. Convention Concerning Indigenous and Tribal Peoples in Independent Countries (ILO Convention No. 169)

*397.* The International Labor Organization (ILO) Convention No. 169, which may also be cited as the Indigenous and Tribal Peoples Convention, also aims to protect the social, economic, and cultural rights of indigenous peoples. Parties assume the responsibility for undertaking action to protect their rights, with the participation of the peoples concerned, and to guarantee respect for their integrity. Indigenous peoples are often closely associated with forests and forests provide habitat and are important to them for economic, social, and cultural reasons. Concerns about conserving and managing forests often coincide with concerns about the survival and integrity of the cultures and knowledge of indigenous peoples.

*398.* Relevant articles in the convention are to be found in the sections that consider land rights (Articles 13–19). Article 14 states that "the rights of ownership and possession of the peoples concerned over the lands which they traditionally occupy shall be recognized." Article 15 provides that the rights of people "to the natural resources pertaining to their lands shall be specially safeguarded," including the right "to participate in the use, management and conservation of these resources" including sharing of benefits and receiving "fair compensation" for damages. Other articles which are relevant include Article 2 giving governments the "responsibility for developing, with the participation of the peoples concerned, coordinated and systematic action to protect the rights of these peoples and to guarantee respect for their integrity"; Article 7, which declares that parties shall "take measures, in co-operation with the peoples concerned, to protect and preserve the environment of territories they inhabit." There is no specific focus within the framework of the ILO convention related to forests, although its implementation program includes activities such as ancestral domain management and environment and natural resource management. Although the convention has been ratified by only fourteen states, it certainly influences national policies and is considered an important instrument on indigenous people in international law.

## §9. International Tropical Timber Agreement

*399.* International Tropical Timber Agreement (ITTA) is a commodity agreement to facilitate the trade in tropical timber and to ensure exports from sustainable sources. Country membership in the International Tropical Timber Organization (ITTO), which administers ITTA, is restricted to states that are either producers or consumers of tropical timber. The agreement first came into force in 1985, but a renegotiated agreement entered into force in 1997. During the renegotiations, the positions of producer and consumer states were sometimes opposed: producers favored extending the scope to cover timber from all sources, in order to bring all forests under the same guidelines as agreed for tropical forests, while consumer countries held the view that broadening the convention to a global scope was beyond its mandate.

*400.* Besides promoting trade, ITTO also deals with environmental concerns and is a source of conflicting interests which hamper effective implementation of some objectives of ITTA. The ITTO Council consists of seventy-five members which account for about 80% of the world's tropical forests and 90% of the international trade in tropical timber. The votes in the council are divided equally between producing and consuming states. Voting share within each group is determined primarily by the respective states' share in the tropical timber trade, although voting share for producing countries also reflects their forest cover. Given this voting structure, ITTO is not necessarily well equipped to safeguard the environment, since those who benefit most from international trade and thus have the largest voting power are likely to be the least enthusiastic about environmental regulations that potentially restrict trade.[85] There has been general reluctance by ITTO producers to make a decision that could be viewed as a trade restriction, whether it involve incentives, labeling or limiting trade in endangered species (Humphreys, 1996).

*401.* The 59th session of the International Tropical Timber Council (ITTC) was convened in Pattaya, Thailand, from 13 to 17 November 2023. In this session, there was agreement to extend ITTA, 2006. Member countries supported the Secretariat in its efforts to position tropical timber in the context of international support for action on climate change and biodiversity loss. The ITTC, the governing body has taken steps toward a decision, by mid-2024, to extend its founding agreement up to 2029. This agreement allowed delegates to buy some time before negotiations toward a new ITTA. ITTO seeks to promote legal trade in tropical timber and encourage the use of wood derived from SFM.

*402.* The Council considered the new European Union Deforestation-Free Regulation (EUDR), which entered into force in 2023. In addition to the "decision to decide" by June 1, 2024 on extending the ITTA from 2006 to 2029, ITTC-59 endorsed projects for SFM and related objectives, adopted its budget and work programme for 2024–2025 with an annual budget of USD 7.1 million, and agreed to a four-year trial period allowing members in arrears to still submit project concept notes for possible funding.

## §10. Agreement Establishing the WTO

*403.* WTO forms the administrative and institutional framework of the revised 1994 GATT and related instruments. The GATT/WTO regime is intended to support and ensure the proper functioning of free trade, while taking into account the protection of the environment. The most important provision in this regard is Article XX of GATT, which includes exceptions to all trade rules for certain purposes such as the protection of animal or plant life and the conservation of exhaustible natural

85. David Hunter, James Salzman & Durwood Zaelke, *International Environmental Law and Policy*, Foundation Press (1998).

resources, subject to the condition that they will not be "applied in a manner which would constitute a means of arbitrary or unjustifiable discrimination ... or a disguised restriction on international trade."

*404.* The GATT/WTO regime is of relevance to forests since it regulates all trade, including timber and timber products, and since trade liberalization can have both positive and negative effects on the exploitation of natural resources. A range of provisions in WTO can accommodate the use of trade measures needed for environmental purposes, as are often included in other environmental treaties. For example, a ban on timber exports for conservation purposes could be consistent with Article XX. In 1998, an Environmental Database was established containing all environment-related notifications to WTO.

*405.* The establishment of WTO's CTE, in 1995, is an attempt to bring environmental and sustainable development issues more into the mainstream of WTO work, but the pace of progress on these issues to date has been rather slow. However, the committee has begun to discuss, or will discuss in the near future, several issues applicable to forests, such as eco-labeling, improved market access to forest products and services, community-based processing and marketing of wood and non-wood forest products, full cost internalization and its application to sustainable forest management, and certification of forest products.

*406.* Hundreds of environmental treaties have been concluded, especially during the past thirty years, on a wide variety of subjects. Yet these have not been negotiated in a systematic way, and coordination among them is lacking. As a result, there are gaps and overlaps in their coverage. Given the number of environmental conventions, there is a noticeable reluctance to negotiate any new treaties, as would be necessary to address the gaps. Instead, the magic of synergistic interaction is often invoked as the solution. Synergy is one of the buzzwords today in international environmental law. The notion is that improved coordination of the implementation of existing conventions would make it possible to cover yet uncharted areas like freshwater resources or river ecosystems. Enhanced harmonization would also resolve conflicts in areas covered by more than one legal instrument—such as conservation of specific species or ecosystems—but is mostly seen as an opportunity to streamline practical issues such as information management, reporting obligations and scientific research. The terms "Increased coordination," "avoidance of duplication," "fostering synergies," "holistic approach" represent the new way of thinking in international environmental law.

## §11. Amendment of Existing Conventions

*407.* There is need of amending existing conventions. For example, ITTA could be extended to include non-tropical timber trade. In practice, however, agreed multilateral instruments are often rather rigid; amendments are difficult to agree on, as they entail a form of renegotiation, which might disintegrate fragile balances within the context of a particular instrument. Furthermore, the focus of a convention is extremely difficult to change: UNFCCC will always consider forests as carbon reservoirs, and a more integrated approach cannot be expected.

## I. Non-legally Binding Instrument

*408.* A specific "under-regulated" function can be singled out and made the subject of an agreement, or of a non-legally binding instrument, which could be more politically convenient to participating states. Possible overlap with existing conventions would then be regulated on the basis of the 1969 Vienna Convention. A comprehensive agreement on forests could provide a way to consider forests holistically, as more than the sum of their functions. Such an agreement would have a unifying influence among the plethora of instruments and initiatives.

*409.* Functions of forests are dispersed over a number of separate international instruments. Some functions receive much more attention than others, and there is a lack of an integrated legal regime that views forests in a holistic way. The current reality is that there is no political will to start negotiations to come to a comprehensive multilateral forest agreement to fill in the gaps, although from a juridical perspective this would be possible and perhaps desirable. However, even the conclusion of a legally binding convention is no guarantee that the commitments will be carried out and will depend on political determination. The views of states are too divergent regarding the extent to which forests can be treated as a common concern of humankind—a global commons—as opposed to the realm of sovereign domain. At this stage, even if a global agreement could be reached, it would only be a marginal framework convention, to be substantiated at a later phase with a protocol, through years of difficult and costly negotiations.

## II. Ecosystem

*410.* An ecosystem consists of the biological community that occurs in some locale and the physical and chemical factors that make up its non-living or abiotic environment. The examples of ecosystems are a pond, a forest, an estuary, a grassland. The boundaries are not fixed in any objective way, although sometimes they seem obvious, as with the shoreline of a small pond.

*411.* The study of ecosystems consists of the study of certain processes that link the living, or biotic, components to the non-living, or abiotic, components. Energy transformations and biogeochemical cycling are the main processes that comprise the field of ecosystem ecology. The ecology is defined as the interactions of organisms with one another and with the environment in which they occur. We can study ecology at the level of the individual, the population, the community, and the ecosystem. Studies of individuals are concerned mostly about physiology, reproduction, development or behavior, and studies of populations usually focus on the habitat and resource needs of individual species, their group behaviors, population growth, and what limits their abundance or causes extinction. Studies of communities examine how populations of many species interact with one another, such as predators and their prey, or competitors that share common needs or resources. Rather than worrying mainly about particular species, one must focus on major functional aspects of the system. These functional aspects include the amount of energy that is produced by photosynthesis, energy or materials flow along the many steps in a food chain, or factors controlling the rate of decomposition of materials or the rate at which nutrients are recycled in the system.

*412*. Usually, biological communities include the "functional groupings." A functional group is a biological category composed of organisms that perform mostly the same kind of function in the system; for example, all the photosynthetic plants or primary producers form a functional group. Membership in the functional group does not depend very much on who the actual players (species) happen to be, but only on what function they perform in the ecosystem.

# Chapter 2. Wildlife Conservation

*413.* Each year, hundreds of millions of plants and animals are caught or harvested from the wild and then sold as food, pets, ornamental plants, leather, medicine, etc. While a great deal of this trade is legal and is not harming wild populations, a worryingly large proportion is illegal and threatens the survival of many endangered species. With overexploitation being the second-largest direct threat to many species after habitat loss, World Wide Fund for Nature (WWF) addresses illegal and unsustainable wildlife trade as a priority issue.

*414.* As per a study evaluating the conservation status of 71,000 animal species has shown a huge disparity between "winners" and "losers." Globally, 48% of species are decreasing, 49% remain stable, and just 3% are rising. Most losses are concentrated in the tropics.

## §1. Wildlife Trade

*415.* People selling or exchanging wild animal and plant resources is really indulging in wildlife trade. It can involve live animals and plants or all kinds of wild animal and plant products. Wildlife trade is easiest to track when it is from one country to another because it must be checked, and often recorded, at Customs checkpoints. People trade wildlife for cash or exchange it for other useful objects—for example, utensils in exchange for wild animal skins. Driving the trade is the end-consumer who has a need or desire for wildlife products, whether for food, construction or clothing.

*416.* The wildlife trade involves hundreds of millions of wild plants and animals from tens of thousands of species. It is estimated that global illegal wildlife trade is worth between USD 20 billion a year, making it one of the most profitable criminal enterprises. Wildlife crime has been linked to drug, human, and arms trafficking, as organized crime groups seek to exploit their established global transit networks. The risks are therefore not only to endangered species and the planet's biodiversity, but to the rule of law, to economies and, as highlighted by this crisis, to health. In February 2020, as a result of COVID-19, the Chinese government introduced emergency measures to limit the trade in wild animals for consumption. But since much of this activity is already illegal, it is unlikely that such a law would eliminate the practice, but rather drive it further underground. There are many voices calling for a permanent and effective ban on wild animal trade. The Financial Action Task Force (FATF) has announced the illegal wildlife trade as a key priority. Financial services institutions should be considering illegal wildlife trade as part of their Know Your Customer (KYC) procedures, and Financial Crime Compliance teams should become familiar with common red flags indicative of the activity. Companies in the global transportation sector need to also be mindful that their services could be misused by illicit actors and exploited through corruption and security loopholes to carry illegal wildlife products increased.

§2. Overexploitation

*417.* The wildlife trade can cause overexploitation to the point where the survival of a species hangs in the balance. Historically, such overexploitation has caused extinctions of severely threatened species and, as human populations have expanded, demand for wildlife has only increased. This has been the case for tigers, rhinoceroses, elephants, and others, but many other species are also affected. Wildlife is vital to the lives of a high proportion of the world's population, often the poorest. Some rural households depend on local wild animals for their meat protein and on local trees for fuel, and both wild animals and plants provide components of traditional medicines used by the majority of people in the world. While many people in developed countries are cushioned from any effects caused by a reduced supply of a particular household item, many people in the developing world depend entirely on the continued availability of local wildlife resources.

*418.* In addition to the impact on human livelihoods caused by the over-harvesting of animals and plants, is the harm caused by overexploitation of species to the living planet in a wider way. Overfishing not only affects individual fishing communities and threatens certain fish species but also causes imbalances in the whole marine system. As human life depends on the existence of a functioning planet Earth, careful and thoughtful use of wildlife species and their habitats is required to avoid not only extinctions but also serious disturbances to the complex web of life.

*419.* Particular problems are associated with illegal wildlife trade, which is usually driven by a demand for rare, protected species which need to be smuggled and/or by a desire to avoid paying duties. In illegal wildlife trade, some species involved are highly endangered, conditions of transport for live animals are likely to be worse, and wildlife is more likely to have been obtained in an environmentally damaging way. The existence of illegal trade is also worrying because it undermines countries' efforts to protect their natural resources.

*420.* Wildlife trade also causes indirect harm through introducing invasive species which then prey on, or compete with, native species. Invasive species are as big a threat to the balance of nature as the direct overexploitation by humans of some species. Many invasive species have been purposely introduced by wildlife traders; examples include the American Mink, the Red-eared Terrapin, and countless plant species. Incidental killing of nontarget species, such as dolphins and seabirds, when they are caught in fishing gear is another menace. It is estimated that over a quarter of the global marine fisheries catch is incidental, unwanted, and discarded. Incidental killing of animals also happens on land when crude traps are set (e.g., for musk deer). These cause damage and death to a variety of animals besides the intended ones.

§3. Geographical Trouble Spots and Role of WWF

*421.* There are certain places in the world where wildlife trade is particularly threatening or where targeted action would be particularly worthwhile. These places are sometimes called "wildlife trade hotspots" and include, for example, China's international borders and the eastern borders of the EU. While these hotspots are trouble areas at present, they also offer opportunities for great conservation success, if action and funds are well focused. There are three key areas where WWF and Wildlife Trade Monitoring Network (TRAFFIC) work to address the threat of the illegal wildlife trade. WWF provides technical and scientific advice to the CITES. WWF and TRAFFIC carry out research on illegal wildlife trade routes, the effects of wildlife trade on particular species, and on deficiencies in wildlife trade laws—information which is essential for CITES members to keep abreast of new trends and react accordingly. This research is used to create new plans for dealing with the illegal wildlife trade and also helps WWF and TRAFFIC promote the inclusion of new species in the CITES appendices or resolutions.

§4. Enforcing Legislation

*422.* It is one thing to ban or limit trade in a particular species, but another to effectively enforce this particularly in DC where equipment, training, and funds for enforcement are often lacking. In addition, many countries still lack strict national legislation and/or appropriate penalties for illegal wildlife trade. To address this challenge, WWF helps countries comply with CITES regulations by helping to develop programs, create regulations, run workshops, assist enforcement efforts, and fund anti-poaching brigades.

§5. Public Education

*423.* One of the most powerful tools of all for addressing illegal and unsustainable wildlife trade is to persuade consumers to make informed choices when buying wildlife-based products. This includes not just the people buying the end product, but also shopkeepers, suppliers, and manufacturers. WWF actively discourages the purchase of certain wildlife goods and encourages the production and purchase of sustainable wildlife goods such as those certified by the Marine Stewardship Council (MSC) and Forest Stewardship Council (FSC). WWF also works hand in hand with many communities around the world, providing practical help to overcome poverty and helping them use their local wildlife in a sustainable way.

§6. Wildlife Crime Control

*424.* Whether a shipment is legal or not can come down to distinguishing species, and there is no easier way to evade the system than to simply claim a protected species is a non-protected lookalike. For this reason, the enhancement of forensic capacity is not only an essential part of law enforcement, but it is at the heart of wildlife protection and wildlife crime control. A wide range of assistance, from the international use of specialized labs to the provision of reference texts and selected samples, can be provided to countries to strengthen response to these crimes. Not every country encounters enough wildlife crime to justify a specialized lab, and universal provision of reference samples would be a major task. In some parts of the world, regional labs may make more sense. For some species, a single international facility could cover the forensic needs of global enforcement. Once wildlife contraband is seized, the effective and universal implementation of international standards is essentially required for the storage, stockpiling, and disposal of protected wildlife products and contraband.

## I. Large-Scale Shipment

*425.* At present, the logistic problems associated with disposing of large illegal wildlife shipments have provided formidable disincentives to enforcement. For example, multi-container loads of rosewood have recently been seized in Hong Kong, China, Singapore, and Sri Lanka. Without the facility to store or dispose of this material, customs authorities will have little capacity to seize more. It is crucial that the provisions provided for in CITES Resolutions are drawn upon to the fullest extent possible to address the challenges that are often associated with large-scale seizures, including by making legislative provision to require the guilty importer or the carrier, or both, to bear related costs. Track and trace technology has been successfully applied to wild source industries like fishing. German buyers of fresh fish, for example, have access to a bar code that allows them to identify exactly where, when, how, and by whom their catch was landed. Similar approaches to other wildlife products could be adopted as industry standards, limiting the scope for the introduction of illegally sourced products. Trade bodies could self-police, since flouting industry standards could give an unfair advantage to competitors. Noncompliant merchandise would be immediately suspect and avoided by legitimate wholesalers, retailers, and consumers.

## II. Law Enforcement Operational Capacity

*426.* The enhancement of law enforcement operational capacity is a very important aspect, and there are gaps in it. Legislation can go some way toward enhancing the profile of wildlife crime, but law enforcement prioritization is the decisive factor. National agencies in source, transit, and destination countries will only prosecute wildlife crime if they have the tools to do so, and this is one area where the international community can assist. Since it appears that the bulk of international wildlife crime enforcement is conducted by customs agents, so they must be enabled and motivated to detect and prevent wildlife trafficking. Although value-intensive items like rhino horn may be air couriered, most volume consignments of illegal wildlife are transported in shipping containers.

## III. Species Identification

*427.* Another difficulty faced in international wildlife law enforcement is species identification. Since the existing controls are species-specific, made from the most threatened species. But the threatened species lists in question are generally limited to domestic species, so there is nothing regulating the possession, use, or sale of the most threatened wildlife products from other parts of the world. Some countries do individually add some foreign wildlife species to their domestic protection lists, such as elephant ivory or rhino horn, on an ad hoc basis. Since protected species lists are dynamic, simply compiling them would seem to pose an insurmountable administrative barrier to extending local protections to foreign species.

*428.* Appendix I of CITES does provide an internationally agreed list of species in need of the highest protection. The CITES Convention is designed to regulate international trade, and it has no role in domestic markets. In theory, CITES parties could detain those in possession of questionable Appendix I products, but, in most, the burden would remain on the state to demonstrate these products were imported illegally. It is possible, however, to reverse the onus, and to require those in possession of Appendix I species to maintain documented proof of their legality through, for example, retention of a copy of the import documentation, or registration in a national database. Even with these protections in place, there will remain wildlife crimes that CITES does not directly address. Poaching, or the illegal taking of wildlife, generally takes place in a single country, and the damage is done whether or not the resulting product is exported.

## IV. Prevention of Poaching

*429.* Poaching often takes place in remote areas of some of the poorest countries in the world, countries with limited capacity to protect wildlife. The international community can also assist with coordinated operations against poachers and their buyers if they extend across borders. Another point of insertion is to influence the practices of those industries making use of wildlife products. Protecting and maintaining wildlife reserves can be an expensive project for DC. Simply setting aside the range has its opportunity costs, as the land could be used to improve the lives of growing populations. International bodies concerned with the preservation of these species should consider an expanded role in helping to maintain them. Finally, corruption plays an important role in wildlife crime. Because officials can transform contraband into legal product with a single piece of documentation, these documents have a large cash value.

*430.* Officials authorizing imports and exports can similarly assure smooth passage, and once inside the destination market, most wildlife products can be sold without question. The officials who control these gateways bear a tremendous responsibility and are therefore subject to considerable scrutiny. The use of audit and oversight techniques should be strengthened. This report has shown that the markets for illegal wildlife are typically transcontinental, and consequently that addressing them is an inherently international affair. Without cooperation, criminals that know no boundaries can easily out-maneuver national law enforcement. Through research, information sharing, joint operations, legal coordination, and technical assistance, the international community can cooperate to protect threatened species, species that can never be replaced.

## Chapter 3. Fisheries

*431.* Developments in the area of fish and fisheries management and law were fostered by the entry into force of the 1995 U.N. FAO Code of Conduct for Responsible Fisheries and the 1995 U.N. Agreement on Straddling Fish Stocks and Highly Migratory Fish Stocks. The U.N. agreement was the first global fisheries agreement requiring a precautionary approach, to be applied to fisheries conservation, management, and exploitation measures. The precautionary approach is listed as one of the general principles applied by states to ensure the achievement of long-term conservation and sustainable use of straddling and highly migratory fish stocks (Article 5(e)). The scope of the principle is not restricted to stocks targeted in the fisheries but encompasses all living marine resources and the marine environment (Article 6(1)). States are subsequently required to take into account the effects on other species of the ecosystem, when adopting conservation measures for the target stocks and could be required to establish measures specially directed at protecting other species or their habitats. The obligation to endorse a precautionary approach in Article 6(2) of the 1995 U.N. Agreement on Straddling Fish Stocks and Highly Migratory Fish Stocks reads as follows: "States shall be more cautious when information is uncertain, unreliable or inadequate."

*432.* Marine fisheries management is intrinsically uncertain arising out from individual fish stocks being harvested, other affected species, and the likely impacts of fishing on the ecosystem of which the species form part. Given the risk of overfishing and the eventual collapse of fish stocks, an explicit precautionary approach encapsulated in both international agreements and national legislations is strongly needed.

*433.* It is not only scientific information about the fish stock in question that is relevant, but states are also to take into account uncertainties relating to environmental and socioeconomic conditions (Article 6(3) (c)). It is important to stress that in contrast to other international instruments, the enactment of precautionary measures is not subject to specific thresholds, such as the threat of serious or irreversible damage. Hence, that agreement signals a significant shift in the burden of proof by creating a presumption in favor of conservation. Therefore, it mirrors a major change in the traditional approach to fisheries management, which has tended to react to management problems only after they reach a crisis level.

*434.* With respect to international jurisdictions, the ITLOS order of August 27, 1999 in the *Southern Bluefin Tuna* cases seems to view the precautionary principle in a more favorable light than decisions by other international courts such as the ICJ or the ECHR. In a case opposing Australia and New Zealand on the one hand and Japan on the other concerning an experimental fishing program for southern bluefin tuna being carried out by the Japanese authorities, ITLOS had stressed the need to carry out a precautionary policy. Although there was scientific uncertainty regarding the conservation measures to be taken, ITLOS held that the principles of prevention and precaution in international law, the parties should "act with prudence and caution to ensure that effective conservation measures are taken to prevent serious harm to the stock of southern bluefin tuna."[86] Further, ITLOS required a risk of "serious harm," not of irreversible damage, to southern bluefin tuna stocks in order to take provisional measures to avert their further deterioration. However, ITLOS avoided bringing further clarification as to the meaning and the status of the principle.

86. *Southern Bluefin Tuna* Cases, 1999.

# Part IX. Soil Erosion, Waste Management

## Chapter 1. Soil Erosion and Land Degradation

*435.* Soil is the earth's fragile skin that anchors all life on earth. It is comprised of countless species that create a dynamic and complex ecosystem and is among the most precious resources to humans. Increased demand for agriculture commodities generates incentives to convert forests and grasslands to farm fields and pastures. The transition to agriculture from natural vegetation often cannot hold onto the soil, and many of these plants, such as coffee, cotton, palm oil, soybean, and wheat, can actually increase soil erosion beyond the soil's ability to maintain itself. Half of the topsoil on the planet has been lost in the last 150 years. In addition to erosion, soil quality is affected by other aspects of agriculture. These impacts include compaction, loss of soil structure, nutrient degradation, and soil salinity. These are very real and at times severe issues.

*436.* Agenda 21 (UNCED, 1992, Chapter 12) emphasizes land degradation through desertification, and the international community, particularly through U.N. organizations, has launched several activities to address it. Other aspects of land degradation receive only a mention in Agenda 21 and are briefly considered in Chapter 10 under the general heading, "Integrated Approach to the Planning and Management of Land Resources." In this sense, the problem of land degradation has been diluted and as such has not received global attention. Though the stated objective in Agenda 21 is, "to strengthen regional and global systematic observation networks linked to the development of national systems for the observation of land degradation and desertification caused both by climate fluctuations and by human impact, and to identify priority areas for action," however the soil science community require mobilization to develop a proactive program.

### §1. Soil Erosion

*437.* The effects of soil erosion go beyond the loss of fertile land. It has led to increased pollution and sedimentation in streams and rivers, clogging these waterways and causing declines in fish and other species. And degraded lands are also often less able to hold onto water, which can worsen flooding. Sustainable land use can help to reduce the impacts of agriculture and livestock, preventing soil degradation and erosion and the loss of valuable land to desertification. The health of soil is a primary concern to farmers and the global community whose livelihoods depend on well-managed agriculture that starts with the dirt beneath our feet. While there are many challenges to maintaining healthy soil, there are also solutions and a dedicated group of people, including WWF, who work to innovate and maintain the fragile skin from which biodiversity springs.

## §2. Land Degradation

*438.* Land degradation, a decline in land quality caused by human activities, has been a major global issue during the twentieth century and perhaps will remain high on the international agenda in the twenty-first century. There are various terms used to state the process of land degradation like soil degradation, land degradation, and desertification. While there is a clear distinction between "soil" and "land" (the term "land" refers to an ecosystem comprising land, landscape, terrain, vegetation, water, climate), there is no clear distinction between the terms "land degradation" and "desertification." Desertification refers to land degradation in arid, semi-arid, and sub-humid areas due to anthropic activities.[87] Many researchers argue that this definition of desertification is too narrow because severe land degradation resulting from anthropic activities can also occur in the temperate humid regions and the humid tropics. The term "degradation" or "desertification" refers to irreversible decline in the "biological potential" of the land which in turn depends on many interacting factors.

*439.* The importance of land degradation among global issues is enhanced because of its impact on world food security and quality of the environment. High population density is not necessarily related to land degradation; it is how a population uses the land that determines the extent of degradation. People can be a major asset in reversing a trend toward degradation. However, they need to be healthy and politically and economically motivated to care for the land, as subsistence agriculture, poverty, and illiteracy can be important causes of land and environmental degradation. The soils are an ecologically important component of the environment, the availability of research and development funds does not match their significance in terms of the cost to society if soils become degraded. The perception that enough is already known about soils, so that generalizations can be made for all soils, is incorrect. There is also a failure to recognize that agriculture is one of the major "stressors" of the environment (Virmani et al., 1994), particularly from a soil degradation point of view.[88] If these attitudes prevail, major catastrophes in the future become more probable.

*440.* The soil is virtually a non-renewable resource and society has an obligation to protect soil, conserve it, or even enhance its quality for future generations. The role of society in sustaining agriculture can be demonstrated, and conversely,

87. M.K. Darkoh, *The Deterioration of the Eenvironment in Africa's Drylands and River Basins* (1995) and UNEP, *Good News in the Fight Against Desertification*, Desertification Control Bulletin (1993).
88. Beinroth et. Al., *Land stresses in Agroecosystems*, Stressed Ecosystem and Sustainable Agriculture, Oxford and IBH (1994).

the role of soil in sustaining society. Land degradation results from mismanagement of land and thus deals with two interlocking systems namely the natural ecosystem and the human social system. Interactions between the two systems determine the success or failure of resource management programs. Land degradation is as much a socioeconomic problem as it is a biophysical problem. Land degradation and economic growth or lack of it are linked to people living in the lower part of the poverty spiral who are in a weak position to provide the stewardship necessary to sustain the resource base. Implementation of mitigation research to manage land degradation can only succeed if land users have control and commitment to maintain the quality of the resources. The land degradation caused by agriculture can be minimized and made compatible with the environment. Land use must match land quality for which appropriate national policies are to be implemented to ensure this occurs to reduce land degradation.

## I. Loss of Productivity

*441.* Land degradation can be considered in terms of the loss of actual or potential productivity or utility as a result of natural or anthropic factors; it is the decline in land quality or reduction in its productivity. In the context of productivity, land degradation results from a mismatch between land quality and land use (Beinroth et al., 1994). Mechanisms that initiate land degradation include physical, chemical, and biological processes.[89] Important among physical processes are a decline in soil structure leading to crusting, compaction, erosion, desertification, environmental pollution, and unsustainable use of natural resources. Significant chemical processes include acidification, leaching, salinization, and fertility depletion. Biological processes include reduction in total and biomass carbon and decline in land biodiversity. The latter comprises important concerns related to eutrophication of surface water, contamination of groundwater, and emissions of trace gases ($CO_2$, $CH_4$, $N_2O$, $NO_x$) from terrestrial/aquatic ecosystems to the atmosphere. Soil structure is the important property that affects all three degradative processes. Thus, land degradation is a biophysical process driven by socioeconomic and political causes.

*442.* Land degradation has an adverse impact on agronomic productivity, the environment, and its effect on food security and the quality of life. Productivity impacts of land degradation are due to a decline in land quality on site where degradation occurs (e.g., erosion) and off-site where sediments are deposited. However, the on-site impacts of land degradation on productivity are easily masked due to use of additional inputs and adoption of improved technology. The relative magnitude of economic losses due to productivity decline versus environmental deterioration also has created a concern. Desertification and land degradation are gradually reducing the productivity of land and the ability of communities to sustain livelihoods.

89. R. Lal, *Tillage Effects on Soil Degradation, Soil Resilience, Soil Quality Ad Sustainability*, Soil Tillage Research (1994).

*443.* The UNCCD pledged to reach land degradation neutrality (LDN) targets by 2030 as a part of the Convention's LDN Strategy. Degraded land is a threat multiplier for communities, as it slowly reduces people's ability to use their land and limits their access to resources. Estimates suggest that if the problem is not addressed, land degradation and desertification will affect 3.2 billion people by 2050. As many as 700 million people in the most affected regions could be left with little option but to migrate by 2050. DC are disproportionately affected by land degradation, with 72% of the world's affected land located in these regions. It is estimated that 1.2 billion people in DC are exposed to climate stress trapping them on degraded agricultural land and excluded them from sustained economic development. The current global food system contributes roughly 25%–30% of all GHG emissions. Climate change, and the extreme weather conditions that are expected to accompany it, will affect all facets of food security by reducing production in many parts of the world, increasing prices and disrupting supply chains. More than 75% of Earth's land area is already degraded, according to the European Commission's World Atlas of Desertification, and more than 90% could become degraded by 2050. The commission's Joint Research Centre found that a total area half of the size of the EU (4.18 million sq.km) is degraded annually, with Africa and Asia being the most affected.

*444.* Factors of land degradation are the biophysical processes and attributes that determine the kind of degradation processes, e.g., erosion, salinization. These include land quality (Eswaran et al., 2000) as affected by its intrinsic properties of climate, terrain and landscape position, climax vegetation, and biodiversity, especially soil biodiversity. Causes of land degradation are the agents that determine the rate of degradation. These are biophysical, socioeconomic, and political forces that influence the effectiveness of processes and factors of land degradation.

## II. Land Sensitive to Degradation

*445.* Depending on inherent characteristics and the climate, lands vary from highly resistant, or stable, to vulnerable and extremely sensitive to degradation. Fragility, extreme sensitivity to degradation processes, may refer to the whole land, a degradation process (e.g., erosion) or a property (e.g., soil structure). Stable or resistant lands do not necessarily resist change. They are in a stable, steady-state condition with the new environment. Under stress, fragile lands degrade to a new steady state, and the altered state is unfavorable to plant growth and less capable of performing environmental regulatory functions.

## III. Economic Impact of Land Degradation

*446.* The soil degradation increases the chance of flooding, as soils that have lost organic matter cannot absorb and retain substantial amounts of water and there is nutrient depletion. A large chunk of farmland is lost due to salinization, mostly caused by the overuse of irrigation in very hot regions. And because degraded soils cannot retain moisture to the same degree as soils rich in organic matter, they are also vulnerable to droughts.

*447.* As per one study, the global annual cost of salt-induced land degradation in irrigated areas is estimated to be EU € 21.3 billion (US$ 27.3 billion) related to lost crop production. The information collected from 118 countries covering 85% of global land area shows that more than 424 million hectares of topsoil and 833 million hectares of subsoil are salt-affected. Thirty crop species provide 90% of food, most of which display severe yield losses under moderate salinity. Irrigating agriculture with saline water will decrease the yield with around 17.3% compared to freshwater irrigation. Estimates predict that 50% of all arable land will become impacted by salinity by 2050. (2023 Wageningen University & Research, https://edepot.wur.nl/632896)

*448.* It is in the context of these global economic and environmental impacts of land degradation, and numerous functions of value to humans that land degradation, desertification, and resilience concepts are relevant.[90] They are also important in developing technologies for reversing land degradation trends and mitigating the greenhouse effect through land and ecosystem restoration. As land resources are essentially non-renewable, it is necessary to adopt a positive approach to sustainable management of these finite resources.

## IV. Land Degradation Processes

*449.* Different processes of land degradation also confound the available statistics on soil and/or land degradation. Principal processes of land degradation include erosion by water and wind, chemical degradation (comprising acidification, salinization, leaching, etc.), and physical degradation (comprising crusting, compaction, hard-setting, etc.). Some lands or landscape units are affected by more than one process, of water and wind erosion, salinization, and crusting or compaction. Unless a clear distinction is made, there is a considerable chance of overlap and double accounting.

## V. Assessment of Land Degradation

*450.* Global assessment of land degradation is not an easy task, and a wide range of methods are used.[91] Therefore, data generated by different methods are not comparable. Further, most statistics refer to the risks of degradation or desertification (based on climatic factors and land use) rather than the actual (present) state of the

90. H. Eswaran, E. Van Den Berg & P. Reich P, *Organic Carbon in soils of the World*, Soil Science Society Am. Journal 192–194 (1993).
91. R. Lal, *Residue Management Conservation Tillage and Soil Restoration for Mitigating Greenhouse Effect by CO $_2$ enrichment*, Soil Tillage Research (1997).

land. The actual degradation may not occur because of judicious land use and advances in land management technologies. Comparison of these data on different estimates shows wide variations because of different methods and criteria used and highlights the importance of developing uniform criteria and standardizing methods of assessment of land degradation.

## §3. Assessing Impact of Land Degradation

*451.* The criteria for designating different classes of land degradation are generally based on land properties. Assessing the productivity effects of land degradation is a challenging task (Lal, 1998). Difficulties in obtaining global estimates of the impact of land degradation on productivity in turn created problems. The data from China show that despite significant differences in cumulative soil loss and water runoff, there were no differences in corn yield. Similar inferences can be drawn with regard to the impact of cumulative soil erosion on the yield of rice in Thailand.

## §4. Desertification

*452.* In 1994, the U.N. established the UNCCD as the sole legally binding international agreement linking environment and development to sustainable land management. The Convention was a response to a call at the U.N. Earth Summit in Rio de Janeiro in 1992 to hold negotiations for an international legal agreement on desertification. The UNCCD set out a definition of desertification in a treaty adopted by parties in 1994. It states that desertification means "land degradation in arid, semi-arid and dry sub-humid areas resulting from various factors, including climatic variations and human activities." The direct causes of desertification can be broadly divided between those relating to how the land is—or is not—managed and those relating to climate change. The former includes factors such as deforestation, overgrazing of livestock, over-cultivation of crops and inappropriate irrigation; the latter includes natural fluctuations in climate and global warming as a result of human-caused GHG emissions.

*453.* A third of the world's land surface is threatened by desertification. Over 4 million square kilometers of land is being degraded every year. Around 120,000 square kilometers are turned into actual desert. The UNCCD 2018–2030 Strategic Framework is a comprehensive global commitment to achieve LDN in order to restore the productivity of vast expanses of degraded land, improve the livelihoods of more than 1.3 billion people, and reduce the impacts of drought on vulnerable populations to build a future that avoids, minimizes, and reverses desertification/ land degradation and mitigates the effects of drought in affected areas at all levels to achieve a land degradation-neutral world consistent with the 2030 Agenda for Sustainable Development.

# Chapter 2. Waste Management

*454.* Waste management is the collection, transportation, disposal or recycling and monitoring of waste. This term is assigned to waste material that is produced through human activity and is managed to avoid its adverse effect on human health and environment. Most of the time, waste is managed to get resources from it which includes all forms of matter, i.e., gaseous, liquid, solid and radioactive matter. The methods for the management of waste may differ for developed and developing nations. For urban and rural populations, industrial and residential areas it does differ as well. The management of waste in metropolitan and rural areas is a general responsibility of the local government.

## §1. Methods for Dumping off Waste

*455.* The main methods of dumping off wastes are landfill, incineration, recycling, biological reprocessing, combustion, etc., which are described below.

### I. Landfill

*456.* Landfill involves burying off the waste and this is the most common and widely practiced method for the disposal of waste around the globe. These landfills are generally conventional with deserted and vacant locations around the cities. In case, landfills or borrow pits are designed carefully, they can serve as economical and quite sanitized methods for waste dumping. However, not much effectively designed and older landfills can cost a big amount to the government not just in terms of money but may create environmental and health issues. The poorly designed landfill's common problems are wind-blown debris and generation of liquid. Landfills can also cause production of gas, which may be hazardous. This gas can be a reason for production of odor, killing surface vegetation and greenhouse effects.

The characteristic, which is a must for an up-to-date landfill, is inclusion of clay or leachate lining. The waste that is deposited is generally compressed for increasing the density and stability, and later it is covered to have it prevented from vermin. One thing, which in addition to modern landfills, is the "gas extraction system" installation. This system is included to have the gas extracted from the borrow pit and used for various purposes.

### II. Incineration

*457.* This is the dumping off method, which involves combustion of waste materials. This sort of dumping off waste materials through incineration and temperature is known as "thermal treatment." This method is utilized to convert waste materials into gas, heat, ash and steam. Incineration is conducted on both individual and industrial scale. This method is used for disposing off all sorts of matters. This is the most practiced method for disposing off perilous material. This, however, is the conflict-ridden method for it causes the emission of perilous gases. Incineration is a common practice in Japan because of scarcity of land, which facilitates by not requiring landfill for waste dumping. Two widely used terms, which are facilitating burning of waste material in furnace and boiler for generation of heat, electricity, and steam, are Waste-to-Energy (WtE) and Energy-from-Waste (EfW). The burning procedure in this method for waste disposal is never perfect, so fear for gas pollutants is mounting. Special concerns have been focused on some extremely importunate organics as dioxins. These organic products are created with the incinerator, and they are causations for serious consequences affecting environment.

### III. Recycling

*458.* Products like PVC, LDEP, PP, and PS are recyclable though they are not collected for recycling. The material, which is composed of a single type, is recyclables and is much easy to work with. However, complex products are difficult to treat and so are complex for recycling.

### IV. Biological Reprocessing

*459.* Waste materials, which come in organic nature are treated through biological reprocessing. The waste materials with organic nature are plant, food and paper products. This reprocessing or recycling of organic matter is put to biological decomposition which later if recycled is used in the form of mulch or compost for landscaping and agricultural purposes. Additionally, the waste gas, which is collected from the process, is used for the production of electricity. The goal behind biological reprocessing is to control and speed up the natural decomposition of organic matter.

A number of composting techniques and methods for digestion are employed depending upon the requirement as if digestion is required for household heaps or industrial materials. There are diverse methods for biological reprocessing like anaerobic and aerobic techniques.

## §2. Recovery of Energy by Combustion

*460.* Waste materials can be combusted for the generation of energy as fuel or other methods, indirect combustion can also be adopted for energy generation. Thermal treatment for recycling purpose included burning of waste for the generation of energy used for household purpose, i.e., cooking and heating while the energy from recycling can also be produced at industrial level from boilers. Among thermal treatments, there are two related kinds i.e., Pyrolysis and gasification. In these methods, materials are heated with little supply of oxygen at high temperature. This process is conducted in sealed vessels with high pressure. In Pyrolysis, the solid is converted into liquid state and liquid is converted into gas. These products of treatment can then be used for the production of energy. The residue that is left behind is generally known as "char," which is further treated for the production of more useable products. In Gasification, the material to be treated is directly converted into synthetic gas (Syn Gas) which has hydrogen and $CO_2$ as its components.

## §3. Reduction and Avoidance Methods

*461.* Another method for the management of the waste material is the avoidance for it being created, and this method is generally named "waste reduction." The avoidance of waste production includes using the second-hand product and repairing the products in place of buying new things. Products are designed for refilling and reusing. Cutting down use of disposable things and producing products that are more complex.

## §4. Waste Handling and Transportation

*462.* Collection of waste material varies from place to place and country to country. Domestic waste collection management works under the supervision of local government or by some private waste management company. Some areas, which are less populated or not much developed, have ceremonial systems for collection of waste. For waste disposal and collection, Curbside collection method, has been adopted in Australia. Almost every residency is endowed with three waste disposal bins, for recyclables, general waste and garden materials. The local municipality provides these bins; however, some of the houses have a compost bin, which is not provided by the municipality. The municipality, for encouraging recycling does provide larger bins for recyclables other than gardening and general waste. The waste which is produced by Municipal, commercial and constructional institutions or bodies is dumped at landfills while recyclables are recycled. Landfills produce gas, which is used for burning as fuel for electricity generation.

*463.* In European countries and some other locations around the globe, waste is collected through a system known as Enavc. This system involves conveying garbage through underground vacuum system. In urban locations in Canada, Curbside collection system is mostly used. Rural areas have their waste disposed by moving it to transfer stations. All collected waste is then disposed off at landfills. Waste management needs education and awareness for global preservation. A declaration known as the "Talloires Declaration" is concerned about the ever-increasing environmental pollution and diminution of natural resources. Education on waste management and pollution is very critical to the perseverance of global health and security of mankind. A number of institutions are working for the promotion of organizations working for this purpose.

§5. WASTE MANAGEMENT LAW

*464.* The development of waste management law has followed a number of different paths around the world. There are a number of reasons for this, and one of the reasons is prevalence of different legal systems in the respective states. There has been a limited specific action on waste management in international law, with two key sources of international law being suggestive of the international waste management law regime and international custom and treaties. International custom ranges from general principle to customary rule, with a customary rule being a strong form of a general principle of law. State sovereignty is considered a customary rule and is represented in Principle 2 of the Rio Declaration. This principle gives states the right to exploit their own natural resources provided they do not cause trans-boundary environmental damage, thus impacting another state's right to exploit its own natural resources. As per principles of state sovereignty, a state cannot only generate waste as abundantly as it wishes, but it can also dispose of its waste in whatever manner it sees fit provided that the waste remains within its territory. The principle of preventative action is one of preventing damage to the environment, and reducing and controlling activities that may cause environmental harm to the neighboring state.

## I. Development of Waste Management Law

*465.* The development of waste management law has taken different directions in different states. Common law states such as the U.S., U.K., and Australia have indicated an aversion to the development based on principle, generally preferring to proceed from a case-by-case consideration of the facts. Such an approach lends itself to a perpetuation of traditions of decentralized management and avoids the development of innovative strategy in favor of optimizing existing conditions. Courts, institutions and legislations all combine to maintain a system where waste management is reduced to a series of technical, environmental pollution control questions. This can be contrasted with the civil law approaches of the Netherlands and Germany, which have been far more comfortable with an approach driven by rationally derived principles. Since the field of waste management is becoming increasingly shorn of its directly observable environmental impacts, this principle-driven approach is fundamental for the realization of far-reaching responses to waste. In civil law systems, the development of a coherent strategy at a national level is more likely than in a common law system.

*466.* The current focus for regulatory discourse surrounding the management of municipal solid waste is one of resource efficiency. Waste management legislators see themselves as having progressed beyond simply managing municipal waste in order to address human health and environmental issues, and now focus upon avoiding waste, and recovering resources from waste that is generated. This transition has varied between states. The American experience of state-based approaches to waste legislation can be contrasted with the European supranational legislative coordination, just as common law "bottom-up" approaches can be contrasted with civil law "top-down" systems.

## §6. Treaties Concerning Waste Management

*467.* The two primary multilateral conventions concerned with the management of waste are the London Convention 1972 and the Basel Convention 1989 and entered into force in May 5,1992. The London Convention is based on the premise that dumping is permitted unless explicitly prohibited. A 1996 protocol reverses the approach of the Convention, prohibiting the dumping of all waste at sea except for a small group of wastes. These wastes are generally inert or generated from sea-based activities such as fishing. The shift from dumping being permitted unless explicitly prohibited, to prohibited unless explicitly permitted is a sign of the growing importance of the precautionary principle. The burden of proof is no longer on demonstrating that the waste will have an impact, rather it is to demonstrate that the waste will not have an impact. The London Convention and its 1996 Protocol demonstrate one trajectory in the development of international waste management law. The Basel Convention continues with this principle but tightens it to a principle of prevention.

### I. The Basel Convention

*468.* The Basel Convention as originally agreed and ratified seeks to control the trans-boundary movement of hazardous waste and "other waste." The Convention prohibits the shipment of hazardous waste to non-parties, as well as prohibiting shipments of waste to states that have prohibited the import of such waste. Where the shipment is not prohibited, the Convention establishes a system of control. It is notable that, with the exception of Antarctica, the Convention does not prohibit any particular hazardous waste destinations.

*469.* The development of waste law internationally follows two potential approaches namely a "bottom-up" consideration of the facts in each case and a "top-down" implementation of broadly adopted principles. The latter approach has been increasingly dominant, both in the case of EU law pushing aside the U.K. common law approaches, and internationally with the assertion of principles of prevention and precaution. It would seem that a principle-driven approach is becoming the standard for waste management law. Notwithstanding this broad trend observed, and acknowledging the current practice of waste management as being somewhat divorced from direct environmental impact, a state's structure and legal history remain significant.

*A. The Waigani Convention*

*470.* The Basel Convention established a global control system for hazardous wastes being shipped from one country to another. States which are parties to the Convention must not trade in hazardous wastes with non-parties, but an exception to this is provided in Article 11 of the Convention, under which parties may enter into agreements or arrangements either with other parties or with non-parties. These agreements can also set out controls which are different from those prescribed by the Convention itself, provided such controls do not reduce the level of environmental protection intended by the Convention.

*471.* The Waigani Convention (Convention to Ban the Importation into Forum Island Countries of Hazardous and Radioactive Wastes and to Control the Transboundary Movement and Management of Hazardous Wastes within the South Pacific Region) is one such agreement entered into force in October 2001. This Convention bans the import of all hazardous and radioactive wastes into South Pacific Forum Island Countries. It also enables Australia to receive hazardous wastes exported from South Pacific Forum Island countries which are not parties to the Basel Convention. There are twenty-four countries within the coverage area of the Waigani Convention.

## II. London Convention on the Prevention of Marine Pollution

*472.* The "Convention on the Prevention of Marine Pollution by Dumping of Wastes and Other Matter 1972" (the "London Convention") was one of the first global conventions to protect the marine environment from human activities and has been in force since 1975. Its objective is to promote the effective control of all sources of marine pollution and to take all practicable steps to prevent pollution of the sea by dumping of wastes. In 1996, the "London Protocol" was adopted to modernize the Convention and, eventually, replace it. The London Protocol entered into force in March 2006. Under the Protocol all dumping is prohibited, but parties may issue permits to allow the dumping of the following specified materials, subject to certain conditions:

- dredged material;
- sewage sludge;
- fish wastes;
- vessels and platforms;
- inert, inorganic geological material (e.g., mining wastes);
- organic material of natural origin;
- bulky items primarily comprising iron, steel and concrete; and
- $CO_2$ streams from carbon dioxide capture processes for sequestration (CCS).

# Part X. Sustainable Development, Global Commons

## Chapter 1. Sustainable Development

*473.* The economic growth has lifted a large number of people out of poverty and has raised the income levels of a large number of people, but it has come at the expense of the environment and poor communities. Through a variety of market, policy, and institutional failures, Earth's natural capital has been used in ways that are economically inefficient and wasteful, without sufficient reckoning of the true costs of resource depletion. The burning of fossil fuels supported rapid growth for decades but set up dangerous consequences, with climate change threatening to roll back decades of development progress.

*474.* Sustainable development recognizes that growth must be both inclusive and environmentally sound to reduce poverty and build shared prosperity for the present population and to continue to meet the needs of future generations. It is efficient with resources and carefully planned to deliver both immediate and long-term benefits for people, planet, and prosperity. The three pillars of sustainable development—economic growth, environmental stewardship, and social inclusion—carry across all sectors of development, from cities facing rapid urbanization to agriculture, infrastructure, energy development and use, water availability, and transportation. Cities are embracing low-carbon growth and public transportation. Farmers are picking up the practices of climate-smart agriculture. Countries are recognizing the value of their natural resources, and industries are realizing how much they can save through energy and supply-chain efficiency.

### §1. Earth Summit

*475.* In 1992, at the UNCED, commonly known as the "Earth Summit," the concept of sustainable development received the approval of over 140 countries. Despite the general agreement, there are hundreds of formulations of sustainable development, each reflecting particular values and priorities. One way sustainable development may be described as "development that meets the need of the present without compromising the ability of future generations to meet their own needs."[92]

92. Brundtland Report, 1987.

Sustainable development requires the integration of three pillars, social justice, economic growth, and environmental protection. However, it is not simply a goal but is also a process as it has significant procedural elements. It ought to be done through empowerment, consultation, impact and risk assessment, the expansion of opportunities and capacities and public participation.

*476.* The principle of sustainable development for the protection and improvement of environment has been unanimously accepted by the world countries as a strategy that caters to the needs of the present without depriving the future generations of their right to available natural resources. It has been rightly said that sustainable development is meant to secure a balance between developmental activities for the benefit of the people and environmental protection and therefore, "it is a guarantee to the present and bequeath to the future generations." The principle of sustainable development seeks to harmonize the conflict between development which may be industrial, economic or social, and right to a healthy environment. In other words, the balance between environmental protection and developmental activities could only be maintained by strictly adhering to the principle of sustainable development.

*477.* Environmental studies have shown that the environment-related problems of developed countries are mainly due to industrial and technological development whereas undeveloped countries have environmental problems because of poverty, over-population, and illiteracy. Thus, encouragement and boost to developmental activities are in the socioeconomic interest of a nation, but this cannot be at the cost of present or future generations, as this will not only affect the present generation but will have its adverse effects on the future generations as well. Therefore, sustainable development is the need of time so that development and environmental protection, both proceed maintaining a balance.

*478.* Development has been recognized as a human right under the Rio Declaration of 1992. But all the countries participating in this summit agreed that economic or industrial development should be carried out in a manner that it does not adversely affect the environment because environmental pollution is a potential danger to human life. It is for this reason that the principle of sustainable development was evolved in this world summit for maintaining a balance between development and environment, and it was realized that both should go hand in hand.

## §2. Defining Sustainable Development

*479.* The principle of sustainable development has evolved on the basic assumption of co-existence of two apparently conflicting notions, i.e., development and environment. But from the practical point of view, ecological, economic, and social aspects of sustainability are inseparable. As William Rees has pointed out that maintenance of ecological integrity has to be accorded primacy over achievement of socioeconomic human needs, thus there should be a convergence between ecological and economic factors in the developmental process. The principle of sustainable development emphasizes two basic needs, first, the need for socioeconomic development, and second, the need for limitation imposed on the environment's capability to cope with the present and future requirements.

*480.* Explaining the interdependence of conservation and sustainable development, the Brundtland Report (1997) pointed out as follows:

> Sustainable development is development that meets the needs of the present without compromising the ability of future generations to meet their own needs … . Sustainable development requires meeting the basic needs of all and extending to all opportunity to satisfy their aspirations for a better life.

## §3. Basic Objectives of Sustainable Development

*481.* The principle of sustainable development seeks to achieve the following three basic objectives:

(1) maintenance production of goods and services for development and efficiency;
(2) conservation and management of neutral resources, including preservation of biodiversity and maintenance of biological integrity;
(3) maintenance and enhancement of the quality of life adopting the principle of equitable distribution of wealth and material resources.

*482.* These objectives may respectively be called as economic, environmental and social objectives of the principle of sustainable development. From the environmental point of view, the objective of the principle of sustainable development centers around three issues, namely, (i) to maintain essential ecological processes; (ii) to preserve genetic diversity; and (iii) to secure sustainable utilization of species and ecosystems.

## §4. Scope and Extent of Sustainable Development

*483.* The concept of sustainable development, as pointed out by the chairperson Ms. Brundtland in her report (popularly called the Brundtland Report), is aimed at meeting the needs of the present without compromising the ability of future generations to meet their own needs. Commenting on sustainable development, the Former President of the World Bank James D. Yolkenson observed, "it is for us to think as to what kind of world we want. Do we want to bequeath a world for our future generation a poorest world wherein innumerable people die of hunger, climate uncertainty, biodiversity at its lowest ebb and social conditions most unstable?" This observation of Yolkenson clearly shows that the central focus of sustainable development is not confined to the present happiness of the people, but it also extends to safeguarding the interests of the coming generations.

*484.* Sustainable development involves a multi-faceted approach, i.e., (i) economic, (ii) human, (iii) environmental, and (iv) technological. It is a process which seeks to bring improvement in the quality of human life along with conservation of the ecological system. Thus, development and environment, both are interdependent and therefore, there cannot be development without protection of environment, nor can there be conservation of environment without development.

## §5. Principles of Sustainable Development

*485.* The principle of sustainable development which received international recognition as a result of Brundtland Commission Report (1987) was overwhelmingly supported by all the nations. Some of the salient principles which underline the concept of sustainable development were spelled out in the Rio Declaration, 1992 and Agenda 21. Therefore, these principles have got to be necessarily followed in order to achieve the objective of sustainable development. These principles are as follows:

(a) Intergenerational equity.
(b) Use and conservation of natural resources.
(c) Environmental protection.
(d) The precautionary principle.
(e) The "Polluter Pays" principle.
(f) Principle of liability to help and cooperate.
(g) Poverty eradication.
(h) Principle of "public trust."

*486.* The principle of intergenerational equity presupposes the right of each generation of human beings to benefit from cultural and natural resources of the past generation as well as the "obligation" to preserve such resources for future generations. The principle emphasizes on conservation of biodiversity resources and renewable sources like forests, water, soil. The principle of intergenerational equity has its genesis in Principles 1 and 2 of the Stockholm Declaration, 1972 wherein environment has been taken as a resource basis for the survival of the present generation and right to be beneficially used by the future generations. Both these principles are reproduced as follows:

> Principle 1.—Man has the fundamental right to freedom, equality and adequate conditions of life, in an environment of quality that permits a life of dignity and well-being, and he bears a solemn responsibility to protect and improve the environment for the present and future generations.
> Principle 2.—The natural resources of the earth, including the air, water, lands, flora and fauna, and especially representative samples of natural ecosystems, must be safeguarded for the benefit of the present and future generations through careful planning and management, as appropriate.

§6. SUSTAINABLE DEVELOPMENT LAW

*487.* Sustainable development law is found at the intersection of three principal fields of international law: international economic law, international environmental law, and international social law. Sustainable development law refers to emerging substantive body of legal instruments, norms, and treaties supported by distinctive procedural elements. In international treaty law, sustainable development is an agreed objective of many international treaties, both at the global and regional levels. As such, sustainable development can be considered part of the "object and purpose" of a growing number of treaties and therefore directly relevant in the interpretation of their provisions. The concept appears, often as an objective or reference in the preamble, in most international statements and declarations related to environmental, social and economic issues since the 1992 Rio de Janeiro Earth Summit. It has also featured as an object and purpose of many international economic, social and environmental treaties involving developed and DC, as a concept which guides the decisions of international courts and tribunals, and the holdings of judges in national courts around the world.

*488.* The sustainable development is part of the object and purpose of many international treaties, including the 1992 UNCBD, its 2000 Cartagena Protocol on Biosafety and its 2010 Nagoya Protocol; the 1992 U.N. Framework Convention on Climate Change and its 1997 Kyoto Protocol; the 1994 U.N. Convention to Combat Desertification and Drought; the 1994 NAFTA; the 1995 Straddling Fish Stocks Agreement of 1982; UNCLOS; the 2000 Cotonou Partnership Agreement between the EU and the African Caribbean and Pacific countries; the 2001 International Treaty on Plant Genetic Resources for Food and Agriculture, and many others. In each treaty, the sustainable development objective is embedded but worded differently and also operationalized differently.

*489.* Paris Agreement (UNFCCC, 2015) can be considered as the first universal legally binding international climate agreement dealing with sustainable development that set the goal of global warming less than 2 and striving to be less than 1.5 degrees Celsius by the end of the century. In November 2021, in the COP26 conference on environmental protection, discussions were held on acting toward achieving the goals of the Paris Agreement and the UNFCCC. One of the major differences is that the UNFCCC process which frames the COP meetings and agreements is supposed to be legally binding in international law, while the procedure driving to, and the outcomes from, the SDGs are voluntary. Climate change is affecting globally and touching all people on the planet. It is increasing the frequency of natural disasters, floods, wild fires, hurricanes, as well as droughts that are becoming more severe due to rising temperatures (SDGs report, 2020). Therefore, most countries have voluntarily started implementing national plans for adaptation to climate change.

## §7. Laws for a Green Economy

*490.* A green economy is considered to result in increased human well-being and social equity, while significantly reducing environmental risks and ecological scarcities. Thus, it is an economy where growth of income and jobs is driven by investments that reduce carbon emissions and pollution, enhance efficiency, and sustain biodiversity and ecosystem services. It is an economic vehicle for sustainable development, and it is a new economic paradigm that can drive growth of income and jobs, without exposing to environmental risk and has strategies to end the persistence of poverty.

*491.* The promotion of green economy requires enabling conditions. National laws and regulatory instruments, as key enabling conditions play a vital role in promoting green economy. They ensure the shared responsibilities of different stakeholders shift funding toward green investment; create or strengthen institutional arrangements for facilitating green economy; provide incentives for the development of green technologies or disincentives for activities that cause harm to the environment; and specify other policy measures for accelerating resource efficiency and green economy.

*492.* There are already many national laws and regulations around the world to support resource efficiency, sustainable production and consumption and promote greening national economy. These new and innovative legislations and regulatory regimes combine traditional command-and-control regulatory measures with new innovative tools including collective public action to change the patterns of production and consumption and economic instruments to shifting funding toward green investment and clean technology development to improve resource efficiency.

*493.* The other emerging markets and least developed countries in their drive to develop and to alleviate poverty have found their national laws and regulations inadequate and unable to address the evolving needs and challenges they are facing in their development efforts. Environmental considerations in relevant policy and legal frameworks are often haphazard, lack needed integration and holistic approaches. As a result, many fast-growing local industries find themselves entering new terrain without proper regulatory frameworks and oversight. Even in countries that have adopted new and innovative legislation and regulatory instruments, there is weak implementation because lack of political will to take strong measures. Further, enforcing agencies lack capacity and power to implement.

## §8. Black Carbon and Short-Lived Climate Forcers

*494.* Black carbon is one of the harmful air pollutants known as Short-Lived Climate Forcers (SLCFs). SLCFs are substances that contribute to global warming but, in contrast to $CO_2$ and other GHG, have a relatively short lifetime in the atmosphere. The main SLCFs apart from black carbon are $O_3$ and its precursors, such as methane. Scientific findings have shown that reducing SLCFs would slow the pace of global warming very quickly, reduce some regional climate impacts, and have significant benefits of reducing air pollution and improving air quality, which in turn have important effects in terms of crop yields and related food security, public health, and development.

*495.* In 2011, UNEP and WMO released the Integrated Assessment of Black Carbon and $O_3$, which assessed the existing science and policy options for addressing SLCFs, and developed an outlook to 2070 which illustrates the benefits of decisive action and the risks to climate, public health and crop yields over the coming decades in the case of inaction. The assessment was accompanied by a Summary for Decision Makers and followed by a Science-Policy Brief which pointed toward the need to move toward a strategy for translating the scientific findings into policy to reduce emissions of SLCFs.[93]

93. https://www.ccacoalition.org/en/resources/integrated-assessment-black-carbon-and-tropospheric-ozone.

# Chapter 2. The Common Heritage of Mankind and Global Commons

## §1. The Common Heritage of Mankind

*496.* The "common heritage of mankind" (CHM) signifies that some resources and localities belong to all humanity, and such resources are available for everyone's use and benefit, taking into account future generations and the needs of DC. When first introduced in the 1960s, the CHM concept remains controversial to this day. Escalating global ecological degradation and ongoing inability to arrest the tragedy of the commons (Hardin, 1968) will ensure the continued relevance of the common heritage concept, despite the difficulties surrounding its acceptance by developed states. Evidence for this can be found in a range of efforts to apply CHM to natural and cultural heritage, marine living resources, Antarctica and global ecological systems such as the atmosphere[94] or climate system.

### I. Emergence of the Principle

*497.* Legal discussion of CHM generally begins with the speech of the Maltese ambassador Mr. Arvid Pardo to the U.N. in 1967. In this speech, he proposed that the seabed and ocean floor beyond national jurisdiction be considered the CHM which triggered the negotiation of the 1982 Law of the Sea Convention (UNCLOS III) and other legal developments that subsequently earned Arvid Pardo the title "father of the law of the sea." But CHM has a much longer history, and Pardo drew upon this in developing CHM as a legal concept for the oceans. Other people, including the writer and environmentalist Elisabeth Mann Borgese (1918–2002) considered CHM an ethical concept central to a new world order, based on new forms of cooperation, economic theory, and philosophy.

*498.* A 1948 draft World Constitution provided that the Earth and its resources were to be the common property of mankind, managed for the good of all. Concern about the use of nuclear technology and resources, for military and peaceful purposes, led to the notion that nuclear resources be collectively owned and managed and not owned by any one state. Traces of CHM are also found in the U.N. Outer Space Treaty (1967), governing state exploration and use of outer space, the moon, and other celestial bodies. CHM, however, achieved prominence in the context of the evolving law of the sea. The 1967 World Peace through Law Conference referred to the high seas as "the common heritage of mankind" and stated that the seabed should be subject to U.N. jurisdiction and control.

---

94. P. Taylor P, *An Ecological Approach to International Law: Responding to the Challenges of Climate Change* (Routledge, London, U.K. 1998).

### II. Influenced Law of Sea

*499.* Concern about the impact of new technologies upon the oceans, militarization and expanding state claims to ownership of parts of the oceans, e.g., continental shelf and EEZs, together with growing economic disparity and associated harm to long-term human security, prompted Arvid Pardo to develop the idea that all ocean space, i.e., surface of the sea, water column, seabed and its subsoil, and living resources, should be declared the CHM, irrespective of existing claims to jurisdiction of states. The intention was to replace the outdated legal concept of "freedom of the high seas" by accepting ocean areas as an international commons. Freedom of the high seas, developed by the Dutch jurist Hugo Grotius (1583–1645), creates an open access regime allowing for its laissez-faire use.

*500.* In contrast, as per CHM concept, ocean space and its resources would be a commons that could not be owned by states beyond a certain limit. As a commons, it would be open to the international community of states, but its use would be subject to international administration and management for the common good of all humanity. Where areas of ocean space and resources existed within national jurisdiction, states would regulate and manage use on behalf of all mankind, not solely for their benefit. This approach recognized the unity of the oceans as ecological systems and rejected both laissez-faire freedom and unfettered state sovereignty. It included efforts to simplify ocean jurisdiction by establishing one single line of demarcation between national and international ocean space (Draft Ocean Space Treaty of 1971) and prevented the tendency of gradually expanding claims to national jurisdiction.

## §2. UNCLOS III

*501.* The 1967 Maltese proposal led to a number of important developments, including the 1970 U.N. General Assembly Declaration of Principles Governing the Sea-Bed and the Ocean Floor and the Subsoil Thereof, beyond the Limits of National Jurisdiction. This declaration set out the legal principles needed to implement the notion that the seabed and its resources are the CHM, and it helped create consensus for the negotiation of a new law of the sea convention, i.e., UNCLOS III, which restricted the application of CHM to a few rocks, e.g., mineral resources such as manganese nodules, sitting on the bottom of the deep seabed.

*502.* Part XI of UNCLOS III deals with the seabed and ocean floor and subsoil thereof (the "Area") beyond the limits of national jurisdiction. Article 136 declares the Area and its resources (only) to be the "common heritage of mankind." The Area and its resources cannot be claimed, appropriated, or owned by any state or person (Article 137). All rights to resources belong to mankind as a whole, with the ISA acting on mankind's behalf (Article 140). The ISA must ensure the equitable sharing of financial and other benefits arising out of activities in the Area, taking into account the needs and interests of developing states and poor states. Promotion of research, transfer of technology to developing states and protection of the marine environment's ecological balance are all important functions of the ISA (Articles 143–145).

*503.* The provisions contained in Part XI of UNCLOS III create an international administration and management regime for only a small part of the international commons (the Area and its resources) leave a major portion uncovered. It has not replaced the freedom of the high seas (Part VII). Therefore, the intended revolution of the law of the sea was not achieved to the satisfactory level. In the 1970s, the most commercially viable mineral resources of this area were thought to be manganese nodules, hence Pardo's view that CHM was reduced in its application to "ugly little rocks lying in the darkest depths of all creation." Despite this serious limitation, the use of CHM was revolutionary.

## §3. 1979 Moon Treaty

*504.* Article 11(1) of the Moon Treaty declares that the moon and its natural resources are the CHM. Disputes concerning the details of an international system for resource exploitation, including provision for equitable benefit sharing, were resolved by deferring the details of a management regime for the future. The Moon Treaty has been ratified by only a few states; nevertheless, it has been used to reject claims to property rights on the basis that it creates a general principle of law, applicable to the whole of the international community and not just states that ratified the treaty.

## §4. Range of CHM

*505.* There are differing opinions with respect to all elements of CHM. This is because; it questions the regimes that apply to resources of global significance, irrespective of where they are situated. It therefore challenges the traditional international law concepts such as acquisition of territory, sovereignty, sovereign equality, and international personality, as well as the allocation of planetary resources and consent-based sources of international law.[95] Further, it has long been recognized that the precedent established for oceans management has the potential to form the basis for the future organization of an increasingly interdependent world.

*506.* Over the years, CHM has been applied to a range of resources and spaces like fisheries, Antarctica, the Arctic landscape, geostationary orbit, genetic resources (the genetic material of plants, animals and life forms, that are of value), and basic food resources. In recent years, UNESCO has supported CHM through a wide range of initiatives, e.g., declarations, conventions, and protocols, that recognize natural and cultural heritage as the CHM. Although difficult to define, "natural and cultural

95. K. Baslar, *The Concept of the Common Heritage of Mankind in International Law* (Kluwer Law International, The Hague, The Netherlands 1997).

heritage" includes tangible and intangible elements, ranging from archaeological sites and historic monuments to cultural phenomena (such as literature, language, and customary practices) and natural systems including islands, biosphere reserves and deserts. One potential new area of application is the human genome. This may prevent the patenting of the human genome by corporate interests. In an ecological and generational context, it is possible to argue that the Earth itself is a global commons shared by each generation and that CHM should "extend to all natural and cultural resources, wherever located, that are internationally important for the well-being of future generations."[96]

*507.* In the short term and from the perspective of state practice and treaty negotiation, the future use of CHM is likely to be limited. International lawyers tend to treat its use—beyond the UNCLOS III and Moon Treaty—as merely political and aspirational. Issues that will shortly test the commitment of states to CHM include the status of marine living resources (of the "Area" and high seas), claims to the seabed under the melting Arctic ice, and the status of oil reserves under the deep seabed. In the context of the oceans, CHM provides the only current alternative to either freedom of use by all states or the acquisition and exercise of sovereign rights.

*508.* CHM also recognizes the interdependence of ecosystems and acknowledges human use. It therefore has much in common with ecosystem management approaches that aim to move away from piecemeal resource-specific management regimes. CHM is also relevant to the wider debate on transforming the role of the state from exclusive focus on protection of national interests to include responsibility to protect ecological systems, wherever they are located, for the benefit of all. States might be reluctant to embrace the possible applications of CHM, but international law is no longer the sole province of states and international lawyers. Global civil society is playing an increasing role in the development of concepts such as CHM. It is linked to renewed interest in cosmopolitanism, global constitutionalism, global ecological citizenship and justice, and the search for shared ethical principles to guide progress toward a more peaceful and sustainable future for all (Earth Charter Initiative 2000). One major use of CHM resources can be investment in bringing sustainable development and protecting environment.

## §5. Global Commons

*509.* The areas which are situated outside of the political reach of any one nation-state are known as Global Commons. The international law identifies four types of global commons namely the High Seas, the Atmosphere, Antarctica, and Outer Space. These areas are considered the CHM—the open access doctrine or the *mare liberum* (free sea for everyone) in the case of the High Seas. Despite efforts

96. Weiss, Edith Brown, *In Fairness to Future Generations: International Law, Common Patrimony and Intergenerational Equity* (Transnational Publishers 1989); P. Taylor, *An Ecological Approach to International Law: Responding to the Challenges of Climate Change* (Routledge, London, U.K. 1998).

by governments or individuals to establish property rights or other forms of control over most natural resources, the Global Commons have remained an exception. The access to some of the resources found within the global commons, except for a few like fisheries, has been difficult, and these resources have historically not been scarce to justify the attempt for exclusive control and access. However, with the advancement of science and technology in recent years, it has made access to resources in the Global Commons easier, leading to an increase in activities to harness them.

## I. Environmental Degradation in Antarctica

*510.* Out of the Global Commons, Antarctica is facing rapid environmental degradation due to pollution emanating from human presence and pressures and the effects of global warming. Furthermore, the doctrine of *mare liberum* (free sea for everyone) allows for the dumping of wastes and overfishing in the high seas. The indication of this trend is that the impact on the resources and the environment of the Global Commons will also most likely worsen. Such a trend of environmental degradation will take its toll on sustainable development and poverty alleviation.

## II. Environmental Issues of Global Commons

*511.* The need to address environmental issues of the global commons has been debated among various stakeholders for a long time. Furthermore, a number of legal and institutional frameworks exist to deal with the environmental issues of the global commons. For example, parts of the UNCLOS are dedicated to environmental management of the world's oceans, and various components of the Antarctic Treaty Systems (ATS) for Antarctica deal with the environment of Antarctica.

## III. Regulatory Issues of Global Commons

*512.* An important legal issue is the fragmentation of legal regulatory frameworks governing the Global Commons. Another problem is that there is no institution evolving and coordinating policies for existing or new environmental issues associated with natural resource exploration or exploitation in the Global Commons. There is also lack of regulatory standards for emerging issues such as bioprospecting, including rights and processes regarding ABS arising from the use of genetic resources. The UNGA had established the Ad Hoc Open-ended Informal Working Group to study issues relating to the conservation and sustainable use of marine biological diversity beyond areas of national jurisdiction to make recommendations to the Secretary-General. Furthermore, the CBD is in the process of developing scientific criteria for biodiversity conservation in areas beyond national jurisdiction.[97]

97. United Nations Environment Programme: http://www.unep.org.

# Part XI. Environmental Crimes, Wars, and Risks

## Chapter 1. Transnational Environmental Crime

*513.* Transnational environmental crimes are activities undertaken by persons acting across national borders, including illegal logging and timber smuggling, animal and its products like hiding and bones smuggling, the black market in ODS, the illegal movement of toxic and hazardous waste and other prohibited chemicals, etc. In addition to the serious environmental consequences, these illegal activities across borders can involve corruption and financial crime, loss of tax revenue, parallel trading with other forms of criminal activity, etc.

*514.* Transnational criminal activities are a central problem for the effective implementation, compliance with and enforcement of environmental law, including MEAs. The implementation of environmental law requires that international legal mechanisms are established and enforced at national level through appropriate legal regimes. Illegal activities challenge enforcement and undermine implementation of environmental law, including MEAs. The illegal activities may have transnational elements and need to be combated through internationally coordinated efforts. Law enforcement cooperation to combat transnational crimes faces obstacles because this relatively new category of crime typically lacks common understandings and approaches between and among states. Environmental crime is a serious problem worldwide in different forms, with some of them being among the most profitable criminal activities in the world. The most common crimes against the environment are connected with the unlawful exploitation of wild fauna and flora, pollution, waste disposal and its trade.

### §1. Environmental Crimes

*515.* With respect to international action on wildlife crime, starting in 2001, the ECOSOC has issued several resolutions that urged Member States to adopt the legislative or other measures necessary for establishing illicit trafficking in protected species of wild fauna and flora as a criminal offense in their domestic legislation; cooperate with United Nations Office on Drugs and Crime (UNODC) with a view to preventing, combating and eradicating trafficking in protected species of wild fauna and flora; promote international cooperation in preventing and combating illicit international trafficking in forest and wildlife resources; and, consider making illicit trafficking in endangered species of wild fauna and flora a "serious crime." In 2013, the Commission on Crime Prevention and Criminal Justice (CCPCJ) adopted a resolution, which was later taken up by ECOSOC,[98] which strongly encouraged Member States, "to take appropriate measures to prevent and combat illicit trafficking in protected species of wild fauna and flora, including the adoption of legislation necessary for the prevention, investigation and prosecution of such trafficking."[99]

*516.* In 2014, the CCPCJ adopted Resolution 23/1, strongly encouraging Member States to make illicit trafficking in forest products, including timber, a serious crime. It also urged them to promote enforcement, research, and technical assistance measures to combat the illicit trafficking of these products. Both resolutions acknowledged and supported the UNODC's Global Programme for Combating Wildlife and Forest Crime, which, since 2013, has delivered technical assistance activities to prevent and combat wildlife and forest crime, raising awareness of wildlife and forest crime among different stakeholders to reduce the demand of protected wild fauna and flora, and improving cooperation, law enforcement and the preventive capacity of Member States to address this crime. The 2013 ECOSOC Resolution included research and asked UNODC, "in consultation with Member States and in cooperation with other competent intergovernmental organizations … to undertake case studies that focus on organized crime networks involved in the illicit trafficking of specific protected species of wild fauna and flora, their parts and derivatives."[100]

*517.* A mechanism for cooperating with "other competent intergovernmental organizations" was found through the International Consortium on Combating Wildlife Crime (ICCWC), launched in November 2010 and bringing together the CITES Secretariat, the International Criminal Police Organization (INTERPOL), UNODC, the World Bank and the World Customs Organization (WCO).[101] In 2015, the General Assembly called upon UNODC, in line with previous mandates and in cooperation with Member States, to "continue to collect information on patterns and flows of illicit trafficking in wildlife and to report thereon,"[102]

98. E/RES/2013/40.
99. ECOSOC Resolution 2001/12, Illicit trafficking in protected species of wild flora and fauna; ECOSOC Resolution 2003/27, Illicit trafficking in protected species of wild flora and fauna; ECOSOC Resolution 2008/25, International cooperation in preventing and combating illicit international trafficking in forest products, including timber, wildlife and other forest biological resources; ECOSOC Resolution 2011/36 Crime prevention and criminal justice responses against illicit trafficking in endangered species of wild fauna and flora.
100. E/RES/2013/40, para. 13.
101. *Ibid.*
102. A/RES/69/314.

## I. Wild Animal Traffic

*518.* Regarded by the INTERPOL as the third largest illegal business in the world—after drug and arms trafficking—wild animal traffic raises a serious threat for the world's biodiversity survival. There are several actors involved in this crime, but consumers are among the most important actors as this crime would disappear if supply and the high prices that people get to pay for them on the black market, ceased to exist. The notable aspect is that more endangered the species is, the higher the price is for it. The most requested species are tropical birds, reptiles (serpents, crocodiles, etc.), arachnids, monkeys (capuchins, chimpanzees, lemurs), and so forth.

## II. Indiscriminate Logging

*519.* Indiscriminate logging not only affects the producing countries, but long-term climatic, economic, and environmental problems will affect most of the countries in the world. For example, the illegal logging in the Amazon forest is projected to lessen rain in northern China and the Midwest U.S. while increasing rain in Northern Europe and Eastern Africa. Apart from the numerous environmental consequences of illegal logging, it can also weaken the economy of poor countries. Illegal logging is said to lower the prices of world timber in the ranges of 7%–16% annually, causing a global revenue loss of about USD 15 billion per year.

## III. Electronic Waste Mismanagement

*520.* The Global E-waste Monitor 2020, in a report produced in collaboration with the UN Environment Program (UNEP), found that a record 53.6 million metric tons of electronic waste were generated last year. Asia produced 24.9 million tons, followed by the Americas (13.1 million tons) and Europe (12 million tons), while Africa and Oceania generated 2.9 and 0.7 million tons, respectively. By 2030, the global total is likely to swell to 74.7 million tons. Out of this only 17.4% of 2019's e-waste was formally collected and recycled. A major portion of this waste is left out of formal recycling, and a good deal of it is illegally exported to Africa, China or India. It is the case of Ghana's rubbish dump, a large electronic waste dump coming from the West. Even though the export of this dangerous waste, including the electronic one, is banned in some places, but the enforcement is very poor.

*521.* The International Electrotechnical Commission (IEC) is working since 2021, on an international standard for the management of electrical and electronic waste. The draft of this standard will be published in 2024. It is working toward environmental protection by providing a step-by-step approach to manage discarded electrical and electronic equipment through methodological steps and decision diagrams to assess product recovery potential.

*522.* The standards so set will prioritize the recovery of functional products and components over the recovery of materials. It will set requirements for recovery processes that protect human and environmental health and avoid, reduce or substitute the use of resources which pose health or environmental risks. While other e-waste standards and legislation mainly focus on waste management solutions and limited recycling, these standards provide a practical approach for implementing the waste hierarchy by giving precedence to repair, refurbishment, and remanufacturing over material recovery, such as recycling.

## IV. Finning

*523.* Shark finning is the act of removing fins from sharks and discarding the still alive shark back into the ocean. This act is prohibited in many countries. Unable to swim effectively, they sink to the bottom of the ocean and die of suffocation or are eaten by other predators. The finning is widespread, and the rapidly expanding and largely unregulated shark fin trade represents one of the most serious threats to shark populations worldwide. Shark finning has caused catastrophic harm to the marine ecosystem. In July 2016, whale sharks were classified as endangered on the IUCN (World Conservation Union) Red List of Threatened Species. Nevertheless, the hunt for them continues.

*524.* Shark finning violates the U.N. FAO's Code of Conduct for Responsible Fisheries, and the practice is contrary to the Organization's International Plan for the Conservation and Management of Sharks. There are approximately 1,000 species of sharks and rays in the world, of which over 30 species are listed under CITES Appendix II for regulated trade. Countries with a coastline are responsible for laws and regulations pertaining to fishing in their waters. Some countries/jurisdictions have enacted full or partial bans on the practice of shark finning—slicing off the fins of the shark at sea (often while the shark is still alive) and discarding the carcass. Still other country/jurisdictions have taken the additional step of enacting complete or partial bans on shark fishing (such that, by inclusion, shark finning is also banned). The U.S. has passed the Shark Fin Sales Elimination Act in December 2022, which went into effect in January 2023. The rule makes it illegal to "possess, buy, sell, or transport shark fins or any product containing shark fins," essentially creating an outright ban on the shark fin trade in the U.S. However, the law still allows people to possess legally obtained shark fins in some circumstances if they have a license or permit.

## V. Dumping in Rivers and Aquifers

*525.* The dumping in rivers and aquifers is caused by companies, factories, and local bodies. Faucal and toxic waste coming from factories is usually dumped in a controlled way, but this is not always the case. In these cases, waste is uncontrollably released into the environment, while at the same time polluting rivers, lakes aquifers, etc. This is a very serious crime because not only it causes the local wildlife to die or get ill but also, as a result of the water leaking into the soil, it finds its way to pollute the surrounding flora as well, affecting the food chain. There are many ways to avoid this waste-dumping problem, such as using sewage collectors or sewage plants, among others.

*526.* There is a need for better understanding of the global problems and existing gaps on transnational or cross-border environmental crime. There must be common approaches to more efficiently and effectively tackle the problem of transnational environmental crime from a legal standpoint. The existing international and national legal and institutional arrangements and law enforcement mechanisms require strengthening and reinforcing to combat transnational environmental crime. The cross-border cooperation in the field of environmental crime requires enhancement.[103]

## §2. UNEP and INTERPOL on Environmental Crime

*527.* The illegal wildlife trade is perhaps one of the most lucrative illegal businesses in the world and ranked as the fourth largest source of criminal earnings, generating up to USD 23 billion annually. UNEP has valued forestry crimes (including illegal logging) as a USD 51–USD 152 billion-per-year industry; illegal fishing estimates run from USD 11–USD 24 billion. The Rise of Environmental Crime finds that weak laws and poorly funded security forces are enabling international criminal networks and armed rebels to profit from a trade that fuels conflicts, devastates ecosystems and is threatening species with extinction. INTERPOL and UNEP have joined to bring to the attention of the world the sheer scale of environmental crime. The vast sums of money generated from these crimes keep sophisticated international criminal gangs in business and fuel insecurity around the world.

*528.* As per INTERPOL, environmental crime is growing at an alarming pace in the world. The complexity of this type of criminality requires a multi-sector response with collaboration across borders. So, there must be strong action, legislation and sanctions at the national and international levels, including measures targeted at disrupting overseas tax havens; an increase in financial support commensurate with the serious threat that environmental crime poses to sustainable development; and economic incentives and alternative livelihoods for those at the bottom of the environmental crime chain. The environmental crime—which includes the illegal trade in wildlife, corporate crime in the forestry sector, the illegal exploitation and sale of gold and other minerals, illegal fisheries, the trafficking of hazardous waste and carbon credit fraud—is growing two to three times faster than global GDP.

*529.* To combat the illegal trade in wildlife, the U.N. system and partners have launched their Wild for Life campaign to mobilize millions to take action against

---

103. *See*: http://www.unep.org

poaching and the trafficking of illegal wildlife products. Already, thousands of people and more than twenty-five ministers have chosen a species to show their commitment to protecting wildlife. The host of this year's World Environment Day, the Government of Angola, has joined the fight, promising to shut down its domestic trade in illegal ivory, toughen border controls and restore its elephant population through conservation measures.

## §3. Organized Criminal Cartels

*530.* The transnational organized criminal networks are using environmental crime to launder drug money. Illegal gold mining in Colombia, for example, is now considered one of the easiest ways to launder money from the country's drug trade. International criminal cartels are also involved in the trafficking of hazardous waste and chemicals, often mis-labeling this type of waste in order to evade law enforcement agencies.

## §4. White-Collar Crime

*531.* There has been a rise in white-collar environmental crime, from the use of shell companies in tax havens to launder money generated from illegal logging to transfer mispricing, hacking and identity theft. Carbon trading is the world's fastest growing commodities market. Carbon credit fraud cases have involved sums of transfers and profits that stretch into the hundreds of millions of dollars.[104]

## §5. Environmental Crime and Response

*532.* The international focus has centered around species, as well as the illegal wildlife trade related to endangered species mainly listed under CITES. However, the wider range of environmental crime from corporate forestry crimes to carbon credit fraud, trafficking hazardous waste or involving threat finance to non-state armed groups and terrorist groups have not yet received a system-wide response. Different needs are to be recognized, and different tools are required depending upon whether environmental crime is a result of poverty and perceptions of restrained livelihood opportunities, or as a source of revenue by non-state armed groups including terrorists and militias, or by organized criminal networks—or a combination.

104. Refer UNEP-INTERPOL REPORT—Value of Environmental Crime up by 26 per cent: http://www.interpol.int/en/news-and events/News/2016/UNEP-INTERPOL-report-value-of-environmental-crime-up-26.

## Chapter 2. Impact of War on Environment

*533.* Military activities are significant contributors to environmental harms like deforestation, pollution and loss of biodiversity and the presence of land mines in large areas. Government's conducting military actions have historically gone unchecked in relation to the related environmental impacts. Yet, increasingly, the wanton destruction of natural resources that military activities often entail has been identified as an area where international laws are needed to prevent environmental impacts. The governments gave little thought to the environmental impacts of their military actions, but a turning point came with the United Nation's Conference on Environment and Development in Rio in 1992 where it was recognized that military activities in the past had caused or contributed to different types of destruction to natural resources, and Chapter 20 of Agenda 21 focused on this specific issue. This was the beginning of legal efforts to regulate and monitor the environmental impacts of military activities. Since then, ongoing meetings on this topic have been held to establish a baseline of environmental norms that should be applicable to all nations or groups engaged in military activities or warfare so as to prevent unnecessary adverse environmental impacts. Consequently, several international agreements now exist which outline the environmental norms that have been developed.[105]

*534.* The twenty-seven legal principles on the Protection of the environment in relation to armed conflicts (PERAC) were passed by the UN General Assembly on December 7, 2022. This was the result of culmination of work by the International Law Commission to better protect the environment during war and occupations. The PERAC principles are extensive and cover important topics such as the rights of Indigenous peoples, the use of natural resources, corporate conduct in conflict zones and the effects of war on marine areas. They do this by bringing together elements of environmental, human rights and security law, as well as existing practices of states and international organizations. One important principle calls on states to make businesses, and subsidiaries, operating in and from their country responsible for harm to the environment and human health caused during wartime. Other principles focus on occupation, introducing the idea that occupiers should use the natural resources of occupied territories in a sustainable way. Existing international humanitarian rules gave the environment limited protection, mainly in the context of international armed conflicts. Environmental harm from conflict leaves communities suffering long after the fighting has stopped.

*535.* The PERAC principles are not legally binding on states, but it is hoped that they will be implemented through national legislation, military training manuals, business guidance, and outreach with non-state armed groups. With respect to implementation, unlike a legally binding international treaty, there is no formal body or process to carry them out and monitor them. But legal experts, academics and

105. http://wedocs.unep.org.

international groups are taking them seriously, and organizations like the International Union for Conservation of Nature are also working on it.

### §1. Collateral Damage to Environment

*536.* Conflicts are typically made up of complex and multiple layers of casualty, ranging from ideologies, politics and personalities to economics and trade. Natural resources, or in environmental parlance "ecosystem goods and services," have also been recognized as one of the potential drivers of conflict. While the human horror and agony of war is more or less captured by the media, the environmental consequences—the "collateral damage"—are scantily or selectively covered or not covered at all.

### §2. Rise in Temperature

*537.* Environmental degradation is aggravated by climate change, which is essentially acting as the motor spinning the scarcity-degradation-conflict cycle ever faster. In Darfur, South Sudan, for example, a major and long-term drop in precipitation, ranging from 16% to 34% in over eighty years, has been recorded with obvious impacts on land quality. Climate change forecast models predict that compared to the 1961–1990 "baseline climate," areas fringing the Sahara, such as Northern Kordofan, are set to experience a 0.5°C to 1.5°C rise in average annual temperatures by 2030 and 2060, respectively, with an average rainfall decline of 5%. The impacts on agriculture are likely to be disastrous with an estimated 70% drop in crop yields. Due to declining rainfall, the spread of the desert which has shifted southwards by an estimated 50 km–200 km since 1930 is expected to continue.

### §3. Direct and Indirect Impact

*538.* Scientific assessment of the environmental effects of conflict is generally categorized as direct and indirect impacts. Direct impacts relate to those occurrences which are physically and lineally linked to military action and which typically arise within the immediate short-term (up to six months), whereas indirect impacts are those that can be attributed to the conflict but which usually interact with a web of factors and only become fully manifest in the medium to longer run. Some examples of direct impacts include environmental contamination from bombing of industrial sites, deliberate natural resource destruction, and military debris and demolition waste from targeted infrastructure.

*539.* Indirect impacts include the environmental footprint of displaced populations, collapse of environmental governance and data vacuum, and lack of funding for environmental protection. At the country level, national response has been variable but on the whole weak. It was rapid and effective in Lebanon, where a coordination cell was established to deal with the oil spill, and international support was successfully mobilized for environmental protection. While in Iraq and Sudan the response has been slow and limited due to weak capacity, it is gradually developing. There has been no coordinated regional reaction, and each country has essentially had to rely on its own resources.

### §4. UNEP Study

*540.* At the international level, the main response to the environmental consequences of conflict has come from the UNEP. In the Gulf War of 1991, it was the first time that UNEP examined the environmental risks of a war, producing a series of desk studies which, however, were curtailed by lack of empirical fieldwork. The defining milestone for UNEP came in 1999 with the publication of its groundbreaking scientific assessment of the Kosovo conflict, which also included for the first time a detailed field-based evaluation of depleted uranium (DU) contamination. Catalyzed by its successful experience in the Balkans, UNEP institutionalized its work in this field by establishing a dedicated Post-Conflict and Disaster Management Branch in 2001 with a global mandate to address the environmental impacts of war. UNEP's scope of work on environment and conflict is centered on supporting post-conflict countries in four main areas: (i) scientific assessment of environmental impacts; (ii) remediation of contaminated "hot spots"; (iii) building and strengthening environmental governance capacity; and (iv) integrating environmental considerations in post-conflict reconstruction and development.

## I. Environmental Diplomacy

*541.* In early 2008, UNEP launched a new program on the role of the environment in peace building with the aim to address the environmental causes of conflict. It will also entail an "environmental diplomacy" component seeking to promote internal reconciliation within conflict-affected countries, as well as catalyzing reengagement with neighbors through dialogue and cooperation on shared ecosystems and resources. Of UNEP's twelve post-conflict assessments, slightly under half have been in the Arab world including Iraq, Lebanon, the Occupied Palestinian Territories, Somalia and Sudan. These reports have by and large succeeded in raising the environment's profile within high-level political agendas, both nationally and internationally. Presenting a synoptic overview of the key environmental challenges facing post-conflict countries, the assessments address the concept of "environment" to include issues that may otherwise be classified under energy, forestry, public health, agriculture, transport, education, etc. It also looks at the environmental history and chronic problems predating the conflict.

*542.* UNEP was unable to field its experts on the ground due to security restrictions, it trained national partners on sampling methodology and field verification to backstop satellite image analysis. Samples were then taken to international laboratories for independent analysis. Overall, the common hallmark of UNEP's reports is their timeliness, accessibility to the non-environmental expert and their attractive visual layout combining photographs, satellite images, maps and graphics.

## II. Environmental Cleanup and Mitigation

*543.* The scientific team of UNEP is deployed to the field working under a military setting, and the international credibility of its scientific findings is high as these are conducted in a transparent manner with the full engagement of national partners. Another practical benefit of these reports is their proven track record in mobilizing donor interest and funding to implement follow-up projects and activities. Drawing on the findings of its assessments, UNEP has designed and delivered environmental cleanup and mitigation measures to reduce direct risks from conflict, such as in Iraq where it collected and secured highly hazardous materials. In Lebanon, UNEP strengthened the government's environmental monitoring system to track contamination levels generated by the conflict. In Darfur, three million trees were replanted to help combat land degradation and alleviate fuel wood shortages around Internally Displaced Persons camps as well as help create the necessary conditions for an eventual return process. Strengthening environmental governance has been UNEP's core activity in post-conflict countries. This has involved capacity-building programs covering a wide spectrum of topics ranging from law and policy development to laboratory training such as in Iraq and Sudan, as well as targeted technical support on specific issues (e.g., hazardous waste) for Palestinian officials.

## III. UNEP Intervention

*544.* In view of the rapid economic growth rates that are characteristic of countries emerging from conflicts such as Sudan and Iraq, UNEP has been providing technical expertise both to the community and to the national authorities to help ensure the environmental sustainability of their interventions and reconstruction investments. UNEP has brokered technical cooperation between Iran and Iraq, Iraq and the Regional Organization for the Protection of the Marine Environment (Kuwait Action Plan), the Palestinian Authority and Israel, and between North and South Sudan.

*545.* Other international organizations have also been extending their support to post-conflict countries to include an environmental component, particularly the UNDP and the World Bank. However, these interventions have largely been on a case-by-case basis and are typically designed with a specific thematic focus (e.g., solid waste, forestry); where the environment in its wider sense is not the driving concern. Moreover, these organizations have a very large portfolio and so do not carry the "environmental flag" in the same way that UNEP does. Nevertheless, they do bring significant resources and expertise to the table, and their long-term in-country presence adds continuity and sustainability to their efforts.

## §5. Peace Building Commission

*546.* In 2005, the U.N. established a Peace building Commission to consider the environmental connection to conflict in its development of integrated recovery strategies. Environment as a sector has also been incorporated in various coordination mechanisms set-up to consolidate the work of international organizations in post-conflict transition settings, such as the U.N. Development Group and Inter-Agency Standing Committee at the global level, and the U.N. Country Team at the country level. Both environmental and conflict-resolution NGOs respond to the specific environmental needs of post-conflict countries and in some cases have proven to be important sources of data and expertise. Some of the key players, include Green Cross International, Greenpeace, International Union for the Conservation of Nature (IUCN) and the WWF for Nature. For instance, Green Cross conducted scientific environmental analysis of the Gulf Wars, while Greenpeace has been monitoring the DU issue and was the first to raise the alarm about the environmental fallout from the ransacking of the nuclear facility in Tuwaitha. Greenpeace was also very quick to deploy assessment teams to Lebanon and Iraq immediately.

# Chapter 3. Environmental Risk Management

*547.* In the beginning of twentieth century, the world population was about 1.6 billion; however, pollution and environmental degradation were common, the problems were local and not widespread. The World as a whole seemed vast, with huge regions keeping natural environment and virtually untouched by its human inhabitants. By mid-century, airplanes and radio broadcasts had begun to shrink distances and brought the communities of the World into greater contact. Industrial growth multiplied the consumption of natural resources and brought issue of environmental pollution in many countries, especially those leaders of the Industrial Revolution. As industrial growth continued, air and water pollution became more and more widespread, as did concern about the cumulative impact of toxic industrial products on living species. All these developments brought the issue of environmental risk management into focus.

*548.* The world population as well as economic activity has increased manyfold. The environmental degradation became a matter of global worries, giving rise to many treaties addressing environmental concerns. The pressures of agricultural and industrial development have begun affecting and extinguishing other species in a rapid rate, and visibly impacting the quality of the soil, forests, oceans, and atmosphere. These pressures are bound to increase in the face of increasing human population, and if economic activity continues its explosive growth, without adequate measures in place to protect the environment. As a consequence, the environmental regulations around the World have become more and more strict, impacting business, social and financial activities.

## §1. Types of Environmental Risks

### I. Difficult to Cover

*549.* Investors and companies are conscious of the ways that environmental issues affect their businesses posing risks, which are difficult to cover, and have to be carefully handled. Regulations related to businesses and the environment constantly improve and change and create uncertainties for companies bringing significant implications for their financial performance. Consumer's reactions and other environmentally motivated actions can create serious non-regulatory risks that may reduce a company's markets or affects its financial strength. But significant rewards are also increasingly available to companies that are able to transform environmental concern into opportunity or competitive advantage. Some companies have recognized new demands for "green" products and developed new niches in the market of goods and services. Some companies have been finding their reputation enhanced and their earnings increased by adopting cleaner production techniques and keeping environmentally adequate facilities. In many industries, environmental issues have implications that can significantly affect companies' financial results.

### II. Affect the Working Conditions

*550.* Environmental risk may arise as a result of public opposition against projects viewed as to have a significant adverse effect on living and working conditions in their localities. Public opposition may stop projects going ahead or may significantly delay their implementation. In this case, actions required to overcome public opposition may impose new and, in some cases, tremendous costs, with significant effects on the project's rate of return. Regulations allowing for public information and participation in projects also cause risk, as failure to conform to such requirements can result in fines, penalties or even revocation of the license which gave the right to continue with the project implementation. Particularly, sensitive projects (involving construction of huge dams, for example) may require efforts to ensure that, while compliance is adequate, public relations are sufficient to permit conclusion without unexpected reactions and consequent delays.

### III. Impacting Supply Chain

*551.* Environmental risk may also arise through customer supply chains, since a customer who produces at an early stage in a supply chain is exposed to changes in the market for the end product. For example, falling car sales will affect manufacturers of auto-parts and tires in the same way. The transmission of business risks in supply chains also applies to environmental risks. Therefore, a customer who produces at an early stage in a supply chain may be vulnerable to the consequences of environmental violations committed by other suppliers or final producers in any part of that supply chain. For example, a customer that supplies a final producer faced with a large expense for remedial work may incur huge losses as a result of that final producer's diminished ability to pay for goods supplied. In the same way, the manufacturer of tires and auto-parts may experience delays if the car producer is obliged to divert funds to face cleanup costs and fines. Similarly, a customer at the end of the supply chain faced with a supplier that goes out of business as a result of an environmental injunction may have to find an alternative source of supply, and possibly pay a higher price for supplies or accept more restrictive or onerous credit terms. In this case, the car producer faces expensive problems if the tire manufacturer goes out of business due to cleanup costs and fines. It is also important to highlight that exporters are especially vulnerable to changes in the supply chain in importing countries. Similarly, foreign regulations can sometimes sweep out suppliers in other countries because of new environmental regulations and standards.

## §2. Methods of Environmental Risk Management

*552.* A good risk management is where the measures taken protect achievement of goals within the accepted tolerance of risk with the lowest cost. Environmental risk management is the process by which risks are identified, appraised, controlled, transferred, and monitored. Environmental risk management may be applied to both individual credit transactions and to aggregate loan and investment portfolios. It minimizes exposure to foreseeable environmental risks, while at the same time providing adequate protection against unforeseeable risks.

*553.* The environmental risk management can help reduce nonperforming assets and improve performance. These procedures include investigation techniques such as due diligence, appraisal techniques, control techniques such as legal covenants and loan agreements, transfers techniques such as risk finance products, routine risk monitoring techniques and specific procedures designed to protect assets during workout and foreclosure operations. Many of these procedures have direct parallels in environmental risk management. The transactions that involve environmental risk are subject to environmental risk management. In practice, however, the institution has to weigh the level of environmental risk within individual transactions against the costs of managing that risk and the likely consequences of failing to manage it.

## I. Environmental Risk Management Culture

*554.* A focus on practical steps to be taken in order to develop an effective environmental risk management system is a way to create and consolidate an environmental risk management culture within the organization. So, the main building blocks of successful environmental risk management are techniques and procedures designed to ensure that environmental risks are managed in a systematic and effective way, while at the same time minimizing overhead and transaction costs which could have a bad effect on competitive position and business performance. Environmental risk management does not constitute an "exact science" and frequently requires credit officers to make judgments on the nature and magnitude of environmental risks which cannot be measured objectively. However, this risk management cannot eradicate environmental risks altogether but can help to minimize exposure to indirect and direct risks, thus reducing potential losses.

## II. Screening

*555.* Environmental screening is the process by which institutions assess whether the level of environmental risk associated with particular transactions is sufficient to justify more rigorous investigative techniques. It is the filtering mechanism for deciding which transactions should be subject to environmental investigations. A common toll in this stage is the sector checklist, which classifies specific industries or activities as representing high, medium, or low environmental impact. Once a company or project matches with the list of risky activities, deeper should be the analysis. In this stage, mandatory EIA can also be identified. Environmental screening is undertaken on the basis of readily available information, collected in the normal course of business.

## §3. Environmental Business Risk Appraisal

*556.* Environmental business risk appraisal focuses on the impact of laws and regulations together with changing supply-chain standards, consumer preferences, and public opinion on a customer's products, markets, and competitive position. Products may be affected by constraints in raw materials caused by changes in environmental regulations or higher required environmental standards. Changes in consumer preferences could cause the company's market or competitive position to drop. So, the institutions incorporate business risk appraisal in their routine due diligence process for credit or other transactions. Typically, business risk appraisal includes an analysis of a customer's business markets, its competitors and competitive strengths and weaknesses, and the capabilities and experience of its management personnel. If feasible and appropriate, environmental business risk appraisal should follow lines of inquiry considering the implications of environmental issues, being the focus of the analysis as given below:

(a) Change in environmental laws and regulations and their implications for a business's products, markets and competitive position.
(b) Change in end-consumer product preferences and their implications for a business's products, markets and competitive position.
(c) Shift in public opinion and opportunities for public participation.
(d) Regulatory change making entire product lines obsolete, for example, asbestos building materials, DDT insecticides, and CFC aerosols.

## §4. Shifting of Environmental Risk

*557.* Shifting of risk has been adopted as the main risk management tool worldwide in the management of risk as a whole. The existence of a developed insurance market has increasingly permitted environmental risk transfer. A growing range of insurance policies is becoming available in the market, covering risk for institutions, their clients and environmental consultants. Essentially institutions can use insurance policies within a risk protection strategy in following areas:

(a) requesting customers to explore policies which protect them against environmental liabilities;
(b) customers to take environmental liability policies naming the financial institution as beneficiary;
(c) taking out first-party policies that transfer the environmental risk of the financial institutions' entire portfolio to the insurers;
(d) the environmental consultants have professional indemnity insurance coverage.

§5. MONITORING ENVIRONMENTAL RISK

*558.* Environmental risk monitoring is the process of maintaining information relating to environmental risks associated with any aspect e.g., of a financial institution's current lending or investment portfolios. Given the dynamic nature of environmental risk and its potential implications, the financial institution put in place basic monitoring procedures to identify new sources of risk at an early stage and wherever necessary review them. Monitoring procedures may range from simple oral inquiries, through more formal types of information disclosure, to new site or plant investigations. Environmental monitoring procedures fall into two basic categories, namely procedures for monitoring environmental risks for individual credits, and procedures for monitoring sources of environmental risk with a broader impact across entire loan and investment portfolios, that is, on multiple transactions.

## I. Review of Individual Transaction

*559.* The simplest form of monitoring involves reviewing the environmental implications of individual transactions through periodic routines checks. Such checks may be conducted periodically as part of normal credit term monitoring procedures. As with other environmental risk management techniques, financial institutions are unlikely to wish to monitor all loans and investment transactions for environmental risk. The emphasis therefore is on the highest-risk transactions as identified during environmental screening and investigations activities. In addition, financial institutions also consider monitoring portfolio environmental risk. Of the two main components to this monitoring activity, the first focuses on sources of environmental risk, for example, changing environmental laws and regulations and changing end-consumer preferences, and their potential impact on a loan and investment portfolio or its high-risk segments.

## II. Watch on Laws and Regulations

*560.* Given the importance of environmental laws and regulations as a source of environmental risk, institutions keep a constant watch on new environmental laws and regulations which may have an impact on existing customers and undermine their credit worthiness. This ongoing process includes developments in all countries of operations and all countries to which their customers export. In most countries, institutions and companies can obtain the basic information for this process simply by placing formal requests with relevant environmental ministries and regulatory agencies. Similar logic applies to monitoring the implications of changing consumer preferences, including preferences of other producers in the supply chain or of end-consumers.

§6. ENVIRONMENTAL POLICY

*561.* Confronted with the growing exposure to environmental risks, business world must be able to respond in a structured and consistent manner. A comprehensive environmental risk management policy is a must for ensuring this aspect. The benefits of having an environmental risk management policy are numerous, and a well-designed policy can provide guidelines for staff and customers about criteria with respect to environmental risk and environmental issues; clarify detailed objectives for staff and customers to explain how the commercial entity intends to achieve its aims, including the specific procedures adopted and the assignment of responsibilities for implementing them, etc. The fundamental requirements of an environmental risk management policy are that it is realistic and cost-effective. If a company is too ambitious in formulating policies, it may find out that they put too much pressure over their resources and place themselves at a competitive disadvantage by imposing unrealistic costs on their transactions. If it is insufficiently ambitious, it may expose itself to unnecessary risks and hence may suffer avoidable losses.

*562.* The exposure to environmental risk varies according to a number of factors, including the precise nature and mix of the services it offers. At the same time, exposure responds to external changes in environmental regulation, supply-chain standards and end-consumer attitudes as demonstrated before. Also, exposure to reputation risk can arise from increased public awareness or negative public opinion. The ability of a commercial entity to respond to environmental risks is a function of its size, the level of expertise in environmental risk management available and its current organization and procedures for risk management as a whole. The potential impact on competitiveness, by introducing environmental risk management techniques and procedures, has to be considered. An important variable which commercial entity adopts is their ability to pass to customers the costs associated with environmental site assessments and audits and even risk transfer costs.

# Part XII. Environment and Human Rights

## Chapter 1. Pollution Free Environment: A Human Right

*563.* Climate change is one of the greatest threats to human rights of the present generation, posing a serious risk to rights to life, health, food, and standard of living across the world. As per UNEP, more than two million annual deaths and a large number of cases of diseases are attributed to pollution. All over the world, people experience the adverse effects of environmental degradation, ecosystems decline, water shortage, fisheries depletion, and natural disasters due to deforestation and unsafe management and disposal of toxic and dangerous wastes. Indigenous peoples suffer directly from the degradation of the ecosystems that they rely upon for their livelihoods. Climate change is escalating many of these negative effects of environmental degradation on human health and well-being and is also causing new ones, including an increase in extreme weather conditions like hurricanes and spread of malaria and other vector-borne diseases. These facts clearly show the close linkages between the environment and the enjoyment of human rights and justify an integrated approach to an environment free from pollution and safeguarding human rights.[106]

### §1. Healthy Environment

*564.* A healthy environment is a prerequisite for the enjoyment of human rights. Thus, the human rights obligations of states include the duty to ensure the level of environmental protection necessary to allow the full exercise of protected rights. Certain human rights, especially access to information, participation in decision-making, and access to justice in environmental matters, are essential to good environmental decision-making which implies that human rights must be implemented in order to ensure environmental protection. The right to a safe, healthy and ecologically balanced environment is a basic human right in itself.

### §2. Stockholm and Rio Declarations

*565.* The Stockholm Declaration, and to a lesser extent the Rio Declaration, show that the link between human rights and dignity and the environment was very

106. Vide, United Nations Environment Programme website, http://www.unep.org.

prominent in the early stages of U.N. efforts to address environmental problems. The international community made efforts to tackle specific environmental problems, with focus being placed on developing policy and legal instruments, both at the international and at national levels, targeted at the environmental problems that were emerging, through a series of MEAs and other mechanisms. Although the foundation of developing such mechanisms laid on the considerations made at the time of the Stockholm Conference, the human rights dimension is not made explicit in most of these instruments.

### §3. Human Rights Council

*566.* Many U.N. bodies have emphasized the need to address the issues of human rights and environment in conjunction. The Commission on Human Rights renamed as the Human Rights Council[107] requested the High Commissioner and invited UNEP, UNDP, and other relevant bodies and organizations, within their respective mandates and approved work programs and budgets, "to continue to coordinate their efforts in activities relating to human rights and the environment in poverty eradication, post-conflict environmental assessment and rehabilitation, disaster prevention, post-disaster assessment and rehabilitation, to take into consideration in their work relevant findings and recommendations of others and to avoid duplication."

## I. Human Rights and Climate Change

*567.* The U.N. reform process called for the integration of human rights in all of the organization's work. In a series of resolutions, the former U.N. Commission on Human Rights and the U.N. Human Rights Council have drawn attention to the relationship between a safe and healthy environment and the enjoyment of human rights. The Human Rights Council in its Resolution 7/23 of March 2008 and Resolution 10/4 of March 2009 focused specifically on human rights and climate change, noting that climate change-related effects have a range of direct and indirect implications for the effective enjoyment of human rights. These resolutions have raised awareness of how fundamental the environment is as a prerequisite to the enjoyment of human rights.

*568.* The climate change caused by human activity has negative impact on and interferes with the full enjoyment of human rights. Climate change affects a wide variety of human rights, including the rights to life, self-determination, development, food, health, water, sanitation and housing. The human rights framework also requires that global efforts to mitigate and adapt to climate change should be guided by relevant human rights norms and principles, including the rights to participation and information, transparency, accountability, equity, and non-discrimination. Principle 15 of the Rio Declaration on Environment and Development calls for states to

107. Paragraph 8 of Resolution 2005/60.

adopt a precautionary approach to environmental harms and act "when there are threats of serious or irreversible damage" even in the absence of full scientific certainty. In the case of climate change, there is no uncertainty. Climate change has already done serious damage. The only uncertainty remaining is how much more damage it will cause. Under these circumstances, urgent preventative action is needed.

## II. Implementation of Human Rights Obligations

*569.* UNEP, the U.N. Office of the High Commissioner for Human Rights, and the U.N. Special Rapporteur on human rights and the environment make efforts to identify, promote good practices relating to the use of human rights obligations and commitments to inform, support and strengthen environmental policymaking, especially in the areas of environmental protection and management. The joint initiative identified practical and concrete examples of good practices where states and other actors have successfully implemented human rights obligations related to environmental protection and management, which could be replicated in other contexts, and which will increase the understanding and awareness of the linkages between human rights and the environment, including providing more clarity on the human rights obligations related to the enjoyment of a safe, clean, sustainable and healthy environment. The good practices were collected at the international, regional, national and subnational levels in collaboration through regional/sub-regional consultations as well as questionnaires and surveys. In the process of identifying such practices and analyzing the practical aspects of the interaction between the two fields of human rights and the environment, UNEP and partners also identified challenges and problems in the balancing of the protection of human rights and the protection of the environment, and identified lessons learned in respect of such interaction, which are available with the good practices identified.[108]

108. *Ibid.*

## Chapter 2. Investment, Human Rights and Environment Protection

*570.* The Human Rights Council in its twenty-sixth session, held on June 26, 2014, adopted resolution 26/9 which established an Open-Ended Intergovernmental Working Group (OEIGWG) on transnational corporations (TNCs) and other business enterprises with respect to human rights. The mandate was to elaborate an international legally binding instrument to provide for international human rights law and on this behalf regulate the activities of TNCs and other business enterprises.

*571.* Four drafts have been developed so far for this treaty. The first draft (known as "Zero Draft") was prepared in 2018. After considering reactions from states and business entities, the Revised Draft was published in July 2019. Again, a second revised draft was published in August 2020, alongside another document explaining the key issues and the structure of the second revised draft. A third revised draft, which is also the latest draft (also referred to as the "Draft Treaty") was published in August 2021.

*572.* The overall purpose of the proposed "Draft Treaty" is to clarify the human rights obligations of transnational business enterprises, and to prevent and mitigate the occurrence of human rights abuses including relating to environment, in the context of business activities by effective mechanisms of monitoring and enforceability. The proposed Draft Treaty would obligate state parties to take all appropriate legal and policy measures to ensure that business enterprises subject to their jurisdiction (including transnational corporations and other business enterprises that undertake activities of transnational character) respect all internationally recognized human rights and prevent and mitigate human rights abuses throughout their operations. The Draft Treaty provides requirements to be fulfilled by state parties, in order to ensure its implementation. State parties are required to amend their legislation where appropriate, so as to be in accordance with the requirements and standards set by the Draft Treaty. This obligation would also include the establishment of adequate monitoring mechanisms to ensure effective implementation of the Draft Treaty.

*573.* The scope of the Draft Treaty is very broad. It would apply to all business activities undertaken by a physical or legal person within a state, including business activities of a transnational character. However, it would permit state parties to establish in their domestic legislation on a non-discriminatory basis to differentiate how business enterprises discharge these obligations commensurate with their size, sector, operational context or the impacts on human rights. The main points of the Draft Treaty are access to remedy for victims, protection and prevention for victims, and the establishment of a committee and international cooperation between states.

§1. International Investment Agreements Addressing Environmental Issues

*574.* For the protection of human rights and environment, IA between investors and Bilateral Investment Treaty (BIT) between states may address human rights and environmental issues and develop a legal framework through which corporate conduct in violation of human rights or environmental law can be taken into account. The IA entered into force or recently signed, appears to take a positive approach toward addressing human rights and environmental issues and acknowledge at least an obligation on investors to make and maintain their investments in accordance with the host State laws and regulations. Further, just for attracting foreign investments, host States should not relax their labor, public health, safety or environmental measures (Iran-Slovakia BIT, 2017, Articles 2 and 10). The new draft of the Dutch Model BIT contains provisions giving power to arbitral tribunals, when deciding on the amount of compensation, to take into account "non-compliance by the investor with its commitments under the UN Guiding Principles on Businesses and Human Rights, and the OECD Guidelines for Multinational Enterprises" (Draft Dutch Model BIT, Article 23). States, as main stakeholders of the Investor State Dispute Settlement (ISDS) system and of investment law, can adopt suitable approaches when negotiating or renegotiating their IA and address their direct concerns about the protection of human rights and the environment within their territory or concerning their nationals.

§2. Issue of Environmental Protection in IA

*575.* At present time, corporations have become, alongside states, actors in the field of public international law whereas most human rights treaties impose obligations upon States and not on non-State actors. However, corporations are often guilty of or, at least, complicit in human rights abuses, including violations of environmental law. A 2006 U.N. interim report regarding corporate violations of human rights noted that human rights abuses take place mostly in low-income countries, with weak governance and a low rule of law index (and high rates of corruption), with most allegations of the worst corporate abuses occurring in the extractive sector.

## I. Corporations: Subject of International Law

*576.* The States have a duty under international law to protect human rights. The corporations can have a reciprocal responsibility to respect those rights as states are no longer the sole actors or participants in the field of public international law. The responsibility of corporations to protect human rights may be found in various guidelines of corporate social responsibility, including the thirty-one "Guiding Principles" prepared by the U.N. Special Representative in 2011 on "Business and

Human Rights." There are also certain codes of conduct, like the U.N. Global Compact, the 2011 OECD Guidelines for Multinational Enterprises, and industry-specific codes of conduct such as "The Voluntary Principles on Security and Human Rights" for the extractive sector.

## II. Jurisdiction of Arbitral Tribunal

*577.* The arbitral tribunals called to discuss issues of human rights and environmental law can do so only if they have jurisdiction to hear claims related to these rights and if the law applicable to the merits covers these matters. There are a variety of dispute resolution provisions in IA, and some offer broad jurisdiction, for example, from limiting jurisdiction to the quantum of compensation for expropriation, to jurisdiction over all disputes concerning investments. A broadly worded jurisdictional clause is helpful for the claimant to bring in arbitration claims related to environmental and human rights issues. The dispute resolution clause must also be broad enough to include counterclaims, reflecting the consent of the parties.

## III. International Law Includes Environmental Norms

*578.* A BIT may contain a list of sources of law for the tribunal to apply, including the BIT itself, the domestic law of the host state, and "principles of international law," or a similar phrase. The question is as to whether "principles of international law" encompass the human rights and environmental norms at issue. There is no consensus on this issue. Some scholars suggest that human rights are part of the applicable law, as they are a "component of international law" (Clara Reiner & Christoph Schreuer, Human Rights and International Investment Arbitration, in Human Rights in International Investment Law and Arbitration, Dupuy et al., eds. 2009, 82, 84–85). Article 42(1) of the International Centre for Settlement of Investment Disputes (ICSID) Convention provides that, in the absence of agreement of the parties on the applicable law, the tribunal "shall apply the law of the Contracting State party to the dispute (including its rules on the conflict of laws) and such rules of international law as may be applicable." In *Von Pezold v. Zimbabwe*, third parties made amicus curiae submission regarding the application of indigenous rights, which they contended were applicable by virtue of the Germany-Zimbabwe BIT's reference to "international law." The tribunal found that the "rules of general international law as may be applicable does not incorporate the entire universe of international law such as international human rights law on indigenous peoples—only the international law relevant to the BIT, such as international law standards for fair and equitable treatment" (*Bernhard von Pezold and Others v. Republic of Zimbabwe*, ICSID Case No. ARB/10/15, Procedural Order No. 2 of June 26, 2012, paras 39, 578).

*579.* To justify actions taken against an investor, a state may rely on an investor's alleged noncompliance with local or international human rights or environmental laws. In *S.D. Myers v. Canada*, Canada relied on the alleged noncompliance of investor with local environmental laws. In *Aven v. Costa Rica*, Costa Rica raised the defense that investors did not follow local environmental laws, justifying measures taken against investors or, alternatively, giving rise to a defense of "unclean hands."

### IV. Environmental Protection Being Subject Matter of Dispute

*580.* The Iron Rhine Arbitration (*Belgium v. Netherlands*) involved activation of the Iron Rhine railway and the entitlement of the Netherlands to insist on Dutch laws pertaining to environmental impact studies. The tribunal held that the environmental impact studies required under Dutch law were applicable to the reactivation of the Iron Rhine, so long as it did not amount to a denial of Belgium's right of transit or rendered the exercise by Belgium of its right of transit unreasonably difficult. In cases between Romania and Energy Group OMV (Austria) (ICC), OMV claimed that the Romanian government failed to reimburse expenses for decontamination of historically polluted locations, which had been privatized, given that the environmental cleanup was provided for in the parties' contract.

### §3. Human Rights and Stabilization Clauses

*581.* The stabilization provisions are kept in contracts so as to protect and keep the benefits available to investor's constant and not affected by change in law. The environmental impact of stabilization clauses found in major investment projects has been brought into focus from time to time. The human rights and environmental and sustainable development activists are ascertaining as to how investor protection may be inconsistent with the protection of human rights. This has drawn attention to investor protections contained in contracts and in bilateral and regional investment treaties. Concerns are being voiced that protection of investor rights in contracts is not being balanced on the one hand with the state duty to regulate investors to protect human rights; and on the other, the investors' responsibility to respect human rights. These concerns were voiced by the Office of the High Commissioner for Human Rights in two recent reports.[109] On balancing investors' rights with obligations, the High Commissioner stated: Investors' rights are instrumental rights. In other words, investors' rights are defined in order to meet some wider goal such as sustainable human development, economic growth, stability, which promote and protect human rights. The conditional nature of investors' rights suggests that they should be balanced with corresponding checks, balances and obligations—toward individuals, the state or the environment. While investment liberalization has focused on the definition of investors' rights, balancing those rights with states' "right to regulate," discussions over investment liberalization have paid less attention to parallel discussions in the U.N., OECD and ILO defining investors' obligations toward individuals. This risks skewing investment liberalization in favor of

109. *Human Rights, Trade and Investment*, Report of the UN High Commissioner for Human Rights, E/CN.4/Sub.2/2003/9(2003).

investors' rights, losing sight of their conditional nature, possibly to the detriment of the rights and interests of other actors.[110] Concerns about stabilization clauses originate from fears that investor protections may infringe on state duties and investor responsibilities toward human rights.

*582.* Thus, the stabilization clauses should not make foreign investments immune from social and environmental laws that come into force after the effective date of the agreement, or require the HG (particularly in hydrocarbon extraction contracts) to compensate the investor for compliance with such laws. The requirement for the HG to pay for compliance is considered wrong in principle, because it denies the state its basic role as legislator with powers different and greater than companies, and furthermore it creates a financial disincentive for the host state, thus hindering the application of dynamic social and environmental standards over the life of a long-term project.[111] A balance is required to be maintained as an investor invests his money for profit, and they weigh pros and cons in the light of their own business efficacy and not in terms of absolute protection of human rights.

*583.* The use of stabilization clauses to deter host states from amending domestic law has led to allegations that they represent an obstacle to sustainable development. In particular, it has been suggested that stabilization clauses may discourage governments from introducing or enforcing laws relating to the protection of human rights, and environmental conservation. Criticism of stabilization clauses has mainly been targeted at projects in the energy and natural resources sectors, where the potential for negative impacts on human rights and the environment is considerable. These are also sectors in which investors are exposed to significant political and economic risks. Their upfront capital investment measured in hundreds of millions or even billions of dollars may only be recovered over a long period of time. The stability of the legal and regulatory framework is very important for investors who risk capital in host states that have a 'volatile legal and institutional system.

110. *Ibid.*

111. *Lifting the Lid on Foreign Investment Contracts: The Real Deal for Sustainable Development, International Institute for Environment and Development* (September 2005), available at www.iied.org; *Heavy Mittal? A State Within a State: The Inequitable Mineral Development Agreement Between the Government of Liberia and Mittal Steel Holdings NV* (October 2006), available at www.globalwitness.org. *See also*, Cotula, Lorenzo, *Stabilization Clauses and the Evolution of Environmental Standards in Foreign Investment Contracts*, 17(1) Yearb. Int. Environ. Law 111–138 (20 06).

# Part XIII. Management of Natural Resources and Environmental Law

*584.* There is an ambition to provide affordable, reliable, sustainable energy for all, free of pollution or of tolerable pollution. A 2023 report by Economic and Social Commission for Asia and the Pacific (ESCAP) of the United Nations showed that 5.3 crore people still lack access to electricity. Out of them, 64 lakh are in India while Myanmar tops the list with 1.47 crore, followed by Pakistan (1.2 crore) and Papua New Guinea (79 lakh).

*585.* In 2022, around 2.3 billion people did not have access to clean cooking facilities and rely on the traditional use of solid biomass, kerosene, or coal as their primary cooking fuel. Household air pollution, mostly from cooking smoke, is linked to around 3.7 million premature deaths a year. The energy crisis and the related inflationary environment in the wake of the Covid-19 pandemic have exposed consumers to a dual threat of reduced income and higher prices of clean cooking fuel. Some countries have implemented policies to counter this trend, although millions, especially in Sub-Saharan Africa, have reverted to traditional use of biomass. This led improvements to slow down between 2020 and 2022.The IEA has released a report 'A Vision for Clean cooking Access for All' providing the latest data and trends on clean cooking as well as a feasible pathway to achieving universal access by 2030.

*586.* Thus, there is a need for provision of one or other sources of energy so as to meet the dream of global sustainable development. In this background, it is important to make efforts so as to put the energy sector on a more secure and sustainable footing so far as environmental protection is concerned.

## Chapter 1. Global Energy Growth and Environment

*587.* The deliberations at COP21[112] (2015 Paris Conference) are sources of guidance on energy policy intentions and the energy-related components and provides a boost to lower-carbon fuels. According to the IEA's new World Energy Outlook 2023, a major shift is underway which will result in a considerably different global energy system by the end of the decade. The phenomenal rise of clean energy technologies such as solar, wind, electric cars, and heat pumps is reshaping how everything is powered from factories and vehicles to home appliances and heating systems. This includes almost ten times as many electric cars on the road worldwide; solar PV generating more electricity than the entire US power system does currently; renewables' share of the global electricity mix nearing 50% up from around 30% today; heat pumps and other electric heating systems outselling fossil fuel boilers globally; and three times as much investment going into new offshore wind projects than into new coal- and gas-fired power plants. The combination of growing momentum behind clean energy technologies and structural economic shifts around the world has major implications for fossil fuels. In this scenario, the share of fossil fuels in global energy supply, which has been stuck for decades at around 80%, declines to 73% by 2030, with global energy-related $CO_2$ emissions peaking by 2025.

*588.* In the present scenario, demand for fossil fuels is set to remain too high to keep within reach the Paris Agreement goal of limiting the rise in average global temperatures to 1.5 °C. This risks not only worsening climate impacts after a year of record-breaking heat but also undermining the security of the energy system, which was built for a cooler world with less extreme weather events. Bending the emissions curve onto a path consistent with 1.5 °C remains possible but very difficult. Despite good clean energy growth based on today's policy settings, global emissions would remain high enough to push up global average temperatures by around 2.4 °C this century, well above the key threshold set out in the Paris Agreement.

112. The international political response to climate change began at the Rio Earth Summit in 1992, where the "Rio Convention" included the adoption of the UN Framework on Climate Change (UNFCCC). This convention set out a framework for action aimed at stabilizing atmospheric concentrations of greenhouse gases (GHGs) to avoid "dangerous anthropogenic interference with the climate system." The UNFCCC which entered into force on Mar. 21, 1994, now has a near-universal membership of 195 parties. The main objective of the annual Conference of Parties (COP) is to review the Convention's implementation. The first COP took place in Berlin in 1995 and meetings since then have included COP3 where the Kyoto Protocol was adopted, COP11 where the Montreal Action Plan was produced, COP15 in Copenhagen and COP17 in Durban where the Green Climate Fund was created. In 2015 COP21, also known as the 2015 Paris Climate Conference.

§1. ENERGY USE AND IMPACT ON ENVIRONMENT

*589.* It is nearly impossible to produce, transport, or consume energy without significant environmental impact. The environmental problems directly related to energy production and consumption include air pollution, climate change, water pollution, thermal pollution, and solid waste disposal. The emission of air pollutants from fossil fuel combustion is the major cause of urban air pollution. Burning fossil fuels is also the main contributor to the emission of GHGs. Different water pollution problems are associated with energy usage. In petroleum-handling operations, there is always a possibility of spilling oil. Coal mining can also pollute water. Changes in groundwater flow produced by mining operations often bring otherwise unpolluted waters into contact with certain mineral materials which are leached from the soil and produce an acid mine drainage. Solid waste is also a by-product of some forms of energy usage. Coal mining requires the removal of large quantities of earth as well as coal.

*590.* Energy use worldwide is expected to grow by one-third to 2040, driven primarily by China, India, Africa, the Middle East, and Southeast Asia, particularly Japan. Non-OECD countries account together for all the increase in global energy use, as demographic and structural economic trends, allied with greater efficiency, reduce collective consumption in OECD countries from the peak reached in 2007. Declines are led by the EU (15% over the period to 2040), Japan (12%) and the U.S. (3%). Global energy consumption will grow by 1.8% in 2024, largely driven by strong demand in Asia. Despite still-high prices and unsolved supply chain disruptions, demand for fossil fuels will reach record levels, but demand for renewable energy will rise by 11%.

## I. Position of China

*591.* There have been conscious efforts in the world including China to shift from polluting energy sources to less polluting or non-polluting energy sources. China has undergone a drastic transformation in recent decades, from a poor Global South country into the world's second largest economy, lifting millions out of poverty in the process. But with that growth has come plenty of emissions. China is on the brink of a new era that will have a major impact on the planet's future environment. According to the Center for Research on Energy and Clean Air (CERA), China's emissions may have peaked in 2023. Its economy is slowing down, its construction sector is weak, wind and solar energy are growing rapidly, and hydropower output will rebound after a series of droughts. As a result, China's carbon emissions are expected to decrease in 2024, a trend that looks set to continue in the years that follow. The International Energy Agency (IEA) reached a similar conclusion in its World Energy Outlook 2023 report. The report predicts that global GHG emissions could peak in 2025, partially driven by what's happening in China. In 2021, the country updated its original Paris Agreement pledge, saying its emission peak would go from around 2030 to "before" it. But China has thus far resisted moving its peak year target closer to 2025.

*592.* At the recently concluded U.N. Climate Change Summit, COP28, in Dubai, China vowed to clarify which year and at what level China's emissions will peak. Given China has committed to peak before 2030, its 2035 goals will feature net emission reduction by default. What China pledges to the U.N. over the coming year will outline the contours of the descent through to 2035, and lay the groundwork for Beijing's broader goal of reaching Net Zero by 2060. China is the only major emitter that will be able to triple its renewable energy installation by the end of this decade. This will be a critical step to force the country away from its addiction to coal. The rapid renewable energy uptake, together with its world-leading electric vehicle and battery storage industries, are becoming major engines for growth in an otherwise weak economy. This shift away from the high-carbon and fossil-fuel energy model provides hope for sustainable growth and meaningful emission reduction over the next decade. The country has compressed the social and economic transformations that took industrialized countries more than a century into that of one generation. Now China needs to join the global trend of demonstrating that decarbonization and prosperity can be achieved at the same time.

## II. Position of India

*593.* India in fact seizes the center of the world energy stage and contributes the single largest share of growth, around one-quarter, in global energy demand. India today is home to one-sixth of the world's population and its sixth-largest economy, but accounts for only 7.3% of global energy use. With policies in place to accelerate the country's modernization and develop its manufacturing base (via the "Make in India" program), population and incomes on the rise and an additional 315 million people anticipated to live in Indian cities by 2040, India is entering a sustained period of rapid growth in energy consumption. Demand for coal in power generation and industry will surge, which will increase the share of coal to almost half of the energy mix and make India the largest source of growth in global coal use. Oil demand increases by more than in any other country. India also steps up its deployment of low-carbon technologies, although uncertainty over the pace at which new large dams or nuclear plants can be built means strong reliance on solar and wind power to deliver on its pledge to have a 40% share of non-fossil fuel capacity in the power sector by 2030.

*594.* India is the world's third-largest emitter of carbon dioxide after China and the U.S., with a booming economy driving electricity demand up by 9.6% in fiscal year 2023. It has been stated that India not going to compromise with the availability of power for growth. Public sector power companies are constructing about 27 GW of thermal plants, almost all coal. However, this is insufficient as at least 80 GW of new capacity to meet future demand, is needed. As per estimates, the share of coal-fired generation in India's power mix will rise to 77% by 2025 before falling to 71% in 2030 and 52% by 2050. India cannot survive without coal as it has no other options.

*595.* Nuclear and hydro take a long time to build, gas is not available, and liquefied natural gas (LNG) is very expensive. India's forte has always been coal as there is indigenous capacity to build it. India's use of natural gas is also growing strongly. In the third quarter of 2023, India's gas demand across all sectors increased 19% year over year to 6,524 MMcf/d, reflecting strong demand from the fertilizer, power and refining sectors. India is one of the fastest growing renewable power markets, with capacity additions of around 15 GW to 20 GW annually. Renewable capacity additions are expected to accelerate further, overtaking coal capacity additions in the next decade. 2035 is the year when transition is expected to happen. The issuance of carbon credits from Indian projects spanning from 2010 to October 2023 totaled 309 million, or 17% of the global market. Over 94% of these credits derived from renewable energy projects.

*596.* In India, a rapidly expanding energy sector could pose serious challenges with water stress and local air pollution. It is only integrated policies on land use and urbanization (the "smart cities" initiative), pollution controls, technology development, and a relentless focus on energy efficiency which can mitigate these risks. A faster pace is essential to reach the 2030 goal of universal energy access to its people.

## §2. Role of Natural Gas in Pollution Control

*597.* Natural gas is replacing more carbon-intensive fuels. It also backs up the integration of renewables which is good for a gradually decarbonizing energy system. A consumption increase of almost 50% makes it the fastest growing of fossil fuels in the world. China and the Middle East are the main centers of gas demand growth, both becoming even larger consumers than the EU, where gas use has not returned to the peak reached in 2010. With gas prices already low in North America, and dragged lower elsewhere by ample supply and contractual linkages to oil prices, there is plenty of competitively priced gas seeking buyers. But the extent of the longer-term expansion is constrained by efficiency policies, notably in the buildings sector, and competition from renewables and (in some countries) from coal in power generation. One-fifth of the projected rise in global demand consists of gas transported over long distances. Thus, an increase in gas consumption can bring down pollution, particularly vehicular pollution at lower levels.

However, emissions of methane, a powerful GHG, along the supply chain dents the environmental credentials of gas if there is no concerted policy action to tackle these leaks. Unconventional gas accounts for some 60% of the growth in global gas supply, but the spread of its development beyond North America, the home of the shale gas revolution, is more gradual and uneven.

## §3. Global Energy Transition

*598.* There are signs that the much-needed global energy transition is underway, but not yet at a pace that leads to a lasting reversal of the trend of rising $CO_2$

emissions. Annual investment in low-carbon technologies increases, but the cumulative USD 7.4 trillion invested in renewable energy to 2040 represents only around 15% of total investment in global energy supply. The steady decarbonization of electricity supply is not matched by a similarly rapid shift in end-use sectors, where it is much more difficult and expensive to displace coal and gas as fuels for industry, or oil as a transport fuel. The net result is that energy policies, as formulated, lead to a slower increase in energy-related $CO_2$ emissions, but not the full de-coupling from economic growth and the absolute decline in emissions necessary to meet the 2°C target. The main action required is progressively reducing the use of the least-efficient coal-fired power plants and banning their construction. Further, investment is to be enhanced in renewable energy technologies in the power sector.

## §4. Subsidies for Renewables

*599.* Globally, fossil fuel subsidies were $7 trillion in 2022 or 7.1% of GDP. Explicit subsidies (undercharging for supply costs) have more than doubled since 2020 but are still only 18% of the total subsidy, while nearly 60% is due to undercharging for global warming and local air pollution. Full fossil fuel price reform would reduce global carbon dioxide emissions to an estimated 43% below baseline levels in 2030 (in line with keeping global warming to 1.5–2° C), while raising revenues worth 3.6% of global GDP and preventing 1.6 million local air pollution deaths per year (Working Paper No. 223/169 dated August 24, 2023 of IMF).

*600.* Further, global renewable energy capacity grew by the fastest pace recorded in the last twenty years in 2023, which put the world within reach of meeting a key climate target by the end of the decade, according to the IEA. The world's renewable energy grew by 50% last year to 510 gigawatts (GW) in 2023, according to figures from the IEA. This growth may make it possible that the global governments meet a pledge agreed at the COP28 climate talks in November to triple renewable energy capacity by 2030 to significantly reduce consumption of fossil fuels.

*601.* It is expected that transition to renewable energy will be accelerated in 2024. There will be an increase in subsidies, tax incentives, and regulatory frameworks will be modified to be more favorable to renewable energy projects. These policies will encourage the adoption of renewable technologies and attracting investments. China continues to lead in renewable energy, aiming to exceed its target of generating 33% of its electricity consumption from renewable sources by 2025, with significant developments in wind energy.

# Chapter 2. Coal and Pollution

*602.* Globally, coal-fired power plants are major contributors to climate change, producing approximately 70% of carbon dioxide emissions attributable to power generation. Coal mining releases large amounts of methane, a highly potent GHG. To avoid catastrophic damage to climate, and to protect local communities and the environment, mining, transporting and burning coal is required to be stopped. All over the world, grassroots advocates and communities are stepping forward to challenge these short-sighted plans. These advocates are challenging permits for coal mines, power plants, and infrastructure, enforcing clean air and water laws that restrict such coal projects, and empowering communities to speak out against coal. Working together, we can mount strong opposition to coal and move toward a more sustainable energy future.

*603.* Coal supplied 36% of electricity generation in 2022. This must drop to 4% by 2030 and then 0% by 2040 so as to limit global warming to 1.5 degrees C (2.7 degrees F) and prevent the catastrophic impacts of the climate crisis. Removing coal from power generation is also critical to decarbonizing other sectors of the economy. It will help ensure that green technologies that run on electricity, like electric vehicles and heat pumps, are powered by cleaner energy sources. While the share of coal used in the global power sector has been gradually ticking down in recent years, it needs to start declining much faster. Developed countries should reach zero coal the soonest, as they're in a stronger financial position than developing nations and are already, for the most part, less reliant on coal. But all countries will require an incredibly swift transition.

## §1. Environmental Impact of Coal

*604.* A large number of environmental problems of different coal-producing countries are associated with the production and combustion of coal. One important impact is acid mine drainage, where acidic runoff is formed through a chemical reaction between water and sulfur-bearing rocks. This runoff contaminates creeks and rivers, diffuses easily and is very difficult to contain. Another significant impact is the practice of mountain top mining. Because the tops of mountains are removed to reveal coal seams, the sediment and waste become valley fill, impacting water quality and resulting in the loss of headwater ecosystems, or the species and environmental processes of the total system that are native to river sources.

*605.* In terms of GHG, mining results in the direct release of methane with a global warming potential twenty-three times higher than $CO_2$, and persist in the atmosphere for decades, particularly from underground mines. The combustion emits common air pollutants, such as $SO_2$, nitrogen oxides, PM, and mercury as well as other heavy metals. These air pollutants have adverse effects on both public health and the environment. Consequently, coal plants use a variety of technologies, such as scrubbers, to reduce most of the pollutants from combustion emissions. The coal combustion residue, referred to as coal ash, contains a broad range of metals, including arsenic, selenium and cadmium. Coal combustion residuals are one of the waste streams generated and require to be managed to prevent environmental impact. Besides, considerable water usage for coal-fired power generation can stress aquifers and watersheds, and in many instances, water is cooled to near ambient levels before being returned to the surroundings to protect ecosystems.

*606.* The environmental challenges of pollution from coal may arise because coal mining itself gives rise to incidences like coal mine accidents, land subsidence, damage to the water sources, mining waste disposal, and air pollution and coal mine accidents. These results in either environmental pollution or landscape changes because of different types of mining. So, the clean processes, or remediation measures, are designed to address environmental pollution. Restoration measures are to be taken to handle landscape change. Reducing these emissions, in the context of increasing use in growing economies, will be a challenge. Development of low-carbon technologies and complementary government policies to drive the deployment of these technologies will be key factors in enabling the use of coal in the future.

*607.* The coal mining wastes can be used as underground fills, or by using it as fuel for power plants or for raw materials to make bricks or other infrastructure materials. The proper use of mined land is determined in terms of local physical and socioeconomical conditions. In European countries, mined lands are reclaimed as forest or grasslands. However, in China, more than 70% of the mined lands are reclaimed for agricultural purposes because the large population and a shortage of farmlands make this necessary. Reconstruction of rural communities or native residential improvement is one important environmental problem arising from coal mining.

## §2. Environmental Concerns and Falling Coal Use

*608.* For more than a century, coal has been used to produce electricity, and it remains the workhorse of the global power sector and a critical part of the world's economy. Coal is the dirtiest, most-polluting fossil fuel, but it has proven difficult for the world to turn its back on this source of energy. Energy research firm Wood Mackenzie has forecasted 2024 as the year when the world's consumption of coal will reach highest level before decreasing.

*609.* However, forecasters have been wrong about coal before. This is not the first-time prediction that the world would reach peak coal demand, same forecast was made in 2013. It has been tough to quit because coal is still the cheapest and most reliable source of electricity in Asian countries. The large-scale solar and battery storage facilities may become the cheapest option after more than a decade from now. It is hard to determine peak coal as there are a number of coal projects in China, India and Southeast Asia that are going to continue. At the COP28 climate summit in Dubai, nearly 200 countries agreed that it was time to begin "transitioning away" from all fossil fuels to combat climate change. The agreement is historic and ground-breaking and comes at a time when the world is consuming oil, natural gas and coal at record levels, highlighting the challenge of actually moving away from fossil fuels.

*610.* Environmental activists at COP28 lobbied for countries to completely phase out fossil fuels by 2050. In North America and most parts of Europe, coal consumption in the electricity sector has been declining. Ontario ended coal use for electricity in 2014, and Canada has legislated the phase-out of coal-fired electricity by 2030. In Alberta, coal power plants produced about half of the province's electricity a decade ago, while currently only two of the facilities still operate and they are set to be converted to natural gas. Once powered primarily by coal, Alberta now gets more electricity from renewables. Those reductions have been offset by the construction of new power plants in other parts of the world, most notably in China, which consumes the majority of coal around the globe.

*611.* Around the world, governments continue to plan new coal-fired power plants and seek to extend the life of existing plants. These facilities rain toxic pollutants and PM on nearby communities, poisoning their air and water. These facilities generally require large amounts of water to operate, jeopardizing access to clean water supplies. In order to meet the 2030 climate targets, the Netherlands is required to emit less $CO_2$. For this reason, on December 22, 2021, it restricted emissions from coal-fired power stations by limiting their operations to no more than 35% of their maximum capacity. It is estimated to result in a reduction in $CO_2$ emissions at coal-fired power stations of approximately 6–7 megatons in the short term. The amendment to the Coal Act came into effect on January 1, 2022 and will apply until the end of 2024. This law implements rules relating to the generation of electricity using coal, in order to organize an effective coal phase out by 2030. Article 2 of the Act prohibits generation of electricity in a production installation using coal. Coal-fired power plants do not have to close down but are allowed to switch to other, cleaner fuels to generate electricity, such as biomass, biofuels, and hydrogen.

## I. Coal to Renewables

*612.* The power sector is leading the charge to decarbonize electricity gains ground in many end-use sectors, making up almost a quarter of final energy consumption by 2040; hence, power sector leads the way toward a decarbonized energy system. Despite reaching an all-time high in production in 2023, global coal demand is expected to decline by 2026, as per a report by the IEA. This decline is to be due to a shift toward renewables and plateauing demand from China. But India would remain the "driving force" for the fuel until that year. The report, released on December 15, 2023 sees the global demand for coal rising by 1.4% in 2023, surpassing 8.5 billion tonnes for the first time. This increase however masks stark differences among regions. While demand in the EU and United States is expected to drop 20% each, it is expected to rise 8% in India and 5% in China in 2023 due to demand for electricity and diminished electrical generation from hydropower. The IEA's expectations of a decline in coal demand is premised not only on a rise in renewable energy capacity but also a change in global climate. The current conditions of drier monsoons in Asia, are expected to turn to better rainfall during 2024-2026. This will translate to greater hydropower output. There has been decline in global coal demand a few times, but they were brief and caused by extraordinary events such as the collapse of the Soviet Union or the COVID-19 crisis. This time appears different, as the decline is more structural, driven by the formidable and sustained expansion of clean energy technologies. The pace at which renewables expand in key Asian economies will dictate what happens next, and much greater efforts are needed to meet international climate targets.

*613.* A steep upward trend in low-cost solar photovoltaic deployment is expected to aid renewable power generation. Further to that, nuclear generation is set to see moderate increases, especially in China, India, and the EU. Against this background, coal-fired generation is likely to be pushed into a downward trajectory from 2024. Currently, a little over half the world's coal demand comes from China. With a major expansion of renewable energy expected, coal demand in the country is expected to fall in 2024 and plateau in 2026. Overall, this will result in a 2.3% fall in global coal demand by 2026.

*614.* Renewables offer a way to align short-term policy action with medium- and long-term energy and climate goals. Renewables are becoming the backbone of national efforts to restart economies after the COVID-19 outbreak. With the right policies in place, falling renewable power costs can shift markets and contribute greatly toward a green recovery.

## §3. Coal and Pollution Problems

*615.* When coal is used, there are various problems of pollution associated with it and which are being described below.

### I. Mining and Radioactivity

*616.* The environmental effect of coal being used as energy includes the effects of obtaining the fuels from mines, using the fuels, and dealing with the wastes following use of the fuel. The effect of coal mining is that normally extensive areas are often disturbed and require subsequent rehabilitation, and in certain situations of geology and climate, acid mine drainage due to oxidation of sulfur can be a problem. Burning any fossil fuel gives rise to $CO_2$. Small amounts of radioactivity are released into the atmosphere from both coal-fired and nuclear power stations. In the case of coal combustion, small quantities of uranium, radium and thorium present in the coal cause the ash to be radioactive. Nuclear power stations and reprocessing plants release small quantities of radioactive gases (e.g., krypton-85 and xenon-133 and iodine-131), which may be detectable in the environment with monitoring and analytical equipment but are never at harmful levels.

### *A. Problem of Radioactive Fly Ash*

*617.* Radioactive fly ash from coal-fired power stations in the past had a much greater environmental impact largely because it was not perceived as a problem and appropriate actions and measures were not taken. Most fly ash is removed from stack gases and mixed with bottom ash before being buried where seepage and run-off can be controlled, or the ash may be used with cement in concrete. Coal combustion has not always been well controlled. Fly ash and bottom ash are often loaded with heavy metals. Fly ash is mostly retained for land disposal, and bottom ash is normally buried also, but not always securely and without effects on groundwater. Waste heat produced due to the intrinsic inefficiency of energy conversion, and hence as a by-product of power generation, is much the same whether coal or uranium is the primary fuel.

## II. Generation of Carbon Dioxide and Sulfur Dioxide

*618.* The main environmental matter relating to power generation is the production of $CO_2$ and $SO_2$ as a result of coal-fired electricity generation. When coal of say 2.5% sulfur is used to produce the electricity for one person in an industrialized country for one year, then about 9 tons of $CO_2$ and 120 kg of $SO_2$ are produced. $SO_2$ emissions arise from the combustion of fossil fuels containing sulfur, as many of them do. Released in large quantities to the atmosphere it can cause (sulfuric) "acid rains" in areas downwind. In the northern hemisphere, many millions of tons of $SO_2$ are released annually from electricity generation, though such pollution has been dramatically reduced from earlier levels.

## §4. Rights of Indigenous People Against Environmental Degradation

*619.* The international law with respect to fossil fuel has evolved toward recognition that indigenous peoples have the right to own, develop, control and use the lands and territories, including the total environment of the lands, air, waters, coastal seas, sea ice, flora and fauna and other resources, including coal which they have traditionally owned or otherwise occupied and used.[113]

## I. Treaty of Point Elliot

*620.* The Treaty of Point Elliot is an example where rights of the indigenous people (called Indians) were recognized in the U.S. Through this Treaty, the tribes

113. *Ibid.*, No. 44.

ceded title to a portion of their ancestral lands in exchange for reservations, payments and a commitment that the Tribe would be able to fish, hunt and gather at all of their "usual and accustomed" places in perpetuity. In one 1906 case, the U.S. Supreme Court observed that these rights were "not much less necessary to the existence of the Indians than the atmosphere they breathed." The fossil fuel export proposals against which the tribes have petitioned will result in dangerous and toxic materials being put into the heart of the tribes' treaty-reserved fishing areas which act as an existential threat to the people who have depended on this landscape since time immemorial.

*621.* Yet another reason to oppose fossil fuel development in the Pacific Northwest is that it perpetuates the centuries-old legacy of exploitation of native peoples and their lands, fish and cultures. Lummi tribal member Jewell James has likened the explosion of coal, oil and gas projects to a twenty-first-century version of the "Trail of Tears." But the region's tribes are writing a new ending to that tragic story, standing in firm opposition to projects that threaten their homes, their way of life, their sacred landscapes and their treaty rights. Recently, the Lummi, a signatory Tribe to the Treaty demanded the U.S. government not to grant permits for a coal terminal adjacent to their reserved area north of Bellingham. The proposed Gateway Pacific Terminal would be established on Lummi sacred land, and a number of the vessels would disturb while passing through fishing areas on their way to load up on coal. The Federal court of U.S. precedent says that where a tribe opposes a project based on its impacts on treaty-reserved fishing, a federal agency cannot authorize anything more than a "de minimis" impact. (That's legalese for "practically nothing.")

## II. Earth Justice Case

*622.* In another instance, Earth justice representing four U.S. tribes, made effort to block a massive tar sands pipeline in Canada that would put treaty fishing areas at risk of catastrophic oil spills. Tribal opposition and impacts to fishing helped convince the state of Oregon to deny a permit for another coal port on the Columbia River. And a small First Nation in British Columbia decided with a unanimous vote to reject more than a billion dollars to allow an LNG terminal to be built on its traditional lands. Communities across the Pacific Northwest have built a passionate and effective movement to stop these projects, and they are winning.

# Chapter 3. Nuclear Energy and Environmental Liability

*623.* The establishment of U.N. and emergence of nuclear power took place almost simultaneously. By its first resolution, the General Assembly established the U.N. Atomic Energy Commission to deal with the problems raised by the discovery of atomic energy. Subsequently, in 1957, the IAEA was established. Based on data reported to the IAEA by December 31, 2019, 450 nuclear power reactors were in operation worldwide, totaling 398.9 GW(e) in net installed capacity, an increase of 2.5 GW(e) since the end of 2018. Nuclear power generated around 10% of the world's electricity in 2019, or almost one-third of all low-carbon electricity, and was set to remain the second-largest source of low-carbon electricity after hydropower. In France, Hungary, Slovakia, and Ukraine, nuclear power even makes up for more than half of the total electricity production. The IAEA works for the safe, secure and peaceful uses of atomic energy and helps ensure the use of nuclear technology for sustainable development. Under the 1968 Treaty on the Non-Proliferation of Nuclear Weapons (NPT), the IAEA conducts on-site inspections to ensure that nuclear materials are used only for peaceful purposes and not for military purposes.

## §1. Treaties on Use of Nuclear Energy

*624.* The U.N. Conference on Disarmament produced the Comprehensive Test Ban Treaty which was adopted in 1996. The Office for Disarmament Affairs promotes nuclear disarmament and non-proliferation. The Committee on the Peaceful Uses of Outer Space produced the 1992 Principles on the use of nuclear power sources in outer space. The U.N. Scientific Committee on the Effects of Atomic Radiation reports on the levels and effects of exposure to ionizing radiation, providing the scientific basis for protection and safety standards worldwide. For addressing the danger of nuclear terrorism, the U.N. has also produced the Convention on the Physical Protection of Nuclear Material (Vienna, 1980), and the Convention (2005). The following treaties are being described keeping in view this background.

### I. Antarctic Treaty 1959

*625.* This treaty in effect demilitarizes the Antarctic continent and bans the testing of any kind of weapon including nuclear on the continent. The Antarctic Treaty was signed in Washington on December 1, 1959, by the twelve countries whose scientists had been active in and around Antarctica during the International Geophysical Year (IGY) of 1957–1958. It entered into force in 1961. Some important provisions of the treaty are that Antarctica shall be used for peaceful purposes only (Article I) Freedom of scientific investigation in Antarctica and cooperation toward that end … shall continue (Article II). Scientific observations and results from Antarctica shall be exchanged and made freely available (Article III).

*626.* Among the signatories of the treaty were seven countries—Argentina, Australia, Chile, France, New Zealand, Norway and the U.K.—with territorial claims, sometimes overlapping. The U.S. and Russia maintain a "basis of claim." All positions are explicitly protected in Article IV, which preserves the *status quo*: "No acts or activities taking place while the present Treaty is in force shall constitute a basis for asserting, supporting or denying a claim to territorial sovereignty in Antarctica or create any rights of sovereignty in Antarctica. No new claim, or enlargement of an existing claim to territorial sovereignty in Antarctica shall be asserted while the present Treaty is in force." To promote the objectives and ensure the observance of the provisions of the treaty, "All areas of Antarctica, including all stations, installations and equipment within those areas … shall be open at all times to inspection" (Article VII).

*627.* The treaty has been recognized as one of the most successful international agreements. Problematic differences over territorial claims have been effectively set aside, and as a disarmament regime, it has been outstandingly successful. The treaty parties remain firmly committed to a system that is still effective in protecting their essential Antarctic interests. The treaty now has fifty-two signatories, twenty-eight are Consultative Parties on the basis of being original signatories or by conducting substantial research there. The treaty also provides that any member of the U.N. can accede to it. The treaty prohibits nuclear explosions and the disposal of radioactive waste. It requires parties to give advance notice of their expeditions; provides for the parties to meet periodically to discuss measures to further the objectives of the treaty; and puts in place a dispute settlement procedure and a mechanism by which the treaty can be modified.

*628.* Since the first Antarctic Treaty Consultative Meeting (ATCM) in 1961, the parties have met frequently, now annually, to discuss issues as diverse as scientific cooperation, measures to protect the environment, and operational issues—and they are committed to taking decisions by consensus. This process has allowed the Antarctic Treaty to evolve into a system with a number of components that meet the special needs of managing activities in the Antarctic. This regime is now known by the broader title of the Antarctic Treaty System, which operates under the umbrella of the annual ATCM. The Antarctic Treaty System comprises the treaty itself and a number of related agreements. It also includes a range of organizations that contribute to the work of the decision-making forums.

*629.* The treaty parties have put in place rules relating to specific issues. The development of these rules through agreements has allowed the implementation of legally binding provisions for the regulation of activities in Antarctica. A number of specialized bodies assist the treaty parties in the conduct of their work. Specific tasks may be directed to these bodies, or they may be invited to provide observers or experts to participate in treaty forums. The Scientific Committee on Antarctic Research (SCAR) coordinates Antarctic research programs and encourages scientific cooperation. The Council of Managers of National Antarctic Programs (COMNAP) comprises the heads of each of the national Antarctic operating agencies.

COMNAP meets annually to exchange logistic information, encourage cooperation, and develop advice to the treaty parties on a range of practical matters.

*630.* The Antarctic Treaty parties have also developed a close relationship with environmental intergovernmental and non-government organizations that represent the broader community interests in conservation. Organizations such as the International Union for the Conservation of Nature, the United Nations Environment Program, and the Antarctic and Southern Ocean Coalition are also invited to the treaty meetings as experts.

## II. Treaty Banning Nuclear Weapon Tests in the Atmosphere, in Outer Space and under Water (Partial Test-Ban Treaty), 1963

*631.* The Test Ban Treaty of 1963 prohibits nuclear weapons tests "or any other nuclear explosion" in the atmosphere, in outer space, and under water. It does not ban underground tests. It prohibits nuclear explosions in the environment if they cause "radioactive debris to be present outside the territorial limits of the State under whose jurisdiction or control" the explosions were conducted. In accepting limitations on testing, the nuclear powers accepted as a common goal "an end to the contamination of man's environment by radioactive substances."

## III. Treaty for the Prohibition of Nuclear Weapons in Latin America and the Caribbean (Treaty of Tlatelolco), 1967

*632.* This treaty prohibits and prevent in the region: (a) the testing, use, manufacture, production, or acquisition of nuclear weapons, by the parties themselves, directly or indirectly and (b) the receipt, storage, installation, deployment, and any form of possession of any nuclear weapons, directly or indirectly, by the parties themselves, by anyone on their behalf, or in any other way. The parties undertake to refrain from engaging in encouraging or authorizing, directly or indirectly, or in any way participating in the testing, use, manufacture, production, possession, or control of any nuclear weapons.

## IV. Outer Space Treaty

*633.* The Treaty on Outer Space namely Treaty on Principles Governing the Activities of States in the Exploration and Use of Outer Space, including the Moon and Other Celestial Bodies (Outer Space Treaty),1967 mandates that outer space be used for peaceful purposes only and that nuclear weapons should not be placed or tested in outer space. This treaty was endorsed by the U.N. General Assembly on December 19, 1966, and opened for signature on January 27, 1967. The treaty came into force on October 10, 1967, after being ratified by the U.S., the Soviet Union, the U.K., and several other countries. Under the terms of the treaty, the parties are prohibited from placing nuclear arms or other weapons of mass destruction in orbit, on the Moon, or on other bodies in space. Nations cannot claim sovereignty over the Moon or other celestial bodies. Nations are responsible for their activities in space, are liable for any damage caused by objects launched into space from their territory, and are bound to assist astronauts in distress. Their space installations and vehicles shall be open, on a reciprocal basis, to representatives of other countries, and all parties agree to conduct outer-space activities openly and in accordance with international law.

## V. Treaty on the Non-Proliferation of Nuclear Weapons, 1968

*634.* The NPT was signed in 1968 by several of the major nuclear and non-nuclear powers pledging their cooperation in stemming the spread of nuclear technology. Although the NPT did not ultimately prevent nuclear proliferation, in the context of the Cold War arms race and mounting international concern about the consequences of nuclear war, the treaty was a major success for advocates of arms control because it set a precedent for international cooperation between nuclear and nonnuclear states to prevent proliferation. The non-NWS agreed not to acquire nuclear weapons and, in exchange, were promised access to and assistance in the peaceful uses of nuclear energy. NWS pledged to carry out negotiations relating to cessation of the nuclear arms race and to nuclear disarmament, and not to assist in any way in the transfer of nuclear weapons to non-NWS.

## VI. Treaty on the Prohibition of the Emplacement of Nuclear Weapons on the Sea-Bed and the Ocean Floor and in the Subsoil Thereof (Sea-Bed Treaty), 1971

*635.* This treaty bans the emplacement of nuclear weapons, or any weapon of mass destruction, on the sea-bed or ocean floor. The final draft of treaty was approved by the UNGA's Resolution 2660 (XXV) on December 7, 1970. It was opened for signature on February 11, 1971 and entered into force on May 18, 1972. The treaty forbids states parties from implanting or placing on the seabed or ocean floor or in the subsoil thereof, beyond a 12-mi territorial zone, any nuclear weapons, or any other types of weapons of mass destruction or structures, launching installations, or any other facilities specifically designed for storing, testing, or using such weapons.

*636.* The treaty allows for verification through observation by the states parties of the activities of other states parties, provided that observation does not interfere with such activities. If after such observation reasonable doubts remain, further procedures for verification may be agreed upon, including inspections. After completion of the further procedures for verification, an appropriate report is circulated to other parties by the Party that initiated such procedures. If consultation and cooperation have not removed the doubts concerning the activities and there remains a serious question concerning fulfillment of the obligations assumed under this treaty, a state party may, in accordance with the provisions of the Charter of the U.N., refer the matter to the Security Council, which may take action in accordance with the Charter. As set forth in Article VII of the Treaty, review conferences have been held every five years in 1977, 1983, and 1989. In 1989, it was agreed that the next review conference would be held no sooner than 1996. In 1992, the Conference on Disarmament informally considered further measures and established no need for a fourth review conference.

## VII. South Pacific Nuclear Free Zone Treaty (Treaty of Rarotonga), 1985

*637.* The Treaty of Rarotonga, the South Pacific Nuclear Free Zone Treaty entered into force on December 11, 1986. The geographic scope of the Rarotonga Treaty is vast, extending from the West coast of Australia to the boundary of the Latin American Nuclear Weapon-Free Zone (NWFZ) in the east, and from the equator to 60 degrees south, where it meets the boundary of the zone established by the Antarctic treaty. The Treaty of Rarotonga contributes to nuclear non-proliferation and disarmament by preventing the placement of nuclear weapons within the South Pacific by Member States (Article 5). The Rarotonga Treaty reinforces, at the regional level, the legally binding commitments that its states parties have made under NPT not to manufacture, possess, acquire or have control of nuclear weapons (Article 3). The Rarotonga Treaty also includes an undertaking by states parties to prevent nuclear testing in their territories (Article 6). A quite distinctive feature of the treaty is its emphasis on keeping the region free of environmental pollution by radioactive wastes and other radioactive matter (Article 7).

## VIII. Southeast Asia Nuclear-Weapon-Free Zone Treaty (Treaty of Bangkok), 1995

*638.* The Treaty on the Southeast Asia Nuclear Weapon-Free Zone, also known as the SEANWFZ Treaty or Bangkok Treaty, was signed on December 15, 1995 by ten Southeast Asian States. The treaty entered into force on March 27, 1997 and was registered with the U.N. on June 27, 1997. It is a key legal instrument in supporting the purposes of ASEAN, which, as per the ASEAN Charter, include preserving Southeast Asia as an NWFZ and free from all other weapons of mass destruction. This treaty established the third NWFZ in the world, following the conclusion of the Treaty of Tlatelolco establishing the NWFZ for the Latin American and Caribbean region in 1967 and the Treaty of Rarotonga, establishing the NWFZ for the South Pacific region in 1985.

*639.* The treaty obliges states parties not to develop, manufacture or otherwise acquire, possess or have control over nuclear weapons, station or transport nuclear weapons, or test or use nuclear weapons. States parties undertake not to discharge radioactive material or wastes at sea, into the atmosphere or on land within the Zone, and not to allow other states to conduct these acts. The treaty commits each state party to use nuclear material and facilities exclusively for peaceful purposes and, prior to embarking on a peaceful nuclear energy programme, to subject that programme to a rigorous nuclear safety assessment conforming to guidelines and standards recommended by the IAEA for the protection of health and minimization of danger to life and property.

## IX. African Nuclear-Weapon-Free Zone Treaty (Treaty of Pelindaba), 1996

*640.* This treaty prohibits research, development, manufacture, stockpiling, acquisition, testing, possession, control, or stationing of nuclear explosive devices by parties to the treaty, as well as assistance to others in such activities, or seeking or receiving assistance in such activities. The treaty also prohibits parties from assisting or encouraging the dumping of radioactive wastes and other radioactive matter within the African zone, and it requires each party to implement or use as guidelines the provisions of the Bamako Convention with respect to the handling of radioactive waste. The treaty requires all parties to apply full IAEA safeguards to their peaceful nuclear activities. The treaty creates the African Commission on Nuclear Energy to monitor compliance and promote the peaceful use of nuclear energy.

## X. Comprehensive Nuclear-Test-Ban Treaty, 1996

*641.* This treaty places a worldwide ban on nuclear test explosions of any kind and in any environment. The CTBT includes a Protocol in three parts: Part I detailing the International Monitoring System (IMS); Part II on On-Site Inspections (OSI); and Part III on Confidence-Building Measures (CBMs). There are also two annexes to the Protocol: Annex 1 detailing the location of various treaty monitoring assets associated with the IMS; and Annex 2 detailing the parameters for screening events. The CTBT bans any nuclear weapon test explosion or any other nuclear explosion. The CTBT is associated with another element in the process of nuclear disarmament: a ban on the production of fissile material for anything other than verified peaceful use. Such a ban imposes a quantitative limit on the amount of nuclear material available for weapons use. That objective is the basis for an initiative at the Conference on Disarmament to negotiate a treaty banning further production of fissile material for weapons purposes—the draft Fissile Material Cut-Off Treaty (FMCT). Taken together, the CTBT and the FMCT are integral components of the nuclear control regime and provide the foundation for eventual nuclear disarmament. The treaty establishes CTBTO, located in Vienna, to ensure the implementation of its provisions, including those provisions for international verification measures.

## XI. International Convention for the Suppression of Acts of Nuclear Terrorism (Nuclear Terrorism Convention), 2005

*642.* This treaty outlines specific acts of nuclear terrorism, aims to protect a broad range of possible targets, bring perpetrators to justice, and promote cooperation among countries. In accordance with Article 2, the Convention applies to acts committed by individuals. Within the meaning of the Convention, any person commits an offence if that person possesses radioactive material or makes or possesses a device with the intent to cause death or serious bodily injury or to cause substantial damage to property or to the environment. The use or threat of use of radioactive material or a device constitutes an offence under the Convention. Any person also commits a crime if that person attempts to commit an offence or participates as an accomplice in the commission of the above acts. The Convention does not apply where the offence is committed within a single state, the alleged offender and the victims are nationals of that state, and no other state has a basis to exercise jurisdiction. The Convention also does not apply to the activities of armed forces during an armed conflict, which are governed by international humanitarian law. Nor does it apply to the activities of military forces in the exercise of their official duties in as much as they are governed by other rules of international law. The Convention does not address the issue of the legality of the use or threat of use of nuclear weapons by states.

### XII. Central Asia Nuclear-Weapon-Free Zone Treaty (Treaty of Semipalatinsk), 2006

*643.* The Central Asian Nuclear-Weapon-Free Zone (CANWFZ) treaty is a binding commitment by Central Asian States (Kazakhstan, Kyrgyzstan, Tajikistan, Turkmenistan, and Uzbekistan) not to manufacture, acquire, test, or possess nuclear weapons. The treaty was signed on September 8, 2006 at the former Semipalatinsk nuclear test site in Kazakhstan, hence the treaty's unofficial name as 'Semipalatinsk Treaty'. The treaty was subsequently ratified by all five Central Asian states and entered into force on March 21, 2009. The treaty was the result of the collective efforts by all five Central Asian States in their common desire to provide security, stability and peace in the region, address environmental concerns and create the necessary conditions for regional development and stability.

## §2. Environmental Friendly Source of Energy

*644.* The nuclear energy has emerged as a clean, emission-free energy alternative at a time when efforts are intensified to combat climate change. It is resulting in more and more countries going for development of nuclear energy for electricity production. In 2019, thirty countries generated nuclear power, and twenty-eight were considering, planning, or actively working to include it in their energy mix. Four of these countries, Bangladesh, Belarus, Turkey and United Arab Emirates, were building their first nuclear plants. The IAEA's projections for global nuclear power capacity in the decades to come depend in part on whether significant new capacity can offset potential reactor retirements. Nuclear energy provided 55% of America's carbon-free electricity in 2019, making it by far the largest domestic source of clean energy. The U.S. being the world's largest producer of nuclear power, generated 809 billion kWh of electricity in 2019—the highest total ever.

Commercial nuclear power plants have supplied around 20% of the nation's electricity each year since 1990. Nuclear power plants are designed to run twenty-four hours a day, seven days a week because they require less maintenance and can operate for longer stretches before refueling (typically every one and a half or two years). The main worry is that this may not lead to proliferation for military purposes and terrorist threats and even its use by terrorists. The nuclear power can play a vital role in reducing GHG that are contributing to global warming.

*645.* Nuclear power is one of the major low-carbon energy sources currently available, and many countries believe that it can help them to address the challenges of ensuring reliable energy supplies while curbing emissions. The differences between pressurized water reactors and boiling water reactors technologies are indiscernible and comparable to other low-carbon energy technologies. Further, studies indicate that gas-cooled and fast reactors have even lower emissions due to higher thermal efficiencies and lower fuel cycle demands, respectively. All low-carbon energy technologies are needed in the years ahead to address the climate challenge. The carbon footprint for nuclear power is very low which is comparable to hydropower and less than any kind of fossil energy, while also providing a constant baseload supply of electricity. If the world is to limit the global temperature increase at an acceptable level, all low-carbon energy sources will be needed to be fully developed, and benefit is derived from them.

*646.* In 1855, Washington Territory Governor and the leaders of a number of Salish Sea tribes signed the Treaty of Point Elliot through which the tribes ceded title to a portion of their ancestral lands in exchange for reservations, payments, and a commitment that the tribe would be able to fish, hunt, and gather at all of their "usual and accustomed" places in perpetuity.[114]

*647.* In one 1906 case, the U.S. Supreme Court tried to capture the centrality of reserved fishing rights to Northwest tribes and said that these rights were "not much less necessary to the existence of the Indians than the atmosphere they breathed." The fossil fuel export proposals—which would put dangerous and toxic materials into the heart of the tribes' treaty-reserved fishing areas—are nothing less than an existential threat to the people who have depended on this landscape since time immemorial.

*648.* The Treaty of Point Elliot represents a legal obligation on the part of the U.S. government to protect a particular way of life. Recently, the Lummi, a signatory tribe to the treaty, demanded the U.S. government to deny permits for a coal terminal adjacent to their reserved area north of Bellingham. The proposed Gateway Pacific Terminal for coal handling would be situated on Lummi sacred land, and a number of the vessels would disturb while passing through fishing areas on

---

114. Hasselman Jan, *A New Front in the Battle Against Coal Export: Treaties*, http://earthjustice.org/blog/2015-july/a-new-front-in-the-battle-against-coal-exports-treaties, accessed on Jul. 27, 2016.

their way to load up on coal.[115] The way for the government to honor this long-standing obligation is to deny the coal port permit. Federal court precedent says that where a tribe opposes a project based on its impacts on treaty-reserved fishing, a federal agency cannot authorize anything more than a "de minimis" impact (That's legalese for "practically nothing.")

*649.* The Lummi's stand against Coal is not isolated. Throughout the region, First Nations and Native American tribes are standing strong against more fossil fuel development. For example, Earth justice which represents four U.S. tribes, made effort to block a massive tar sands pipeline in Canada that would put treaty fishing areas at risk of catastrophic oil spills. Tribal opposition and impacts to fishing helped convince the state of Oregon to deny a permit for another coal port on the Columbia River. And a small First Nation in British Columbia stunned the world with a unanimous vote to reject more than a billion dollars to allow an LNG terminal to be built on its traditional lands. Communities across the Pacific Northwest have built a passionate and effective movement to stop these projects, and they are winning.[116]

*650.* The question now is whether the government will keep the 160-year-old promise embodied in the Treaty of Point Elliot by rejecting the coal port.[117]

115. *Ibid.*
116. *Ibid.*
117. *Ibid.*

## Chapter 4. Electricity and Pollution

*651.* The production of electricity must have regard to minimizing environmental pollution and public health effect. With nuclear power, the focus is on uranium mining and nuclear wastes. The health and environmental costs of nuclear power are very low relative to the main alternatives like electricity generation through coal. Environmental and health consequences of electricity generation are important issues, alongside the affordability of the power which is produced. Environmental and health consequences are usually seen as external costs—those which are quantifiable but do not appear in the utility's accounts. Hence, they are not passed on to the consumer but are borne by society at large. They include particularly the effects of air pollution on human health, crop yields and buildings, as well as occupational disease and accidents. Though they are even harder to quantify and evaluate than the others, external costs also include effects on ecosystems and the impact of global warming.

*652.* Production of electricity from any form of primary energy has some environmental effect and some risk. A balanced assessment of nuclear power requires comparison of its environmental effects with those of the principal alternative, coal-fired electricity generation, as well as with other energy options. That comparison needs to recognize that waste and decommissioning costs are internalized in nuclear power economics much more fully than, for example, with coal-fired power generation.

### §1. Coal Used for Electricity Generation

*653.* The environmental effect of coal being used for electricity generation includes the effects of obtaining the fuels from mines, using the fuels, and dealing with the wastes following use of the fuel. At a mine, ordinary operating procedures normally ensure that there is no significant water or air pollution.

### §2. Nuclear Power Stations

#### I. Nuclear Waste

*654.* The solid high-level waste from nuclear power stations is hot and very radioactive, so it must be isolated from people and the environment indefinitely. It is stored for forty to fifty years while the radioactivity decays to less than 1% of its original level. Then it is finally disposed of deep underground and well away from the biosphere. In more than fifty decades of civil nuclear power experience, nuclear wastes have not caused any serious health or environmental problems nor posed any real risks to people. There has been no pollution or plausible hazard from such material routinely removed from power stations and nor is any likely, either short- or very long-term, Intermediate-level waste (radioactive but not requiring cooling) is placed in underground repositories, not necessarily deep, with little delay. Low-level waste is generally buried more conventionally. Radioactive fly ash from coal-fired power stations had a much greater environmental impact largely because it was not perceived as a problem and appropriate action and measures were not taken. Today most fly ash is removed from stack gases and mixed with bottom ash before being buried where seepage and runoff can be controlled, or the ash may be used with cement in concrete.

*655.* Nuclear wastes are certainly a significant part of the nuclear power picture and need to be managed and disposed properly. Alternatives for power generation are not without challenges, and for a variety of reasons they—particularly those from coal combustion—have not always been well controlled. Fly ash particularly, but also bottom ash, are often loaded with heavy metals. Fly ash is mostly retained for land disposal today, and bottom ash is normally buried, but not always securely and without effects on groundwater. Waste heat produced due to the intrinsic inefficiency of energy conversion, and hence as a by-product of power generation, is much the same whether coal or uranium is the primary fuel. The thermal efficiency of coal-fired power stations ranges up to a possible 40%, with newer ones typically giving better than 35%. That of nuclear stations mostly ranges from 29% to 38% with the common light water reactor today giving about 34%.

## II. Nuclear Power Plant Accident

*656.* A number of measures have been taken for safety at nuclear plants to avoid nuclear disasters/accidents. Many nuclear accidents/disasters have taken place, and some of them are discussed in the following paragraphs.

### *A. Three Mile Island (1979)—U.S.A.*

*657.* The partial meltdown of Unit 2 (TMI-2) reactor at Three Mile Island nuclear power plant in March 1979 resulted in the most serious accident in U.S. history. The accident was classified under Level 5 of the International Nuclear Event Scale (INES).

### *B. Chernobyl (1986)—Ukraine (USSR)*

*658.* The world's worst nuclear power plant accident took place in April 1986 at Chernobyl nuclear power plant in Ukraine due to the release of a fraction of reactor core material. The radiation was released into the atmosphere over much of Europe causing the death of 31 people and leaving many more suffering from the effects of radiation. The efforts to control the contamination and ward off the disaster involved more than 500,000 workers and have still not been entirely completed.

### C. *Fukushima Daiichi (2011)—Japan*

*659.* Fukushima Daiichi nuclear disaster was caused by the large tsunamis resulting from the Tohoku earthquake in March 2011. The tsunami waves destroyed most of the safety and power systems, except for one diesel generator at Unit 6. This caused the loss of cooling for the reactor cores, resulting in meltdowns at three reactors. This was followed by the release of significant amounts of radioactive materials contaminating the surroundings. The hydrogen explosions that occurred at the facility further damaged the concrete outer structure and caused the evacuation of occupants within the 20 km zone. There were no reports of casualties due to radiation exposure.

## §3. Pollution and Preference of Energy Source

*660.* There is no reason for preferring one fuel over the other on account of the amount of waste heat and consequent water requirements for cooling. This is the case whether power station cooling is by water from a stream or estuary, or using atmospheric cooling towers which evaporate water. However, it is noteworthy that whereas coal-fired power plants tend to be located near a source of coal, nuclear plants can be sited according to cooling requirements, and can more readily make use of lake or seawater for direct cooling. Hence, they are less likely to require expensive cooling towers or to deplete supplies of fresh water for evaporative cooling. For a given level of thermal efficiency and size of plant, the cooling requirements for a nuclear plant are slightly greater as it does not lose heat up the stack with combustion products. In any case, the dumped heat need not always be "waste." In colder climates, district heating and agricultural uses are increasingly found. In France, the waste heat from a nuclear plant is used for a crocodile farm. Any such use of waste heat decreases the extent to which local fogs result from its release to the environment in winter. In dryer climates, the rejected heat can be used for desalination to provide potable water.

## §4. Coal-Fired Electricity Generation

*661.* The acid rain (rainwater having a pH of 4 and lower) in north eastern U.S. and Scandinavia causes ecological changes and economic loss. In the U.K. and the U.S., electric power utilities at first sought to minimize this by increasing their use of natural gas. It is possible to remove a lot of the $SO_2$ from coal stack gases using flue gas desulfurization equipment, but the cost is considerable. Power utilities have spent many billions of dollars on this. On the other hand, between 1980 and 1986, $SO_2$ emissions in France were halved simply by replacing fossil fuel power stations with nuclear ones. At the same time, electricity production increased 40%, and France became a significant exporter of electricity.

NOx from fossil fuel power stations operating at high temperatures are also an environmental problem, regardless of the fuel source. If high levels of hydrocarbons are present in the air, nitrogen oxides react with these in sunlight to form photochemical smog. Moreover, NOx have an adverse effect on the Earth's ozone layer, increasing the amount of ultraviolet light reaching the Earth's surface.

## §5. Radiation

*662.* Traditionally, occupational health risks have been measured in terms of immediate accident, especially fatality rates. However, today, and particularly in relation to nuclear power, there is an increased emphasis on less obvious or delayed effects of exposure to cancer-inducing substances and radiation. Many occupational accident statistics have been generated over the last fifty years of civil nuclear power in North America and Europe. These can be compared with those from coal-fired and other electricity generation. All show that nuclear is distinctly the safer means of electric power generation in this respect. A major reason for coal showing up unfavorably is the huge amount of it which must be mined and transported to supply even a single large power station—some 20,000 times as much coal as uranium from the mine.

# Part XIV. Environmental Jurisprudence

*663.* Environmental jurisprudence has drawn its knowledge base from different disciplines of studies like basic sciences, earth science and Common Law jurisprudence. The concern is more with enforcement "rights," because environmental pollution may affect individuals as well as the public at large. Therefore, if pollution is termed as either a wrong or a crime, it requires different understanding of law because of its very nature, wherein the study of environmental jurisprudence gains importance. There are a number of principles at national and international levels that are at the core of most environmental legal protection systems. In order to achieve sustainable development, environmental protection constitutes an integral part of the development process and cannot be considered in isolation from it. The result has been an infusion of environmental principles and norms into nearly every branch of international law. In the decade after the Rio Conference, environmental concerns encountered increasing competition on the international agenda from economic globalization, emphasis on free trade, and the development crises of poor countries. The decades of legal developments have led to the emergence of basic principles of environmental protection that are recognized in international and national law. These have informed the development of environmental law by giving meaning to concepts not contained in formal legal instruments. The key environmental principles developed over the past several decades have crystallized into principles.

*664.* The design and application of modern environmental law have been shaped by principles and concepts like precautionary principle, prevention, polluter pays, etc. outlined in publications "Our Common Future (1987)," published by the World Commission on Environment and Development, and the Earth Summit's Rio Declaration (1992). These principles are being applied in real-life situations, whereas some other concepts are evolving and through development may assume the shape of principles.

*665.* ICJ in a case decided in 2018 (Certain Activities Carried Out by Nicaragua in the Border Area (*Costa Rica v. Nicaragua*) Compensation Owed by the Republic of Nicaragua to the Republic of Costa Rica (2018)) recognized conservation interests and ecosystem services.

*666.* There was a territory dispute between Costa Rica and Nicaragua over a 3 km area of wetland in the northern part of Isla Portillas. In 2010, Costa Rica instituted proceedings with ICJ against the Republic of Nicaragua for unlawful incursion, occupation, and use of Costa Rican territory, including claims of serious damage to protected rainforests and wetlands. The environmental damage claim arose from Nicaragua's activities in excavating a canoe (channel) for navigational purposes, which entailed removal of trees and vegetation. Nicaragua responded by instituting proceedings against Costa Rica in 2011 claiming violations of Nicaraguan sovereignty and major environmental damage arising from a road construction works by Costa Rica along the border area between the two countries. In 2013, the court joined the two cases. In 2015, the court decided the sovereignty dispute in favor of Costa Rica rendering Nicaragua's activities unlawful under international law, which gave rise to an obligation of reparation by Nicaragua. Costa Rica claimed compensation for two categories of damages: quantifiable environmental damages caused by Nicaragua in excavation of the 2010 canoe and 2013 eastern canoe; and costs and expenses incurred due to Nicaragua's unlawful activities, including expenses to monitor and remedy the environmental damage so caused. Nicaragua countered that Costa Rica was only entitled to "material damages" which are damage to property or other interests of Costa Rica that can be assessed in financial terms.

*667.* On the question of compensation, the court identified the legal principles of international law for the determination of compensation. The first is the well-settled principle of international law that a breach of an obligation gives rise to an obligation to make reparation in adequate form. There was no dispute between the parties that damage to the environment was compensable under international law. What is significant is that court recognized ecosystem services as part of the compensable damage to the environment, including both direct and indirect services. The court stated that "damage to the environment, and the consequent impairment or loss of the ability of the environment to provide goods and services, is compensable under international law," which may include indemnification for such impairment or loss or payment for restoration of the damaged environment. In light of Nicaragua's wrongful acts, the court concluded that Nicaragua had an obligation to make full reparation for environmental damages caused. The court stated that the lack of certainty as to the extent of damage did not preclude awarding compensation for the impairment or loss of environmental goods and services. The court stated its view that "damage to the environment, and the consequent impairment or the loss of the ability of the environment to provide goods and services is compensable under international law."

*668.* The court also developed a method of valuation of environmental damage "from the perspective of the ecosystem as a whole," which is an overall assessment of the impairment or loss of environmental goods or services rather than separate valuation of each different category. The court included in its "overall assessment" approach the removal of trees, which the court found to be the greatest damage to the environment, wetlands, and the capacity of the area for natural regeneration.

*669.* The court awarded USD 120,000.00 to Costa Rica for the impairment or loss of environmental goods and services of the area in question. In addition, the court rejected Costa Rica's claim of USD 54,925.69 to replace the lower quality soil used by Nicaragua. However, the court awarded in full Costa Rica's claim of USD 2,708.39 to compensate for measures taken to restore the wetland. The court also assessed claims by Costa Rica for costs and expenses incurred as a result of Nicaragua's unlawful activities in the disputed territory, which included the costs of surveillance of the area, monitoring the protected areas, and also costs for the construction of dyke as a measure to prevent irreparable harm to the environment from the excavations of the canoes. Most significant thing is that for the first time the 72-year-old ICJ decided an environmental compensation case. The court has recognized the important value of biological diversity and its services.

## Chapter 1. Precautionary Principle

*670.* Starting in the 1990s, the precautionary principle within the space of a decade has a meteoric rise and, as a result, this principle has been able to establish itself as a new general principle of international law (de Sadeleer, 2002: 91–223). In addition, it has come to occupy an uncontested position not only in international but also in EC law, as well as in several European countries (particularly in France) and other countries of the world, to the point where it overshadowed the principle of prevention. The precautionary principle has been applied in a wide array of areas ranging from classical environmental issues relating to nature, water, air, etc.; or concerning wider areas such as food safety (mad cow disease, the spread of genetically modified organisms (GMOs), etc.) as well as health issues.

*671.* The Precautionary principle has been defined in many ways in legal orders and case law applications; however, the principle can be understood in a variety of ways. Under preventive approach, the decision-maker intervenes provided that the threats to the environment are tangible. Pursuant to the precautionary principle, authorities are prepared to tackle risks for which there is no definitive proof that there is a link of causation between the suspected activity and the harm or whether the suspected damage will materialize. In other words, precaution means that the absence of scientific certainty—or conversely the scientific uncertainty—as to the existence or the extent of a risk should henceforward no longer delay the adoption of preventative measures to protect the environment. The principle can be understood as the expression of a philosophy of anticipated action, not requiring that the entire corpus of scientific proof be collated in order for a public authority to be able to adopt a preventive measure.

*672.* In case of operator's civil liability, it can be imposed provided that the victim is able to shed light on the link of causation between the operator's behavior and the ensuing damage. A WTO member will be able to enact a food safety measure provided that its regulatory choice is based upon clear scientific evidence resulting from a risk assessment. This presupposes continuous recourse to scientific expertise, with experts being able to provide flawless data to both courts and decision-makers. However, precaution provides for the possibility to act while uncertainties have not yet been cleared up. Praised by some, disparaged by others, the principle is no stranger to controversy. In particular, its implementation in the field of food safety has sparked off heated debates. Discussions about its status and functions have greatly intensified with respect to WTO trade issues.

*673.* There are two widely referred definitions of the Precautionary Principle. One of the most important expressions of the Precautionary Principle internationally is in the Rio Declaration from the 1992 UNCED, also known as Agenda 21. The declaration stated: "In order to protect the environment, the precautionary approach shall be widely applied by states according to their capabilities. Where there are threats of serious or irreversible damage, lack of full scientific certainty shall not be used as a reason for postponing cost effective measures to prevent environmental degradation."

*674.* The second definition is based on 1998 Wingspread Statement on the Precautionary Principle and it states: "When an activity raises threats of harm to human health or the environment, precautionary measures should be taken even if some cause and effect relationships are not fully established scientifically. The process of applying the precautionary principle must be open, informed and democratic and must include potentially affected parties. It must also involve an examination of the full range of alternatives, including no action. In this context the proponent of an activity, rather than the public, should bear the burden of proof."

## §1. Precaution in Response to the Limitations of Science

*675.* The scientific understanding is the major factor around which environmental law is organized. Several factors explain why science is much more in evidence in environment law than in other branches of the law. First, scientists detect, identify, and set out the ecological problems to which the law must respond. Second, environmental crises are mainly perceived through scientific descriptions of physical world. Science is often called upon to play a decisive role in judicial procedures. Scientists thus play a decisive role in the conception and implementation of environmental law throughout the world. The regulations adopted in this field are based on scientific calculations, computations, or affirmations. As a matter of fact, the rise of new technologies has caused a new generation of risks to emerge (CFCs, POPs, GMOs, hormone-disrupting chemicals, electromagnetic fields, etc.).

*676.* Pollution brings a challenge to the ability of science to anticipate and prevent harm. These risks are fundamentally different from traditional industrial risks. First, their impacts are much wider and diffused. Second, they are permeated with uncertainty. It is also difficult to determine the damages they may provoke, in terms of localization, of degree of damage between the first exposure and the actual impact of damage, frequency, duration, nature, and scale. Uncertainty may impinge upon one of these factors whereas there is no definitive definition of uncertainty. The following examples are illustrative of the ways in which uncertainty pervades the risk assessment process:

(a) *Insufficiency*: for instance, the various scientific disciplines involved in assessing the risk are not sufficiently developed to explain the cause-and-effect relationship.
(b) *Inconclusiveness*: the realities of science dictate that the scientists, whatever the quality of their investigations, will never be able to eliminate some uncertainties.
(c) *Imprecision*: may be caused by the fact that the data to analyze the risks are not available or are out-of-date, information not available, measurement errors, contradictions, ambiguity, etc.

*677.* The precaution aims to bridge the gap between scientists working on the frontiers of scientific knowledge and decision-makers willing to act to determine how safe is safe enough. In other words, precaution is testament to a new relationship with science, where it is consulted less for the knowledge which it has to offer than for the doubts and concerns which it is in a position to raise.

## §2. Methodological Observations

*678.* So far, the precautionary principle has been embroiled with controversies, critics being confused as to the scope and the status of the principle. The distinction between prevention and precaution can be explained. A dividing line could be drawn between the two principles. The prevention is based on the concept of certain risk, precaution is distinguished by the intrusion of uncertainty. Accordingly, the question is no longer merely how to prevent assessable, calculable and certain risks, but rather how to anticipate risks permeated by a high level of uncertainty. As a matter of policy, envisaging anticipatory action in response to uncertainty, precaution represents an additional milestone in risk reduction. In other words, precaution urges prevention forward in the hope of closing the gap that always exists between decision-making and the mastery of risk. Second, variations in terminology have emerged, reflecting the considerable controversy surrounding the principle.

*679.* Disputes have arisen as to whether precaution should be labeled as a "principle" or merely as "an approach."[118] This debate reflects different perceptions as to the suitable regulatory response to avoid environmental and health damages amid uncertainties. As per one approach, precaution is not legally binding. To avoid the more extreme versions of the precautionary principle, which press for greater environmental protection, some—including, among others, U.S. policymakers—prefer to use the term "precautionary approach" rather than "precautionary principle"; the latter term is preferred by the EC institutions and some of its Member States. The various provisions of international agreements enshrining precaution mirror this variation. For instance, in the 1992 Rio Declaration on Environment and Development, the 1996 Protocol to the London Dumping Convention and the 2001 Stockholm POPs Convention, the principle is called an "approach," while the "approach" became a principle in the 1992 OSPAR Convention, the 1992 Helsinki Convention on the Protection of the Marine Environment of the Baltic Sea Area and in the Barcelona Convention to Protect the Mediterranean Convention. Furthermore, to make matters even more complex, in the field of waste management, the 1991 Bamako Convention uses both the terms "precautionary approach" and "precautionary principle" in the same provision (Article 4.3(f)). Lastly, the Cartagena Protocol on Biosafety (CPB) refers to the "precautionary approach" in its preamble, but uses terminology that clearly reflects the same basic rationale for application of the precautionary principle in Articles 10 and 11. Thus from a legal point of view, the question remains whether precaution could become a principle of customary law in international law, on the one hand, and a general principle of environmental law at the national level on the other hand.

118. J. Peel, *Precaution: A Matter of Principle, Approach or Process?,* 5 Melb. J. Int'l. L. 483–501 (2004).

## §3. The Formulations of the Principle in the Different Environmental Sectors

*680.* Precaution has slowly been permeating various fields of international law, whether through the declaration of public policy objectives (soft law), agreements (hard law) or judicial interpretation (case law). Since the 1992 Rio Conference, it has been taken up in the majority of bilateral and multilateral international treaties relating to environmental protection. At present, the precautionary principle can be found in large number of multilateral treaties, covering a wide range of environmental issues ranging from air pollution to waste management.[119] Given that the principle is applied in a variety of contexts, its formulation often differs from agreement to agreement.

### I. Policy Documents

*681.* The precautionary principle has been established as a general principle of environmental policy in various soft-law declarations adopted by the UNECE (Bergen, May 16, 1990), the Governing Council of the UNEP,[120] the Council of Ministers of the Organization of African Unity (Addis-Ababa, 1990), the Ministerial Conference on the Environment of the U.N. Economic and Social Commission for Asia and the Pacific (Bangkok, 1990), and the Environment Ministers of the OECD (1991). It was eventually accorded universal recognition at the U.N. Conference on Environment and Development. Recognized in Agenda 21 of June 16, 1992, the principle was defined in the nonbinding 1992 Declaration on Environment and Development, which declares that in order to protect the environment, the precautionary approach shall be widely applied by states according to their capabilities. Where there are threats of serious or irreversible damage, lack of full scientific certainty shall not be used as a reason for postponing cost-effective measures to prevent environmental degradation (Principle 15).

*682.* No doubt the environmental law operates in areas with high levels of scientific uncertainty but in many activities, which entail some change to the environment, it is impossible to determine precisely what effects the activity will have on the quality of the environment or on human health. Often available scientific evidence provides cause for concern but does not give conclusive information. In such scenarios, risk assessment compels to strike a balance between the need to protect health and environment on the one hand and the advantages of strict restrictions that may turn out to be unwarranted on the other hand. It is in this context the role for Precautionary Principle emerges.

119. *See* Marr 2003; Trouwborst 2002; Douma 2003; de Sadeleer (ed.) 2007.
120. UNEP Governing Council Decision 15/27, 1989, on the Precautionary Approach to Marine Pollution.

*683.* The Precautionary Principle continues to be applied widely across sectors both internationally and nationally. The nature and scope of its application have varied widely according to the context and sector within which it has been applied. "Precautionary Principle" plays a significant role in determining whether developmental process is sustainable or not. "Precautionary Principle" underlies sustainable development which requires that the developmental activity must be stopped and prevented if it causes serious and irreversible environmental damage. The emergence of Precautionary Principle marks a shift in the international environmental jurisprudence—a shift from assimilative capacity principle to Precautionary Principle.

## §4. Better Safe Than Sorry

*684.* The Precautionary Principle is a tool for making better health and environmental decisions. It aims to prevent harm from the outset rather than manage it after the fact. In common language, this means "better safe than sorry." The Precautionary Principle denotes a duty to prevent harm, when it is within our power to do so, even when all the evidence is not in.[121] Thus, the "precautionary principle" is a notion which supports taking protective action before there is complete scientific proof of a risk; that is, action should not be delayed simply because full scientific information is lacking.

*685.* The Precautionary Principle conveys the common sense-based advice to err on the side of caution. The principle intends to prevent harm to humans, environment, and ecosystem at large. When the impacts of a particular activity—such as emission of hazardous substances—are not completely clear, the general presumption is to let the activities go ahead until the uncertainty is resolved. The Precautionary Principle counters such general presumptions. When there is uncertainty regarding the impacts of an activity, the Precautionary Principle advocates action to anticipate and avert environmental harm. Thus, the Precautionary Principle favors monitoring, preventing and/or mitigating uncertain potential threats.

*686.* "Precautionary Principle" plays a significant role in determining whether developmental process is sustainable or not. "Precautionary principle" underlies sustainable development, which requires that the developmental activity must be stopped and prevented if it causes serious and irreversible environmental damage. The emergence of Precautionary Principle marks a shift in the international environmental jurisprudence—a shift from assimilative capacity principle to Precautionary Principle.

*687.* Important expressions of the Precautionary Principle internationally are included in the Rio Declaration from the 1992 UNCED, also known as Agenda 21. The declaration stated: "In order to protect the environment, the precautionary approach shall be widely applied by states according to their capabilities. Where

121. http://ccsuniversity.ac.in.

there are threats of serious or irreversible damage, lack of full scientific certainty shall not be used as a reason for postponing cost effective measures to prevent environmental degradation."

## §5. Assimilative Capacity Principle

*688.* Assimilative capacity principle underlies early legal measures to protect the environment. Before the Stockholm Conference 1972, the concept of "Assimilative Capacity" has been recognized at the international level. As per this concept, the natural environment has the capacity to absorb the ill effects of the pollution, but beyond a certain limit, the pollution may cause damage to the environment requiring efforts to repair it. Principle 6 of the Stockholm Declaration contains assimilative capacity principle which assumes that science could provide the policymakers with the necessary information and means to avoid encroaching upon the capacity of the environment to assimilate impacts, and it presumes that relevant technical expertise would be available when environmental harm is predicted, and there would be sufficient time to act in order to avoid such harm.

### I. Shift from Assimilative Capacity to Precautionary Principle

*689.* The uncertainty of scientific proof and its changing frontiers from time to time have led to great changes in the environmental concepts during the period between the Stockholm Conference of 1972 and the Rio Conference of 1992. Earlier the concept was based on the assimilative capacity rule as revealed from Principle 6 of the Stockholm Declaration. So, Precautionary Principle is a principle which ensures that a substance or activity posing a threat to the environment is prevented from adversely affecting it, even if there is no conclusive scientific proof that particular substance or activity will certainly lead to the environmental damage.

## §6. Origin and History of the Precautionary Principle

*690.* The Precautionary Principle is a narrower concept than merely looking for safety. Precautionary "thinking" has a much longer history. The Late Lessons from Early Warnings report (2001) mentions the example of Dr. John Snow who in 1854 recommended removing the handle of a London water pump in order to stop a cholera epidemic. The evidence for the causal link between the spread of cholera and contact with the water pump was weak and not a proof beyond reasonable doubt. The report then mentions a series of other examples, such as asbestos, where a precautionary approach could have saved many lives if early warnings of potential (at the time unproven but still reducible) harm had been taken more seriously.

*691.* The Precautionary Principle, however, dates from the 1970s. Some scholars mention Swedish and some a German origin of the Precautionary Principle. The term "Precautionary Principle" had its origin in the German word *Vorsorgeprinzip.*[122] In Germany, the Precautionary Principle ("Vorsorgeprinzip") may be traced back to the first draft of a bill (1970) aimed at securing clean air. The law was passed in 1974 and covered all potential sources of air pollution, noise, vibrations and similar processes. The most unambiguous elaboration of the Precautionary Principle in German environmental policy is from a later date and reads: "Responsibility towards future generations commands that the natural foundations of life are preserved and that irreversible types of damage, such as the decline of forests, must be avoided." Thus, the principle of precaution commands that the damages done to the natural environment should be avoided in advance and in accordance with opportunity and possibility.

## §7. Basic Features of Precautionary Principle

*692.* The Precautionary Principle represents a paradigm shift in decision-making. It allows for four key elements that can prevent irreversible damage to people and nature.[123]

### I. Anticipatory Action

*693.* There is a duty to take anticipatory action to prevent harm. Government, business, and community groups, as well as the general public, share this responsibility.

### II. Right to Know

*694.* The community has a right to know complete and accurate information on potential human health and environmental impacts associated with the selection of products, services, operations, or plans. The burden to supply this information lies with the proponent, not with the general public.

### III. Alternatives Assessment

*695.* An obligation exists to examine a full range of alternatives and select the alternative with the least potential impact on human health and the environment, including the alternative of doing nothing.

122. An alternative translation of this word would mean "foresight principle"—which could have given an active and positive impression, as against the reactive and perhaps negative connotation attached with precaution.
123. http://.ncbi.nlm.nih.gov.

### IV. Full Cost Accounting

*696.* When evaluating potential alternatives, there is a duty to consider all the reasonably foreseeable costs, including raw materials, manufacturing, transportation, use, cleanup, eventual disposal, and health costs even if such costs are not reflected in the initial price. Short- and long-term benefits and time thresholds should also be considered when making decisions.

### V. Participatory Decision Process

*697.* Decisions applying the Precautionary Principle must be transparent, participatory, and informed by the best available scientific investigation and other relevant information.

## §8. Need of Precautionary Principle

*698.* The effects of careless and harmful activities have accumulated over the years. Humans and the rest of the natural world have a limited capacity to absorb and overcome this harm. There are plenty of warning signs: Chronic diseases and conditions affect more than 100 million men, women, and children in the World—more than a third of the population. Cancer, asthma, Alzheimer's disease, autism, birth defects, developmental disabilities, diabetes, endometriosis, infertility, multiple sclerosis, and Parkinson's disease are becoming increasingly common.

*699.* In laboratory animals, wildlife, and humans, considerable evidence documents a link between levels of environmental contamination and malignancies, birth defects, reproductive problems, impaired behavior, and impaired immune system function. Scientists' growing understanding of how biological systems develop and function leads to similar conclusions. Other warning signs are the dying off of plant and animal species, the destruction of ecosystems, the depletion of stratospheric ozone, and the likelihood of global warming. Serious, evident effects such as endocrine disruption, climate change, cancer, and the disappearance of species can seldom be linked decisively to a single cause.

## §9. Precautionary Principle in Practice

*700.* Several MEAs refer to precautionary principle in some form but rarely provide elaboration into specific guidance. Similarly, several national-level environmental initiatives invoke the precautionary principle. Here, a brief overview of some such initiatives is provided.

## I. Multilateral Environmental Agreements

*701.* Montreal Protocol on Substances that Deplete the Ozone Layer, 1987 contains that "Parties to this Protocol, determined to protect the ozone layer by taking precautionary measures to control equitably total global emissions of substances that deplete it." The Rio Declaration on Environment and Development, 1992 says "In order to protect the environment the precautionary approach shall be widely applied by states according to their capabilities." Article 3.3 of the U.N. Framework Convention on Climate Change, 1992 says, "The Parties should take precautionary measures to anticipate, prevent or minimize the causes of climate change and mitigate its adverse effects." The CBD, 1992 does not directly use the term "precaution" but interprets the "serious and irreversible" harm referred in the Rio Declaration in the context of biodiversity. It states, "where there is a threat of significant reduction or loss of biological diversity, lack of full scientific certainty should not be used as a reason for postponing measures to avoid or minimize such a threat."

*702.* The Maastricht Treaty of EU, 1992 says that "Community policy on the environment must aim at a high level of protection and be based on the precautionary principle, as well as on the principle that preventive action should be taken, that environmental damage should be rectified at source and that the polluter should pay." The Cartagena Protocol on Biosafety, 2000 embodies that "In accordance with the precautionary approach the objective of this Protocol is to contribute to ensuring an adequate level of protection in the field of the safe transfer, handling and use of living modified organisms resulting from modern biotechnology that may have adverse effects on the conservation and sustainable use of biological diversity, taking into account risks to human health, and specifically focusing on trans-boundary movements." The Stockholm Convention on POPs, 2001 states, "Mindful of the precautionary approach as set forth in Principle 15 of the Rio Declaration on Environment and Development, the objective of this Convention is to protect health and environment from persistent organic pollutants." This treaty operationalizes precaution with explicit reference to it in the preamble, provisions for adding POPs, and determination of best available technologies.

## II. National Experiences

### *A. Asia*

*703.* In Asia, even though several countries have adopted well-drafted environmental and biodiversity laws, reference to "precautionary principle" is missing. For instance, Malaysia's National Biodiversity Policy makes explicit reference to the CBD (1992) but refrains from using the term "precautionary principle." Similarly, other countries in the region, Vietnam, Indonesia, and Lao PDR also do not directly invoke precautionary principle in their laws. On the other hand, in several countries (e.g., India and Pakistan), the highest judicial authority has cited "precautionary principle" in its judgments.

*B. Africa*

*704.* Several countries have made explicit reference to "precautionary principle" in their laws. Examples include the 1997 Mozambique Environment Legislation, the 1996 General Environmental Law of Cameroon, and South Africa's National Environmental Management Act.

*C. Latin America*

*705.* Many countries in this region have incorporated precaution as guiding principle in their national environmental laws. Examples include general and biodiversity-related environmental laws in Argentina, Peru, Costa Rica and Ecuador.

*D. Australia*

*706.* The precautionary principle is deeply rooted in Australia's environmental policy, as reflected in the Intergovernmental Agreement on Environment of 1992, and the Commonwealth Environment Protection and Biodiversity Conservation Act of 1999. As mentioned above, precaution is deeply entrenched in the environmental legislations of several European countries. On the other hand, in the U.S., precaution is rarely stated explicitly in any of its laws. However, the precautionary principles are well entrenched in several protection acts such as Endangered Species Act of 1973 and the Wild Bird Conservation Act of 1992.

# Chapter 2. Polluter Pays

*707.* The "polluter pays" principle is a globally accepted practice, according to which those who produce pollution should bear the costs of managing it so as to prevent damage to human health or the environment. For instance, a factory that produces a potentially poisonous substance as a by-product of its activities is usually held responsible for its safe and proper disposal. This principle is applied by most of the regulations of pollution affecting land, water and air. In U.K. law, pollution is defined as contamination of the land, water, or air by harmful or potentially harmful substances. Part of a set of broader principles to guide sustainable development worldwide (formally known as the 1992 Rio Declaration), the PPP has also been applied more specifically to emissions of GHG which cause climate change. The "polluter pays" principle can be implemented through carbon price which imposes a charge on the emission of GHG equivalent to the corresponding potential cost caused through future climate change. In this way, a financial incentive is created for a factory, for instance, to minimize its costs by reducing emissions.

## §1. Basic Concept

*708.* As per "polluter pays principle," whoever is responsible for damage to the environment should bear the costs associated with it. Few people could disagree with the proposition that those who cause damage or harm to others should "pay" for those damages. The polluters are forced to bear the costs of their activities, and this factor also enhances economic efficiency. Appropriately applied, policies based on a PPP should enable to protect the environment without sacrificing the efficiency of a free-market economic system.

## §2. Polluter Pays: Interpretation

*709.* An interpretation of the PPP would define pollution as any by-product of a production or consumption process that harms or otherwise violates the property rights of others. The polluter would be the person, company, or other organization whose activities are generating that by-product. The payment should equal the damage and has to be made to the person or persons being harmed. Inanimate objects and the environment do not incur costs, people do. It is not merely the physical property that is being damaged, but the interests of the owner are being affected. However, most advocates of PPP rarely talk about harm to people. Instead, they redefine the concepts of cost and damage to apply to things rather than to people. Polluters are said to be those who "damage" or impose "costs" on the environment. Thus, environmentalists define a "polluter" far more broadly, not as someone who is harming others, but as someone who is simply using his own property and resources in a way that offends the environmentalists. Because, in such cases, there are no victims to compensate, the amount to be paid is determined by the extent to which it will deter the politically disfavored activity. The payment (whether there are real victims or not) typically goes to the government in the form of a tax. In such cases, the PPP is used to promote an environmental agenda rather than to ensure that real polluters pay compensation to real victims of their activities.

## §3. Taxing All Consumption and Production Activities

*710.* Ultimately since almost all human activity involves altering and affecting the natural environment, the PPP as defined by its most vocal proponents can be invoked as a justification for taxing all consumption and production activities. The use of "market-based instruments" to enforce these arbitrary curtailments of the use of property is often justified on the grounds of "economic efficiency." Instruments such as tradable emissions permits are said to result in less misdirection of resources than command-and-control solutions to pollution problems. However, when the fundamental concept of pollution is misguided, and the target reductions are made arbitrarily without the benefit of market signals as to the costs of production or the wishes of the consumers, no instrument is efficient. Environmental problems occur because there is a conflict over the use of a resource. When we think of damage to property, we are not simply speaking about the alteration of one or another of its physical aspects, we are in fact tying that property to an owner and the uses that he or she may have planned for it.

## §4. Who Should Be Paid

*711.* In order to decide who the polluter is and who should be paid, one must first know who has rights to the resource, use of which is in dispute. There are situations where ownership is in dispute or property rights are undefined. These problems need to be clarified, either in the courts, as is typically the case when there are disputes over property rights, or legislatively, as may be necessary when rights are completely undefined, as might be the case with rivers, the ocean, etc. Unfortunately, the PPP that is currently guiding public policy has lost the concept that environmental problems are essentially about interpersonal conflicts over the use of property. The notion of property rights as the rights that human beings have to property have been replaced with the idea that somehow the property itself has rights that are being violated by productive human activity.

*712.* These errors lead to the illogical definition of a polluter as someone who causes damage to, or imposes costs, not on others, but on the environment. Since the environment cannot be compensated directly, this makes for an excuse to impose taxes on the offending parties, which, of course are to be used to "undo the damage." Ultimately though, these "payments" enhance the incomes of a host of government bureaucrats, consultants, and lawyers, all of whom benefit from the process. The PPP as it is currently being advocated may end up being a wealth transfer from nonpolluters to politically well-connected non-victims.

*713.* A property rights-based PPP, if implemented, would solve many of these problems by enforcing existing property rights and providing principled guidance for the privatization of currently non-owned resources by courts and legislatures. It will be much easier for lawmakers and adjudicators of disputes to move in the right direction once the problem is clearly identified.

# Chapter 3. Prevention

*714.* In the spirit of prevention is better than cure, preventing environmental harm is cheaper, easier, and less environmentally dangerous than reacting to environmental harm that has already taken place. The prevention principle is the fundamental notion behind laws regulating the generation, transportation, treatment, storage, and disposal of hazardous waste and laws regulating the use of pesticides. The principle was the foundation of the Basel Convention on the Control of Transboundary Movements of Hazardous Wastes and their Disposal (1989), which sought to minimize the production of hazardous waste and to combat illegal dumping. The prevention principle was also an important element of the EC's Third Environmental Action Programme, which was adopted in 1983.

## §1. Problems with Prevention

*715.* Curative measures may take care of environmental damage, but they come too late to avert it. In contrast, preventive measures do not depend on the appearance of ecological problems; they anticipate damage or, where it has already occurred, try to ensure it does not spread. In any case, common sense dictates timely prevention of environmental damage to the greatest extent possible, particularly when it is likely to be irreversible or too insidious or diffuse to be effectively dealt with through civil liability. However, the outlines of the preventive principle are difficult to discern; it gives rise to so many questions that any attempt at interpretation calls for constant clarification.

## §2. Prevention Embodied in Rio Principle 2

*716.* The interaction between the principle and the obligation not to cause environmental damage to the environment of other states or to areas beyond national jurisdiction Pursuant to Principle 2 of the 1992 Rio Declaration on Environment and Development, states have "the responsibility to ensure that activities within their jurisdiction or control do not cause damage to the environment of other states or of areas beyond the limits of their national jurisdiction." This can be seen as a manifestation of the principle of prevention.[124] Rio's Principle 2 has been incorporated, for instance, into the Preamble of the UNFCCC. Rio's Principle 2 is widely recognized to reflect a rule of CIL, placing preventive duties on the right of states to carry out activities within their territory or under their jurisdiction[125] Accordingly, states find themselves bound by a due diligence requirement to prevent trans-boundary pollution. In other words, the state must have failed to show due diligence if it is to be held liable. However, customary law does not specify what diligent conduct

124. N. De Sadeleer, *Environmental Principles: From Political Slogans to Legal Rules* (OUP, Oxford 2002).

125. P. Sands, *Principles of International Environmental Law, Manchester* (Manchester University Press 1995) and P. Sounders, *A Nation of Home Owners* 190 (Routledge 1990).

entails or what concrete measures states are required to take in order to fulfill their duties under Rio's Principle 2. Indeed, the obligation to prevent trans-boundary harm is subject to a variety of interpretations as to what preventive actions may be required of a state, as well as what amount of damage is to be prevented.

## §3. Formulations of the Principle in the Different Environmental Sectors

*717.* Prevention cannot be ensured merely by setting general rules whose credibility depends on the effective implementation of state liability. The basis for the preventive principle in international law can be sought in multilateral and bilateral conventions intended to ensure environmental protection rather than in international state liability. The proliferation of preventive mechanisms found in such conventions (EIAs, notification procedures, exchange of data on the impact of harmful activities, etc.) plays a crucial role in implementing the duty of diligence to prevent trans-boundary harm and therefore giving substance to the principle of prevention. In addition, the preventive principle is implicitly or explicitly set out by an extensive body of international treaties and related instruments (Sands, 1995: 196), the subjects of which include:

- the marine environment (for instance, UNCLOS, 1982: Articles 194(1)(2), 195, 192, 196, 204, 207, 208, 209, 210, 211, 212);
- the management of high seas fisheries (for instance, Article 5 of the 1995 U.N. Fish Stocks Agreement);
- the protection of rivers (for instance, Article 21 of the 1997 New York Convention on the Law Relating to the Uses of International Watercourses for Purposes other than Navigation);
- climate (for instance, UNFCCC, 1992: Article 3(3));
- the ozone layer (for instance, Article 2(2)(b) of the 1985 Vienna Convention for the Protection of the Ozone Layer);
- waste management (for instance, Article 4(2)(c) of the 1989 Basel Convention on the Control of Trans-boundary Movements of Hazardous Wastes and their Disposal);
- biodiversity (for instance, Article 14 of the 1992 CBD);
- vulnerable ecosystems such as the Antarctic and the Alps (for instance, Article 3(2) of the 1991 Madrid Protocol on Environmental Protection to the Antarctic Treaty, Article 2 of the 1991 Salzburg Convention on the Protection of the Alps);
- trans-boundary environmental risk assessment (for instance, the 1991 Espoo Convention on EIA in a Trans boundary Context; Article 3(1) of the 1992 Helsinki Convention on the Trans boundary Effects of Industrial Accidents).

The stringency of preventive obligations will largely depend on the nature of the instrument (soft law or hard law) and the relevant provision, for example, reference to the preventive principle in a preamble fulfills an interpretative function, while its inclusion in an operative provision is binding.

## Chapter 4. Integration Principle

*718.* Together with the precautionary principle, the principle of sustainable development and other principles, the integration principle constitutes an attempt to fill pre-existing gaps and to function as a "closing norm" in the normative system of international environmental law. The goal of integration principle is that "all economic and social developments should have environmental requirements built fully into their planning and execution." Principle 4 of the 1992 Rio Declaration on Environment and Development, envisages that "in order to achieve sustainable development, environmental protection shall constitute an integral part of the development process and cannot be considered in isolation from it." Clear authority for the proposition that the integration principle applies to Member States can be found in treaties that bind the Community and its Member States. For instance, Article 3(4) of the Climate Change Convention stipulates that "Policies and measures to protect the climate system against human-induced change ... should be integrated with national development programmes."

*719.* As per this principle, environmental requirements "must be integrated in sectoral policies." A large number of treaties have incorporated, either expressly or implicitly, the integration principle. This does not necessarily mean that the integration principle is a general principle of international law. It is noticeable that the ICJ in its judgment in the *Gabcíkovo-Nagymaros* (Hungary/Slovakia) case referred to the principle of sustainable development as a "concept" rather than as a principle.[126] This appraisal invoked a critical dissent by Judge Weeramantry, who considered the word "concept" to be something of an understatement. Judge Weeramantry argued that authority and precedent do allow us to speak of sustainable development as a principle.[127] The court apparently disagreed. It may well be that the court would take a similarly reluctant position when asked to apply the integration principle. After all, authority for the integration principle is hardly stronger than that for the more general principle of sustainable development.

*720.* In view of the variety of sources in which the integration principle has been included, partly legal and partly nonlegal, Phillip Sands in his textbook on international environmental law included the integration principle as a principle of international environmental law (1995, pp. 205–206). According to him, the integration principle fulfills a variety of legally relevant functions, which do not seem to hinge on a formal legal status of the principle.

*721.* As a policy or objective, the integration principle fulfills an important function. Arguments of policy provide reasons for legislative bodies to develop the law in order to further the objective. Similarly, one could consider many provisions of international environmental law as a form of application or implementation of the

126. 32 ILM 1247 (1993).
127. *Ibid.*, para. AC.

integration policy. The principle does not have any autonomous normative meaning, but it refers to other applicable rules. For a proper understanding of this construction, it is necessary to distinguish between situations where the principle addresses the Community and where it addresses states. In this construction, the integration principle does not have any autonomous normative meaning. Further, it essentially is a rule of reference. It refers to environmental protection requirements that are defined by other norms—not by the integration principle itself. The integration principle in itself does not force any other change in the balance between environmental protection and economic development.

*722.* The integration principle would mean that states have to incorporate requirements presented by other environmental rules in their development policies.

*723.* States would be obliged to comply with the norms of international law that apply to them. The integration principle cannot change this and surely does not render applicable norms that otherwise would not apply. It does not ask the Community or the Member States to apply prior agreed norms to their development policies, but to integrate "the environment," or "environmental interests" into development policies. This is the form in which the integration principle was incorporated in Principle 4 of the Rio Declaration. This states, "environmental protection shall constitute an integral part of the development process." This construction has an autonomous normative identity. It requires integration of environmental interests that in themselves are not contained in legal principles or norms. In this respect, the integration principle goes beyond the normative structure of existing international law.

*724.* In this context are the proceedings in Case 321/95 (*Greenpeace v. Commission*) concerning the legality of decisions taken by the Commission pursuant to Council Regulation 1787/84 on the European Regional Development Fund.[128] In these decisions, the Commission granted Spain financial assistance for the construction of two electric power stations in the Canary Islands. A number of plaintiffs, including Greenpeace, argued that the decisions of the Commission were not in keeping with Community law, in particular, the requirements for EIA. The court declined to hear the case for lack of *locus standi*. But the advocate stated that the treaty provisions concerning the environment—including the integration principle—"are not mere proclamations of principle."[129] He stated that the integration principle "appears to impose on the Community institutions a specific and clear obligation which could be deemed to produce direct effect in the Community legal order."[130] He continued to state that this obligation has not remained a "dead letter" but has been imported into secondary Community law.

*725.* In international law, the basic authority of states is governed by what commonly is called the Lotus principle. In the "Lotus" decision, the PCIJ addressed its

128. 1998 ECR I 1651.
129. *Ibid.*, para. 62.
130. *Ibid.*

inquiry to the question: "whether or not under international law there is a principle which would have prohibited Turkey, in the circumstances of the case before the Court, from prosecuting Lieutenant Demons."[131] The court held that in the absence of such a principle or of a specific rule to which it had expressly consented, the authority of a state could not be limited. This holding is often implicitly extrapolated to other areas of law, including environmental law. The argument is then that the discretionary authority of state is only limited when there is a specific rule of law that curtails their authority. If there were no such rule, freedom would reign.

*726.* While the Lotus holding has often been criticized, it appears that it rightly depicts the normative structure of international environmental law. States have accepted many more or less specific environmental norms. Directives, regulations, and treaties govern certain activities and do not govern others. For instance, the Habitat Directive protects only certain species and habitats but not other species and habitats. Thus, international environmental law leaves gaps that are not, or not expressly, governed by special norms. In such gaps, the Member States can make their policy decisions unhindered.

*727.* The integration principle has a procedural and a more substantive component. With regard to the procedural function, the principle requires, that interests of environmental protection are considered in decision-making process. Of course, this requirement overlaps with the already applicable requirement of EIA. It can, however, have a procedural significance in those cases where these requirements do not apply. Whereas the question to what extent such interests should be given protection generally lies beyond judicial scrutiny, the requirement that such interest should be considered in a procedural sense is a requirement that can be applied by courts and other supervisory mechanisms.

*728.* The integration principle provides a means of balancing two competing norms. Consideration of conflicting norms that protect development, on the one hand, and the environment, on the other, can be aided and given focus by introducing the integration principle. In this respect, the principle can fulfill a similar function as the principle of sustainable development. The principle of sustainable development is free agents, which may in principle be combined with any other rules, modifying that rule which establishes the relationship between other, primary norms. It is in this sense that the ICJ used the term of sustainable development in the *Gabcíkovo-Nagymaros* case. The court argued that "the need to reconcile economic development with protection of the environment is aptly expressed in the concept of sustainable development,"[132] and subsequently formulated a way to achieve that reconciliation.

*729.* The integration principle plays three distinct roles in international environmental law. First, it serves as an objective that underlies and inspires more specific

131. PCIJ Series A, No. 10, p. 21.
132. 32 ILM 1247 (1993) para. 140.

environmental law. As such, the principle is unobjectionable, though not distinguishable from environmental policy. Second, the integration principle can, as a rule of reference, be used as a vehicle to encourage the Community and other international institutions to comply with relevant norms of international law in their various activities. Third, the integration principle may be considered as an autonomous normative principle. Whether it will play that role depends upon the identification of normative space and the development of criteria to evaluate integration. This is an area where much depends upon the energies and activities of interested actors to make the principle effective and practicable.

## Chapter 5. Sustainable Development Principle

*730.* Sustainable development is economic planning that attempts to foster economic growth while preserving the quality of the environment for future generations. Despite its enormous popularity in the last two decades of the twentieth century, the concept of sustainable development proved difficult to apply in many cases, primarily because the results of long-term sustainability analyzes depend on the particular resources focused upon. For example, a forest that will provide a sustained yield of timber in perpetuity may not support native bird populations, and a mineral deposit that will eventually be exhausted may nevertheless support more or less sustainable communities.

*731.* Sustainability was the focus of the 1992 Earth Summit and later was central to a multitude of environmental studies. One of the most important areas of the law of sustainable development is ecotourism. Although tourism poses the threat of environmental harm from pollution and the overuse of natural resources, it also can create economic incentives for the preservation of the environment and increase awareness of unique and fragile ecosystems throughout the world. In 1995, the World Conference on Sustainable Tourism held on the island of Lanzarote in the Canary Islands, adopted a charter that encouraged the development of laws that would promote the dual goals of economic development through tourism and protection of the environment. Two years later, in the Malé Declaration on Sustainable Tourism, twenty-seven Asian-Pacific countries pledged themselves to a set of principles that included fostering awareness of environmental ethics in tourism, reducing waste, promoting natural and cultural diversity, and supporting local economies and local community involvement. Highlighting the growing importance of sustainable tourism, the World Tourism Organization declared 2002 as the International Year of Ecotourism.

## Chapter 6. The Public Participation Principle

*732.* Decisions about environmental protection integrate the views of the public. Generally, government decisions to set environmental standards for specific types of pollution, to permit significant environmentally damaging activities, or to preserve significant resources are made only after such decisions have been formally and publicly announced and the public has been given the opportunity to influence the decision through written comments or hearings. In many countries, citizens may challenge in court or before administrative bodies government decisions affecting the environment. These citizen lawsuits are an important component of environmental decision-making at both the national and the international levels.

*733.* Public participation in environmental decision-making has been facilitated in many countries by laws that mandate extensive public access to government information on the environment. Similar measures at the international level include the Rio Declaration and the 1998 Århus Convention, which committed the forty European signatory states to increase the environmental information available to the public and to enhance the public's ability to participate in government decisions that affect the environment. The Internet has become a primary vehicle for disseminating environmental information to the public.

# Chapter 7. Proximity Principle

*734.* The Proximity Principle highlights a need to treat and/or dispose of wastes in reasonable proximity to their point of generation. The principle works to minimize the environmental impact and cost of waste transport. As per this principle, most waste should be treated and managed within the region in which it is generated provided there are no unacceptable adverse effects—on people, the environment or transportation systems. However, it may not be feasible or practical to treat certain wastes (e.g., special or hazardous wastes) close to its source of arising or within the region in which it is generated and to be taken elsewhere for disposal. The proximity principle reduces risks and social costs of long-distance transportation of waste. Risks identified included heavy vehicle traffic and congestion, fuel consumption, carbon emissions, traffic accidents, waste spillages and contamination. Significant financial savings that could be made by waste operators transporting the waste to places where the disposal fee per ton is significantly less due to the particular facility operator.

*735.* The restricted solid waste can be transported to the place closest to the origin of the waste that can be lawfully used for its disposal. The restrictive provisions with respect to disposal of waste have a "polluter-pays" likeness, whereby the social costs caused by long-distance transportation of waste are taken into account, and waste generators are held responsible for its safe disposal and managing it to prevent additional impacts on human health or the environment.

*736.* The proximity principle will likely have significant commercial and competition ramifications for people operating in the waste industry for two reasons. First, it will shrink the potential client base for many waste disposal facility/landfill operators, particularly those operating in remote rural locations. Second, it will reduce competition between landfill operators.

# Part XV. Means of Implementation and Compliance

## Chapter 1. Implementation and Enforcement

### §1. Command and Control

*737.* For enforcement purposes, most environmental laws fall into a category of law known as "command and control." These laws typically involve three elements:

(1) identification of a type of environmentally harmful activity;
(2) imposition of specific conditions or standards on that activity; and
(3) prohibition of forms of the activity that fail to comply with the imposed conditions or standards.

The most obvious forms of regulated activity involve actual discharges of pollutants into the environment (e.g., air, water, and groundwater pollution). However, environmental laws also regulate activities that entail a significant risk of discharging harmful pollutants (e.g., the transportation of hazardous waste, the sale of pesticides, and logging). For actual discharges, environmental laws generally prescribe specific thresholds of allowable pollution; for activities that create a risk of discharge, environmental laws generally establish management practices to reduce that risk.

*738.* The standards imposed on actual discharges generally come in two forms: (1) environmental quality, or ambient, standards, which fix the maximum amount of the regulated pollutant or pollutants tolerated in the receiving body of air or water, and (2) emission, or discharge, standards, which regulate the amount of the pollutant or pollutants that any "source" may discharge into the environment. Most comprehensive environmental laws impose both environmental quality and discharge standards and endeavor to coordinate their use to achieve a stated environmental-quality goal. Environmental-quality goals can be either numerical or narrative. Numerical targets set a specific allowable quantity of a pollutant (e.g., 10 µg of carbon monoxide per cubic meter of air measured over an eight-hour period). Narrative standards require that the receiving body of air or water be suitable for a specific use (e.g., swimming). The management practices prescribed for activities that create a risk of discharge are diverse and context-specific regulated by command-and-control legislation. The environmentally harmful trade is also regulated by command-and-control legislation.

*739.* Among the most-developed regulations are those on trade in wildlife. The CITES, 1973 authorizes signatories to the convention to designate species "threatened with extinction, which are or may be affected by trade." Once a plant or animal species has been designated as endangered, countries generally are bound to prohibit import or export of that species except in specific limited circumstances. In 1989, listing of the African elephant as a protected species effectively prohibited most trade in African ivory, which was subsequently banned by Kenya and the EC. Despite these measures, some countries either failed to prohibit ivory imports (e.g., Japan) or refused to prohibit ivory exports (e.g., Botswana, Namibia, South Africa, and Zimbabwe), and elephants continued to face danger from poachers and smugglers.

## §2. Environmental Assessment Mandates

*740.* EA mandates are significant forms of environmental law. Such mandates generally perform three functions: (1) identification of a level or threshold of potential environmental impact at which a contemplated action is significant enough to require the preparation of an assessment, (2) establishment of specific goals for the assessment mandated, and (3) setting of requirements to ensure that the assessment will be considered in determining whether to proceed with the action as originally contemplated or to pursue an alternative action. Unlike command-and-control regulations, which may directly limit discharges into the environment, mandated EAs protect the environment indirectly by increasing the quantity and quality of publicly available information on the environmental consequences of contemplated actions. This information potentially improves the decision-making of government officials and increases the public's involvement in the creation of environmental policy.

*741.* There are forums where international environmental disputes can be adjudicated, such as national courts, the ICJ, and international arbitration tribunals. These forums, however, generally require that the disputing parties being states voluntarily submit to the jurisdiction of the court or panel. In addition, even when these forums obtain jurisdiction over an international environmental dispute, they have to rely on the cooperation of national governments to enforce rulings. For economic, policy and political reasons, this cooperation is often withheld.

## §3. Compliance Through Bans and Incentives

*742.* The use of economic instruments and trade bans to create incentives for environmental protection is a popular form of environmental law. The incentives include pollution taxes, subsidies for clean technologies and practices, and the creation of markets in either environmental protection or pollution. Denmark, The Netherlands, and Sweden, for example, impose taxes on $CO_2$ emissions. By the

1990s, "tradable allowance schemes," which permit companies to buy and sell "pollution credits," or legal rights to produce specified amounts of pollution, had been implemented in the U.S. This was designed to reduce overall $SO_2$ emissions by fossil-fuel-fired power plants. According to proponents, the program would provide financial rewards to cleaner plants, which could sell their unneeded credits on the market, and allow dirtier plants to stay in business while they converted to cleaner technologies.

*743.* The economic incentives and trade bans to encourage compliance have also been included in IEAs. For example, the Montreal Protocol, the Framework Convention on Climate Change, and the Biodiversity Convention provide economic incentives in the form of technical assistance, technology transfers, and money to build the administrative capacity of national environmental agencies. These incentives have been of particular value in promoting the involvement and compliance of DC—part of the Rio bargain between northern (developed) and southern (developing) countries. The GEF, a new international funding institution, also provides money for training, equipment, and enforcement related to environmental protection measures. Some recent IEAs, such as the Biodiversity Convention, have designated the GEF as their exclusive funding mechanism.

## §4. Set-Aside Schemes

*744.* Another method of environmental protection is the laws requiring setting aside of lands and waters in their natural state. In the U.S., for example, the vast majority of the land owned by the federal government (about one-third of the total land area of the country) can be developed only with the approval of a federal agency. Europe has an extensive network of national parks and preserves on both public and private land, and there are extensive national parks in southern and eastern Africa in which wildlife is protected. Arguably, the large body of law that regulates use of public lands and publicly held resources is "environmental law." Some, however, maintain that it is not.

*745.* Many areas of law can be characterized as both "set aside" and regulatory. For example, international efforts to preserve wetlands have focused on setting aside areas of ecological value, including wetlands, and on regulating their use. The Ramsar Convention provides that wetlands are a significant "economic, cultural, scientific and recreational" resource, and a section of the Clean Water Act, the primary U.S. law for the protection of wetlands, contains a prohibition against unpermitted discharges of "dredge and fill material" into any "waters of the United States."

## Chapter 2. Institutions and Bodies for Enforcement

*746.* As per a report published on November 22, 2023, by the UNEP, there is growing attention to specialized environmental enforcement. Specialized environmental courts and tribunals in at least sixty-seven countries have given access to foreign plaintiffs, whose rights are violated at home by transnational entities domiciled within the courts' jurisdictions. At least thirty-nine countries have a national or subnational judicial training institute with environmental law in their curriculum, and nine countries have made environmental law a mandatory component of legal training. Further, technology has revolutionized environmental enforcement, as demonstrated by satellites, drones, Artificial intelligence (AI), and citizen science, improving detection of illegal activities, from deforestation and illegal dumping of waste to wildlife poaching.

*747.* There being no international body to directly enforce international environmental law, the task of direct enforcement is left to the member nations, whose governments propose, adopt, and implement environmental policies. Sometimes, the implementing national legislation is identical to the international agreement. For example, Canada implemented the Migratory Birds Treaty (with the U.S.) by adopting the Migratory Birds Treaty Act. Because the language of this act is identical to the language in the treaty, the law is basically a legislative codification of the international agreement. Other times, however, the IEA is of a general nature, and national governments draft and implement more specific laws. For instance, in 1989, the International Convention on Trans-boundary Movement of Hazardous Waste was signed in Basel, Switzerland. This convention forbids the export of hazardous wastes to countries that lack "adequate means to dispose of them." Under the terms of the convention, signatory nations are called upon to draft their own more specific national laws to implement this pledge.

### §1. Agreements Establishing Institutions

*748.* Some environmental agreements have established international institutions that can directly impose trade sanctions (such as the Montreal Protocol) or have authorized Member States to impose trade sanctions against violating parties (such as the International Convention for the Regulation of Whaling). For instance, in response to Japan's violation of the International Whaling Commission's whaling moratorium, the U.S. threatened to restrict Japanese fishing vessel activity in U.S. territorial waters. Japan elected to accede to the whaling moratorium rather than suffer any such restrictions. However, the type of sanctions envisioned under the Montreal Protocol and International Whaling Commission are procedurally very difficult to impose.

§2. Commission on Sustainable Development

*749.* Although international institutions are generally not responsible for directly implementing and enforcing international environmental law, they often play important monitoring, informational, and diplomatic roles in this regard. Four agendas were adopted at the 1992 Convention on Environment and Development at Rio de Janeiro which created a new international body, the CSD. The CSD meets yearly at the U.N. in New York to review and advance the implementation of Agenda 21—an enormous and complex mandate. Most global agreements, such as the Biodiversity Convention and the Framework Convention on Climate Change, are implemented by an annual or biennial COP. These COPs lack the power to bring enforcement actions against either governments or private parties. They help monitor national compliance by requiring member nations to submit annual reports. Through meetings and publications, COPs also provide a forum to discuss and debate issues associated with the implementation of the agreement. There are other institutions similar in function to the CSDs and the COPs. The North American Commission on Environmental Cooperation (NACEC) based in Montreal, Canada, monitors compliance with the North American Agreement on Environmental Cooperation (NAAEC), one of the side agreements under NAFTA.

§3. European Environmental Agency

*750.* The European Environmental Agency, based in Copenhagen, Denmark, monitors the compliance of individual European countries with environmental directives adopted by the EU. Although the CSD, COPs, NACEC, and the European Environmental Agency indicate that the international community is trying to improve compliance with environmental agreements, there is still a lack of effective implementation and enforcement. A 1992 study by the U.S. General Accounting Office concluded that IEAs lack adequate procedures to monitor and ensure compliance. Countries have become skilled in negotiating IEAs, but they are much less skilled at making the agreement operate effectively.

§4. Jurisdiction for Disputes

*751.* Enforcement and jurisdiction may be defined as a court's ability to hear a complaint (jurisdiction for dispute) and impose its decision. If the subject matter of the case is not within the scope of a court's jurisdiction, or if one of the parties, either the one bringing the case (plaintiff) or the one against whom it is brought (defendant) is not within a court's jurisdiction, the court will not hear the dispute. This is particularly relevant to international environmental law for a number of reasons. First and foremost, if a treaty or convention does not specify an international forum that has jurisdiction on subject matter, often the only place to bring a suit with respect to that treaty is in the Member State's domestic court system. This then presents two additional hurdles. If the Member State being sued, does not have domestic implementing legislation in place to hear the dispute, there will be no forum available. Even in the event that the domestic legislation provides for suits of this nature, the judges who decide the case are residents of the country against which it is brought, and the resulting potential conflicts of interest are obvious. With respect to parties, only nations are bound by treaties and conventions and not private individuals.

*752.* Disputes between states concerning international environmental law can be heard in the ICJ provided the dispute is between states that have declared that the ICJ has compulsory jurisdiction. The ICJ is a court of general jurisdiction that provides Advisory Opinions and decides contentious cases. Interstate litigation is based on the remedial principle of "State Responsibility" or international tort law. The ICJ is only able to determine disputes between states: individuals and other non-state actors are not able to be parties to a dispute. Environmental protection disputes between states and non-state actors such as individuals, communities, and corporations can also be heard in international human rights courts such as the ECHR and the African Commission of Human and Peoples' Rights.

*753.* In international forums, such as the ICJ, countries must consent to being sued in order to preserve their sovereignty. Thus, it is generally not possible to sue a country against its will. When it is an International Environmental Law TNC, not a country that has violated an international agreement, it is nearly impossible to sue a country for not enforcing its laws against a TNC or for not enacting sufficient implementing legislation. The final difficulty is the question as to who may bring a suit. Often, only countries may sue countries, not individual citizens and NGOs. This has huge repercussions in that the environmental harm must be large and notorious for a country to even notice it. Second, for a country to have a stake in the outcome of the subject matter, some harm may have to cross the borders of the violating country into the country that is suing. Finally, even if trans-boundary harm does exist, the issue of causation, especially in the environmental field, is often impossible to demonstrate and prove with any certainty.

## §5. Difference in Compliance

*754.* In all the fields of international law, no country is ever in perfect compliance with every international obligation. Another factor is that some countries are substantially more powerful than others. This may seem self-evident and unimportant, until one considers that suing another country may expose the plaintiff country to retaliatory actions. In spite of this political reality, however, Mexico successfully challenged the U.S. in the WTO in the *Tuna Dolphin* Case, and several Asian countries successfully challenged the U.S. over their efforts to compel shrimp-exporting countries to harvest shrimp without harming turtles. The entirety of international law, beyond the environmental field, remains largely unenforceable without the consent of the states. Even if a treaty or convention provides for specific substantive measures to be taken by a country (which is not always the case, since many treaties merely provide frameworks), and even if a forum for litigation or dispute resolution is specified or sanctions by Member States for noncompliance are authorized, a country cannot be forced to do what it is not willing to do. One can sanction the country, order damages, restrict trade, or, most frequently, declare noncompliance, but beyond that, if a country does not comply, there is very little to be done. Countries usually accept or avoid international environmental obligations because it is in their economic self-interest to do so.

# Chapter 3. Environmental Impact Assessment

*755.* The EIA has developed as a main tool to ensure environmental and social sustainability, which is used by government and other stakeholders for effective pollution management. EIA enhances public participation and transparency for stakeholders to enable them to take informed decision. In addition, EIA, in conjunction with monitoring tools and recourse mechanisms, allows the gathering of information on environmental quality and provides a venue for expression and discussion of different shades of opinion.

## §1. Enforcement of EIA

*756.* The EA process incorporates the following main stages:

(a) screening: to determine applicability and level of detail of an EIA;
(b) scoping: during which are identified and the terms of reference for the EIA are completed;
(c) detailing: preparation of the EA report, including identification of impacts, evaluation of alternatives, and design of mitigation measures;
(d) transparency: public participation and disclosure; and
(e) final Action: the preparation of the environmental management plan.

*757.* The U.S. was the first country to introduce EA as part of the NEPA in 1969 as a tool leading to implementation of NEPA policies. The EA process had two objectives: ensure that decision-makers are making informed choices regarding impacts on the environment and open the process to citizen involvement. EIA also became an important instrument for environmental sustainability for multilateral international development agencies, including the World Bank.

## §2. Nature of EIA

*758.* A country's legal system and its political, administrative, and cultural context play an important role in shaping that country's EIA system and account for differences in EIA systems among countries. As a result, the use of EIA as a tool varies among countries from its consideration as an administrative process that helps incorporate environmental and social concerns of different stakeholders into the decision-making of authorities. Underlying the value of EIA is the view that environmental decision-making processes are strengthened when the responsible authority can systematically incorporate the views and opinions of all relevant stakeholders regarding the decision at hand and implement them. An alternative vision of EIA considers this instrument as an environmental management tool that helps control the environmental impacts of a broad range of projects, such as in Brazil where authorities often establish design and operational conditions through the

EIA process (World Bank, 2008), or Guatemala (World Bank, 2006c) and Nepal (World Bank, 2007b), where EIA became the main policy instrument to minimize or mitigate environmental impacts.

## §3. Screening

*759.* There are two general methods for environmental screening namely prescriptive and standardized. They are defined through positive or negative lists in legislation and regulations, and discretionary or customized approaches where indicative guidance is relied upon to determine requirements for EIA on an individual or case-by-case basis. Screening tools include positive lists that identify activities that require EIA and the negative lists identifying activities excluded from EIA requirement. Screening could also include analysis of impacts and risks, such as in the U.S., where EIA applies to those investment activities which pose a significant negative impact.

## §4. Scope of EIA Study

*760.* Identifying the scope of an EIA study is an important aspect of the EIA process. There is a wide difference worldwide in the manner and method of identifying the scope. In some instances, EIA scope is determined through either formal or informal consultations; or defined by the legal framework without providing opportunities for public input. Terms of reference for EIA are then prepared based on results of consultations, legal requirements, or based on generic terms of reference. An important factor in determining the scope of an EIA is drawing the boundary of the impacts of the proposed activity issues that are addressed through the EIA process, and making sure that issues that remain outside of this boundary are addressed by other instruments such as Strategic Environmental Assessment (SEA), cumulative impact assessment study, and land use planning.

## §5. Preparations, Approval, and Supervision

*761.* Supervision of the EIA falls either on the sectoral agency, or on the environmental agency, or is a responsibility shared by sectoral and environmental agencies. The environment agency's role generally ranges from review and provision of comments about the adequacy of the analysis and the impact on the environment, ensuring public participation in the EIA, to the approval of the EIA, including prior approval of the terms of the reference through the screening and scoping stages. Moreover, in many countries, agencies at the local level are responsible for supervising EIA preparation. For example, in Pakistan, the federal EPA has jurisdiction over all EIAs, but often delegates its power to provincial EPAs, resulting in provincial authorities having jurisdiction for the vast majority of EIA cases except those involving federal land, military projects, and trans-border or trans-provincial impacts (World Bank, 2006d).

*762.* Many agencies establish registers for consultants, or technical specialists, or firms that carry out EIA, and some seek to issue certifications or provide learning courses for EIA practitioners in attempts to improve EIA quality.[133] Project proponents, together with the consultants often hired by them to prepare EIA, have significant effects on EIA's quality and objectivity. The capacity of EIA practitioners has often been cited as an important factor in the quality of EIAs, alongside resources allocated to EIAs by proponents.[134]

## §6. Public Participation and Public Disclosure

*763.* Countries vary widely in the extent to which EIA relies on public participation, ranging from countries where opening the decision-making process to citizen involvement is one of the main purposes of EIA, to countries where public participation and involvement in the EIA process are not required by EIA regulations. Most countries fall in between, with regulations that require public involvement at various stages of the EIA process.[135] EIA systems vary in terms of how technical the EIA process is perceived to be, from those where it is seen as a technical process left to technical experts, to systems where the EIA process is considered as more participatory with respect to public involvement. Similarly, disclosure of EIA varies between countries where disclosure of EIA is mandatory, to countries where there is no legal requirement for disclosure of EIA, or where there are legal requirements that are not enforced in practice.

## §7. Prerequisite Factors for EIA

*764.* In designing or modifying the EIA system, it is important to have clarity regarding the purpose of the EIA and what it should and could accomplish within the broader policy framework. It is seen whether the need is for a technical report focused on preparation of mitigation measures for the identified impacts, or instead for a tool to open the decision-making process to public involvement. An overall regulatory framework within which the EIA tool is anchored should be established. This framework is an important element in the successful application and use of EIA (United Nations University (UNU) 2011).

## §8. Advantages and Limitations of EIA

*765.* The advantages and limitations of EIA process and its study are very important in the present world scenario where some countries are at the critical stage of pollution levels requiring emergency measures. These are described below.

133. World Bank 2006a; 2006c; 2006f.

134. O. Nadeem & R. Hameed, *Evaluation of Environmental Impact Assessment System in Pakistan*, Department of City and Regional Planning, University of Engineering and Technology, Lahore, Pakistan, 2008.

135. At screening, scoping, EA preparation, and before and after government decisions.

## I. Public Discussion and Participation

*766.* One major strength and outstanding feature of EIA in many countries is increased public discussion and participation (COWI 2009). However, in practice a number of limitations are also associated with it. In some instances where public participation is required by EIA legislation, such participation could be limited in practice. For example, the law in India required that a public hearing is conducted; however, NGOs often considered the public hearing as a staged process that appeared to involve citizens when the decision had already been made. In response, the 2006 EIA notification changed the requirement from public hearing to public consultation in an attempt to force project proponents to proactively seek the views of affected communities. In other instances, where projects are only discussed openly for their potential environmental merits and shortcomings, but not for social or economic ones, public discussion could focus on allegedly environmental problems when there are underlying social or economic reasons for delaying or stopping a project (World Bank, 2006e).

## II. EIA and Achieving Environmental Management Objectives

*767.* EIA is to be used in conjunction with other policy tools and should not be over-emphasized for achieving environmental management objectives. For example, in El Salvador, the National Environment Law (1998) introduced nine instruments of environmental policy including, among others, environmental zoning, environmental evaluation, environmental information and public participation, and economic and financial incentives. However, the implementation of the environmental policy focused on the EIA, and this led to over-burdening the tool. Further development of other instruments was recommended to complement a comprehensive environmental policy (World Bank, 2006b). South Africa, where EIA is applied within the framework of an integrated environmental management system, the Strategic Plan for the Environment Sector has called for developing a broader "toolkit" of environmental impact management approaches and instruments in addition to EIA in order to address the issue of over-reliance on EIA.[136]

## III. Time-Intensive Process

*768.* An effective screening system is important to ensure that the EIA does not become a prerequisite for too many activities, thus limiting the responsible authority's ability to adequately assess important projects and weakening the legitimacy of EIA. For example, in Colombia, the lack of a screening procedure resulted in an EIA being required for any project, regardless of the intensity and magnitude of its potential impacts, location, the sensitivity of the surrounding area, or public opinion regarding the project. Lack of screening has led to a situation where the EIA

136. P. Tarr, *Regional Workshop on SEA in Southern Africa, New Partnership for Africa's Development NEPAD and Environmental Assessment,* 7 Afr. J. Envtl. Assessment & Mgmt. 1–13 (2003).

regulations become a hurdle to projects and add little value to the environmental planning and management processes for which they were intended (World Bank, 2007a).

## IV. Potential for Rent-Seeking

*769.* Where the EIA is linked to the licensing process, it may become a tool for rent-seeking and could be a source of illegal influence on the responsible authorities. For example, in Bangladesh, the Environment Conservation Act (1995) required environmental clearance for development projects, but it also reserved the right to the government to waive the clearance requirement. This provided the incentive for project proponents to exert influence on the government to avoid this requirement. Because public consultation and public participation were limited, these two forces were precluded from countering the illegal influence, and they were blocked from providing an incentive for the effective identification and mitigation of potential environmental impacts (World, Bank 2006a).

## V. Interaction with Other Tools and Possible Substitutes

*770.* EIA is more effective when applied in combination with other policy tools and mechanisms for environmental management, such as environmental regulations, standards, enforcement, and monitoring systems; land use planning; and market-based incentives. In many legal systems, the judiciary provides an important avenue for recourse. Furthermore, public participation is enhanced through tools that promote access to information, advocacy, and participation in decision-making, and ability to complain and access to legal recourse.

*771.* In many legal systems, the approval of an EIA is a requirement for environmental licensing, and the two tools are closely linked. In countries where EIA is regarded as an environmental management tool, it is often linked to the licensing process, and approval of the EIA is made a prerequisite for granting a license. For example, in Jordan, the approval of an EIA is a prerequisite for all licenses or permits required prior to construction (World Bank, 2010). On the other hand, in the U.S., EIA is not linked to environmental permitting but is rather a way to open the decision-making process to public scrutiny. For permitting purposes, the U.S. system relies on other instruments such as zoning plans, standards, and regulations. Risk assessment may also feed health-issue considerations into the EIA process for projects requiring thorough examination of risks to human health and could either proceed separately of EIA or be integrated within the EIA process.[137]

*772.* Despite these risks and limitations, EIA remains a very useful and important tool for two reasons. First, it keeps developers of new projects to be serious and

137. O. Demidova & A. Cherp, *Risk Assessment for Improved Treatment of Health Considerations in EIA*, 24(4) Env't Impact Assessment Rev. 411–429 (2005), ISSN 0195-9255; CODEN EIARDK.

to take environmental impacts and risks into account. Second, it allows or may allow governments and society to analyze projects in depth. Yet this is an expensive process with regard to both inputs and time. Even when studies are of excellent quality, the process may reach wrong conclusions because EIA takes the project's effects into account but may lack in considering cumulative effects. Thus, EIA should be applied selectively, but also apply in conjunction with other tools that take cumulative effects into consideration.

# Selected Bibliography


Convention on Biological Diversity, http://www.cbd.int/.

Dinah, Shelton & Kiss Alexandre. *Judicial Handbook on Environmental Law*. United Nations Environment Programme, ISBN 92-8007-2555-6.

Environmental Risk Analysis by Financial Institutions—A Review of Global Practice, UNEP, 2016.

Environmental Crime Convergence, Research Report, June, 2023, Prepared by Earth League International and John Jay College of Criminal Justice.

Environmental Security Strategic Plan 2017–2020, by INTERPOL.

Hunter, David. 'International Environmental Law'. ABA 19(1) (January 5, 2021), https://www.americanbar.org/groups/public_education/publications/insights-on-law-and-society/volume-19/insights-vol--19---issue-1/international-environmental-law/.

https://www.un.org/ruleoflaw/thematic-areas/land-property-environment/environmental-law/.

Norouzi, Nima, & Elham Ataei. "Covid-19 Crisis and Environmental Law: Opportunities and Challenges." *Hasanuddin Law Review* 7(1) (2021): 46–60.

The Global E-waste Monitor 2020, www.globalewaste.org/.

United Nations Environment Programme, http://www.unep.org/.

World Wildlife Crime Report. 'Trafficking in Protected Species', 2020, UNODC.

## Selected Bibliography

# Index

*The numbers here refer to paragraph numbers.*

# Index

# Index

www.ingramcontent.com/pod-product-compliance
Lightning Source LLC
LaVergne TN
LVHW011115300926
849160LV00008B/384

* 9 7 8 9 4 0 3 5 3 3 0 8 7 *